Contributions to Management Science

More information about this series at http://www.springer.com/series/1505

Vanessa Ratten • Vitor Braga •
Carla Susana Marques
Editors

Knowledge, Learning and Innovation

Research Insights on Cross-Sector Collaborations

Springer

Editors
Vanessa Ratten
La Trobe University
Melbourne, Victoria
Australia

Vitor Braga
Polytechnic Institute of Porto
Porto, Portugal

Carla Susana Marques
University of Trás-os-Montes
and Alto Do
Vila Real, Portugal

ISSN 1431-1941 ISSN 2197-716X (electronic)
Contributions to Management Science
ISBN 978-3-319-59281-7 ISBN 978-3-319-59282-4 (eBook)
DOI 10.1007/978-3-319-59282-4

Library of Congress Control Number: 2017951228

Printed on acid-free paper

This Springer imprint is published by Springer Nature
The registered company is Springer International Publishing AG
The registered company address is: Gewerbestrasse 11, 6330 Cham, Switzerland

Acknowledgements

Editing this research book about knowledge, learning, and innovation has taken a long time but is well worth the effort. Originally, the idea for this book came together because of the joint interests of the coeditors in how cross-sector collaboration is affecting firms in terms of their entrepreneurial capabilities and internationalization. There is a current trend toward cross-sector collaboration, and this can take a variety of different forms depending on the cultural and social context of the firms involved. We thank the authors who, coming from a diverse range of countries contributed with chapters to this book, and to the peer reviewers. Each of the coeditors would like to thank the following. Vanessa thanks her family including her mum Kaye, dad David, and brothers Hamish and Stuart. Carla and Vitor also thank their family.

This work is supported by European Structural and Investment Funds in the FEDER component, through the Operational Competitiveness and Internationalization Programme (COMPETE 2020) (Project No. 006971 (UID/SOC/04011); Funding Reference: POCI-01-0145-FEDER-006971), and national funds, through the FCT-Portuguese Foundation for Science and Technology under the project UID/SOC/04011/2013.

Preface

For a long time, business survival has been determined by processes of knowledge, learning, and innovation. This triangular association is critical for the competitiveness of firms, but it is also a rather complex field. The processes of knowledge, learning, and innovation are both intra-firm and inter-firm processes. Achieving the competitiveness in a competitive world requires firms to master the ability to exploit the advantages arising from both intra-firm and inter-firm processes.

So far, the dominant note in the academia is that knowledge, learning, and innovation are processes that are looked from either an intra-firm or an inter-firm perspective. However, the interplay between them is critical for understanding the complex world where businesses take place. In addition, in many studies, such an approach is also seen from inside a particular industry. However, cross-sector collaboration can also be a source of innovation and a place for sharing knowledge and learning processes.

In light of such perspectives, this book is an attempt to bring together different perspectives on knowledge, learning, and innovation in order to trigger the willingness, in the academia, to contribute further with insights that allow us to deepen the knowledge on such processes and, on the other hand, to provide businesses with perspectives that may support their collaboration decision-making in order to foster inter- and intra-firm learning, innovation, and knowledge creation.

One important aspect of learning and innovation is related to the association between the firm and the customer, as a valuable provider of a critical asset for business—information. Such relationship is a different perspective on cross-sector collaboration as it is based on collaboration between business and its customers. The co-creation of knowledge, many times through virtual platforms, provides important insights for the improvement of products, and it is strongly influenced by opinion leadership. On a different perspective, global consumers do add competitive advantage as the selection of global marketing strategies may influence the outcome of the link between firms and intellectual capital. Such customer relationship is important to the extent that it determines the potential re-visit of the customer and its potential in adding value to the firm.

Knowledge and learning, from an intra-firm perspective, is strongly supported by the resource based theory, where the firm is seen as a place where different assets (human and physical) collaborate toward the creation of value and share an identity and common goals. This is particularly important in the case of family business, where social ties and human capital display different characteristics and impress, to the business, particular features on the creation of knowledge and innovation. Such processes also support different forms of internationalization. This is strongly associated with the potential existence of agency problems (often present on inter-firm collaboration) that can be strongly reduced in the case of family business of inter-firm family collaboration.

In addition to the traditional view of inter-firm collaboration, the informal economy may also be an interesting aspect of knowledge sharing and innovation, many times triggered or hindered by the levels of literacy and education, as much as other physical infrastructures to support entrepreneurship and innovation. As often associated with the informal economy (although not necessarily) the gender entrepreneurship also adds important insights for this book, as the network of female entrepreneurs, as much as the enforcement/implementation have significant effects on firm performance.

This book sheds light on the less obvious aspects of collaboration as the source of knowledge creation leading to innovation. Gender perspectives, intra-firm collaboration, and relational marketing are some of the aspects explored in this book, as other (different) forms of collaboration leading to knowledge, learning, and innovation.

Melbourne, Australia — Vanessa Ratten
Porto, Portugal — Vitor Braga
Vila Real, Portugal — Carla Susana Marques
April 2017

Contents

List of Editors and Contributors

Editors

Vanessa Ratten is an Associate Professor at La Trobe University, Australia. She completed her PhD at the UQ Business School, the University of Queensland, Australia. She is currently the program coordinator of the entrepreneurship and innovation degrees at the La Trobe Business School and teaches innovation, entrepreneurship, marketing, and management courses. She has previously been on the business faculties of Deakin University, the University of Queensland, Queensland University of Technology, and Duquesne University. Her research interests are international entrepreneurship, sport entrepreneurship, and technology innovation.

Vitor Braga is an Associate Professor at the School of Technology and Management at the Porto Polytechnic and a researcher at the Centre for Innovation and Research in Business Sciences and Information Systems. He holds a PhD from Middlesex University Business School on Business Co-operation. His research interests also include international business, family business, entrepreneurship and innovation, and economic geography. He is the director of the Business Sciences BSc and the MSc in International Management and the head of the Business Sciences department.

Carla Susana Marques has a PhD in Management. She is Assistant Professor in the University of Tras-os-Montes e Alto Douro (UTAD) and Coordinator of the "Innovation, Markets and Organization" research group in UTAD's Centre for Transdisciplinary Development Studies. Her research on innovation and entrepreneurship has been presented at numerous international conferences and published in international journals. Her most recent research projects have covered issues relating to women entrepreneurship, youth employment strategies, and entrepreneurship education.

Contributors

Lutfije Ademi is currently working at International Trade Support Service, as marketing manager. She pursued a degree in business administration at the Faculty of Business and Economics. She continued her postgraduate studies enrolling in the program—Master of Marketing at South East European University in Tetovo, Macedonia.

Ogechi Adeola teaches Marketing Management at Lagos Business School. She holds a doctorate in Business Administration (DBA) and an MBA from Manchester Business School and a law degree from the University of Nigeria. She has been a guest speaker and discussant at local and international conferences, including the Lagos Chamber of Commerce and Industry (LCCI) business clinic, West African Power Industry Convention (WAPIC), and Yale Africa-China Conference. She has published academic papers in top scholarly journals. Adeola currently serves as Associate Dean of Business Administration at the University of the People, an accredited online institution, headquartered in Pasadena, California, USA.

Noor Hazlina Ahmad PhD is a Professor at the School of Management Universiti Sains Malaysia. She teaches entrepreneurship and organisational behaviour related subjects. Her research interests are in the areas of Entrepreneurship, SMEs and Organisational Behaviour. She has published her work in high impact journals such as Journal of Small Business Management, Journal of Business Ethics, Management Decision, Social Indicators Research and many more. Currently, she serves as the President of the Asian Academy of Management and sits on the editorial board of the Asian Academy of Management Journal.

Grisna Anggadwita obtained her Bachelor's degree from the Department of Electrical and Communications, Telkom Institute of Technology Bandung, Indonesia. She continued her graduate studies in Management Science at the School of Business and Management, Bandung Institute of Technology, Indonesia. She received a scholarship from Tanoto Foundation when she continued her study. She became a Research Assistant in interest group of Entrepreneurial and Technology Management in the School of Business and Management, ITB. Currently, she joined as a Lecturer at the Faculty of Economic and Business, Telkom University, Indonesia. Her research interests include technology management, women entrepreneurship, business incubator, and innovation management.

Börje Boers, PhD, is a Senior Lecturer at the School of Business, University of Skovde, Skovde, Sweden. His research interests concern family firms, organizational identity, and entrepreneurship. He is a member of the research group of Strategic Entrepreneurship at the University of Skovde and affiliated member at the Centre for Family Enterprise and Ownership at Jonkoping International Business School, Jonkoping, Sweden.

Qiuhong Boers MSc in Communication, Gothenburg University, Sweden, and MA language and Culture in Europe, Linkoping University, Sweden. As a native Chinese, Qiuhong is interested in intercultural communication, in particular the communication of cultural, professional, and gender identity.

Alexandra Braga has a PhD in Management. She is a Assistant Professor at the School of Technology and Management, Polytechnic of Porto, and Researcher in the Centre for Transdisciplinary Development Studies and in the Centre for Research and Innovation in Business Sciences and Information Systems. Her research on innovation and knowledge management has been presented at numerous international conferences, and she has published in various international journals.

Mathilde Bru is a postgraduate student at the ESC Rennes School of Business. She holds a Master of Science in International Marketing from the ESC Rennes School of Business. She is currently conducting academic research in the field of co-creation and the role of lead users and opinion leaders.

Mustafa Fedai Cavus received his PhD degree from Selcuk University, Turkey. He is a full-time professor of management and strategy at the Faculty of Economics and Administrative Sciences, Department of Management Information Systems, Osmaniye Korkut Ata University, in Turkey. His research interests include organizational behavior, human resource management, and small business.

Carlo Drago is an Assistant Professor in probability and mathematical statistics at the University "Niccolò Cusano" (Italy), where he teaches Probability and Statistics. He received the PhD in Statistics at the University of Napoli "Federico II". He has been visiting lecturer at the University of Porto (Portugal) and visiting scholar at the Universidad Pontificia Comillas de Madrid (Spain). His research interests focus on network analysis, analysis of time series, nonparametric statistics and symbolic data analysis. He has published in journals such *as Cliometrica, Applied Health Economics and Health Policy, Physica A, International Review of Law and Economics.*

Olaniyi Evans is a consultant, lecturer, author, and the founder of Analystman, a Lagos-based company specialized in research solutions and data analysis. Prior to founding Analystman, Evans managed a wide variety of research project types and sizes at the Lagos Business School. He also designed and taught several economics modules at the University of Lagos. In addition, Evans is the author of *How to Get a First-class Degree*, *The Psychology of First-class Students*, and *The Art of Research.* He holds BSc (first-class) and MSc (distinction) degrees in Economics from the University of Lagos, where he is currently a doctoral student.

Gianluca Ginesti is a Lecturer in accounting at the University of Naples of "Federico II" (Italy) and he obtained the PhD in accounting and business administration at the University of Campania "Luigi Vanvitelli" (Italy). He has been visiting scholar at the Bangor Business School—Bangor University (United Kingdom). Dr. Ginesti has published in journals such as *Journal of Accounting and Public Policy, Corporate Governance: The International Journal of Business in Society, Financial Reporting and Finance Research Letters*. His research interests focus on financial reporting complexity, international financial reporting standard (IFRS) and corporate governance.

Ratih Hurriyati is a Professor of Marketing Management at the University of Education, Indonesia. She has research interests in business, management, marketing, service management, and strategic entrepreneurship.

Cici Xiao He She received her PhD in international business from the University of Otago, New Zealand. Her main research area is international business. She is now a postdoc research fellow at the University of Otago and degree program manager at Overseas Education Colleague of Shanghai Jiao Tong University.

Afam Icha-Ituma is a Reader in Management Studies at FUNAI (Federal University Ndufu-Alike, Ikwo), Nigeria. Prior to joining FUNAI, he held a number of academic positions in the UK, including Lecturer at Brunel University, Academic Consultant at Mountbatten Institute, and Senior Lecturer at Bournemouth University. He has been a Visiting Research Fellow at Kingston Business School (UK), the University of Leiden (Netherlands), and the University of Lisbon. His work has been published in a number of Journals including Human Relations, International Human Resource Management Journal, Personnel Review, Career Development International, and International Journal of Management Education.

Paul Igwe is a Lecturer at the University of South Wales UK—Faculty of Business and Society where he has responsibility for teaching and leading modules across Entrepreneurship, International Business, and Economics modules. Prior to his current role, Paul undertook postdoctorate position combining research and teaching at the University of Plymouth between 2013 and 2016 (where he obtained his MSc and PhD degrees). Under this role, he undertook three external funded research projects. Paul's research interest includes—SMEs start-up and strategies, family and gender issues in entrepreneurship, household savings and investments behavior, and entrepreneurship in the developing economies.

Ayse Gokcen Kapusuz graduated from the Nigde University, Faculty of Economics and Administrative Sciences, Department of Business, Nigde, Turkey, 2008. She graduated with a PhD from Osmaniye Korkut Atta University, Osmaniye/Turkey in June 2016. Now she is working as an academician in Adiyaman

University, Turkey. Her research focuses on human resource management and organizational behavior.

Masoud Karami has a PhD in Marketing with a focus on Iranian consumer's cultural value from the University of Tehran, Iran. Recently, he is doing his second PhD in International Entrepreneurship at the Department of Marketing at the University of Otago, New Zealand. He has published in journals such as the Journal of Islamic Marketing and Advances in International Management.

Norris Krueger is a leading authority on entrepreneurial cognition and its application to entrepreneurial learning and training. For example, he is leading efforts to apply neuroscience to entrepreneurship research. He is the most cited author on entrepreneurial intentions and a leading consultant on developing entrepreneurs. He researches and speaks on building entrepreneurship training programs.

Carmem Leal has a PhD in Management. She is an assistant professor of knowledge management at the University of Trás-os-Montes and Alto Douro (UTAD). She is currently a researcher at the Centre for Transdisciplinary Development Studies (CETRAD). Her research on knowledge management and intellectual capital has been presented at numerous international conferences. At the moment, her research focuses on knowledge management within enterprises' performance.

Marlene Loureiro has a PhD in Communication Sciences. She is an assistant professor of Communication Sciences at the University of Trás-os-Montes and Alto Douro (UTAD). She is currently a researcher at LABCOM.IFP—Communication, Philosophy and Humanities Research Unit of University of Beira Interior. At the moment, her research focuses on organizational and interpersonal communication and gender studies.

Bachruddin Saleh Luturlean is a researcher in the School of Economic and Business, Telkom University, Bandung, Indonesia.

Riccardo Macchioni is a Full Professor in accounting at the University of Campania "Luigi Vanvitelli" (Italy), where he teaches in undergraduate and postgraduate modules on financial accounting. Professor Macchioni has published several monographs in theme of accounting and in journals such as *Accounting Forum, Financial Reporting* and *Italian Accounting Review* (RIREA). His research interests focus on financial reporting, generally accepted accounting principles and international financial reporting standard (IFRS).

Robert Newbery is a Senior Lecturer in Enterprise and Innovation and has worked extensively in Asia, Africa, Europe, and North America. He has founded and run a number of entrepreneurial businesses having a PhD, MSc, MBA, and BSc. He is Principal Investigator for a Comic Relief funded project "Scaling innovative rural distribution for farmer inputs" in Kenya and is developing the Rural Business

Network development concept with colleagues internationally. Robert is particularly interested in how entrepreneurship is being used for development in both the "Global North" and "Global South."

Michael Z. Ngoasong is a Lecturer in Management at Open University. His current and main research is focused on development entrepreneurship, digital entrepreneurship, and women's social entrepreneurship in developing countries, with a strong regional focus on Sub-Saharan Africa. After receiving a PhD from the University of Nottingham, he worked as an academic at Coventry University London Campus, where he taught and researched international business and management. His research has been published in leading journals such as Strategic Change: Briefings in Entrepreneurial Finance, Human Resources Development International, Annals of Tourism Research, Tourism Management, and Energy Policy.

Ramo Palalić is an Assistant Professor at the Faculty of Business and Administration, Management Department, International University of Sarajevo, Bosnia and Herzegovina. He teaches in both undergraduate and postgraduate level in the area of entrepreneurship and small business management, marketing, and international management. His research interest covers entrepreneurship, small and medium enterprises, leadership, and marketing.

Nazmiye Ulku Pekkan completed her license degree at Anadolu University Business Administration Faculty. Graduated from Kahramanmaras Sutcu Imam University Business Administration with thesis Master Program in 2012. She worked as a lecturer at Toros University between 2014 and 2016 in Turkey.

Veland Ramadani is an Associate Professor at South East European University, Republic of Macedonia, where he teaches both undergraduate and postgraduate courses in entrepreneurship and small business management. His research interests include entrepreneurship, small business management, entrepreneurial marketing, and business development. He has authored around 80 research articles and 16 books. He services on the editorial and review boards of several journals from the field of entrepreneurship and management.

Zaiben Nisah Mohd Rashid obtained her MBA from the Graduate School of Business, Universiti Sains Malaysia. Her research interests are in the areas of Entrepreneurship and SMEs, particularly looking into the performance of women entrepreneurs.

Laurent Scaringella is an assistant professor and director of the Master of Science in International Marketing at the ESC Rennes School of Business. He holds two BSc degrees, one from Turku Polytechnics and another from Université Pierre Mendès France. He holds MIB and DBA degrees from Grenoble Ecole de Management. He was involved in several projects funded by the European Commission during the course of his doctoral studies. He is a Visiting Scholar at the

Haas School of Business at the University of California, Berkeley. He has published articles in journals such as Technological Forecasting and Social Change, the Journal of Engineering and Technology Management, the International Journal of Entrepreneurship and Small Business, the International Journal of Entrepreneurship and Innovation Management, European Journal of Innovation Management, and the Journal of Organization Design

Pi-Shen Seet is Professor of Entrepreneurship and Innovation in the Management discipline at Edith Cowan University's School of Business and Law. He conducts research and supervises research students in entrepreneurship, innovation, family business, international business and human resource management. He has held positions at Flinders University and University of Adelaide. A Philosophy, Politics and Economics graduate from Oxford University, he completed his PhD at the Judge Business School, University of Cambridge. He is visiting scholar at the Nanyang Technopreneurship Centre, Nanyang Technological University, Singapore and the Joint Research Center for Sino-Foreign Family Business, School of Management and Economics, Beijing Institute of Technology.

Yuliani Suseno, PhD, is a senior lecturer at Edith Cowan University, Perth, Australia. She received her PhD from the UQ Business School, The University of Queensland, Australia.

Pattanee Susomrith PhD lectures in Organisational Behaviour and Human Resource Management units at Edith Cowan University, School of Business and Law, in Western Australia. She is also a member of the Faculty's Centre for Innovation Practice and a professional member of the Australian Human Resource Institute. Her research interests include workplace learning in small and medium enterprises, human resource outsourcing, innovation, and employee turnover.

Lili Adi Wibowo is a Professor at the Indonesia University of Education, Bandung, Indonesia.

Shang Zhengang got his Bachelor's Degree of Economics from Dongbei University of Finance and Economics and Master's Degree of Management from Hohai University. He is studying the Doctoral of Business Administration at the University of Otago.

Mr. Shang published several papers of international business and finance and a book of continual education. His research area covers the transformation of organization, leadership, and innovation of enterprises. He is one of the founders and executive dean of Overseas Education College (OEC) of Shanghai Jiao Tong University. OEC has provided the training programs for more than 80,000 Chinese managers and entrepreneurs. Recently, OEC becomes the top-list continual education college in China.

Knowledge, Learning and Innovation: Research into Cross-Sector Collaboration

Vanessa Ratten, Carla Susana Marques, and Vitor Braga

Abstract This introductory chapter discusses the role of knowledge, learning and innovation in terms of research into cross-sector collaboration. An essential part of this collaboration is entrepreneurship, which links knowledge, learning and innovation. An overview of the main trends within the innovation field is examined that highlights the interdisciplinary perspective of studies around the learning organization and knowledge management. This helps to stress how firms and individuals need to be entrepreneurial when engaging in cross-sector collaboration. The chapter concludes with an overview of the chapters in this book and suggestions about the practical importance of knowledge, learning and innovation is cross-sector collaboration.

Keywords Knowledge • Learning • Innovation • Cross-sector collaboration • Entrepreneurship

1 Introduction

This chapter focuses on the links between knowledge, learning and innovation by examining the entrepreneurship involved in cross-sector collaborations. Innovation is evident in a variety of cross-sector collaborations but most derive from the sharing of knowledge between individuals or organizations. Baregheh, Rowley, and Sambrook (2009: 1323) state "as marketplaces become more dynamic, interest in innovation, its processes and management has escalated". This has resulted in innovation being at the core of global competitiveness and it plays a central role in

V. Ratten (✉)
La Trobe University, Melbourne, VIC, Australia
e-mail: v.ratten@latrobe.edu.au

C.S. Marques
University of Tras-os-Montes e Alto Douro, Vila Real, Portugal
e-mail: smarques@utad.pt

V. Braga
Polytechnic Institute of Porto, Porto, Portugal
e-mail: vbraga@estgf.ipp.pt

V. Ratten et al. (eds.), *Knowledge, Learning and Innovation*, Contributions to Management Science, DOI 10.1007/978-3-319-59282-4_1

collaborations. In this book, we define innovation broadly by suggesting it represents creative change that has a positive impact on society. This enables a focus on how knowledge and learning lead to strategic renewal in the form of organizational and individual change.

Ettlie and Reza (1992) suggest the most common types of innovation include new organizational forms, processes, products, services and technology. Thus, the wide ranging types of innovation mean that it is important to understand the precursors as a way of identifying the successful way knowledge is transformed. As the word 'innovation' is hard to define it means there is some overlap with the concepts of knowledge and learning. However, we define knowledge as information that can be used for a specific purpose and is learnt through collaboration. This means that at the heart of innovation is an organizational perspective that utilises the internal and external changing business environment (Damanpour, 1991).

An early definition of innovation is proposed by Kimberly (1981: 108) who suggests three statges: "innovation as a process, innovation as discrete item including products, programs or services; and innovation as an attribute of organizations". Most discussions around innovation involve the role of newness to changing business practices. Some definitions of innovation link it explicitly to knowledge. Knowledge can take a variety of forms but often involves commercial, design, management and technical activities (Rothwell, 1992). When an innovation is utilized there needs to be a degree of entrepreneurship in terms of its marketing or practical application. Baregheh et al. (2009) suggests that the innovation process has six steps: stages, social, means, nature, type and aim. In the stages process, ideas are created and generated using information and knowledge. These ideas are then implemented into the marketplace depending on their suitability and cost. Afterwards the ideas are developed into products or services that are then adopted into the market. In the social stage, the ideas are disseminated to a group of stakeholders including customers, employees and organizations. This helps to develop a social system around the idea and how it can enter into the market. Sometimes this might include the use of other firms and developers who can collaborate for beneficial reasons. In the means stage, the ideas are then discussed in terms of creative capabilities. This helps create inventions often using technological innovation. The nature stage involves nurturing the ideas in terms of looking at ways to improve them (Ratten, 2016). This might happen organically as ideas gestate in the marketplace. At other times there may need to be a strategic intervention in terms of changing the innovation to suit the market.

The type stage involves focusing on the kind of innovation that is under development such as product, service, process or technological (Ratten, 2011). Finally, the last stage involves examining the aim of the innovation to see how it can succeed, differentiate and compete in the marketplace (Ratten, 2012). Therefore, it can be argued that innovation is similar to learning and knowledge but each has its distinct meaning (Ferreira, Fernandes, & Ratten, 2016). As business management is becoming more interdisciplinary it helps to focus on innovation as a way of leveraging collaborative efforts (Gerguri-Rashiti, Ramadani, Abazi-Alili, Dana, & Ratten, 2017).

In this chapter, we suggest that cross-sector collaboration is facilitated by knowledge, learning and innovation. This helps researchers and practitioners encourage more collaboration by closely investigating how they use knowledge. An important contribution of this book is that it develops a better understanding of the linkages between knowledge, learning and innovation in order to arrive at a conclusion that entrepreneurship is involved in all forms.

2 Overview of Chapters

This first chapter of the book by the co-editors Vanessa Ratten, Carla Susana Marques and Vitor Braga has discussed the role of knowledge, learning and innovation in cross-sector collaboration. The second chapter by Noor Ahmad, Yuliani Suseno, Pi-Shen Seet, Pattanee Susomrith and Zaiben Rashid discusses the linkage between entrepreneurial competences and learning in an emerging economies context. This is helpful to understand the way women entrepreneurs access learning in order to facilitate innovation in the form of firm performance. The third chapter by Mathilde Bru and Laurent Scaringella discusses the role of knowledge and innovation in the form of co-creation. The importance of opinion leaders in harnessing the learning obtained in an organizational context is discussed. The fourth chapter by Vanessa Ratten, Carmem Leal, Marlene Loureiro, Rui Silva and Alexandra Braga examines the role of knowledge and innovation in Portuguese enterprises. This is helpful in understanding the role of cross-sector collaborations in a European setting. The fifth chapter by Masoud Karami and Cici Xiao He discusses social ties and human capital, which are an important part of knowledge sharing. This is important particularly for the internationalization of small and medium sized enterprises who utilize their knowledge for global competitiveness. The sixth chapter Ayse Gokcen Kapusuz, Mustafa Fedai Cavus and Nazmiye Ulku Pekkan discusses the role of knowledge in the form of social entrepeneurship. This is important in facilitating learning about how individuals and communities can give better social support particularly to females in business. The seventh chapter by Paul Igwe, Robert Newbery and Afam Icha-Ituma discusses the entrepreneurship challenges, which often occur when knowledge is shared through cross-sector partnerships. The eighth chapter by Qiuhong Boers and Börje Boers examines the role of professional identities, which is important in the knowledge economy. Increasingly female entrepreneurs are learning about ways they can succeed in business and this often occurs as a result of knowledge acquisition. The ninth chapter by Veland Ramadani, Lutfije Ademi, Vanessa Ratten, Ramo Palalić and Norris Krueger focuses on the role of knowledge creation and relationship marketing in family businesses. This is important as family firms in particular learn through relationships about important market developments. The tenth chapter by Ogechi Adeola, Michael Ngoasong, and Olaniyi Evans examines how people learn and share knowledge based on their gender. This is an interesting research avenue to take as it influences business developments in family businesses.

The eleventh chapter by Gianluca Ginesti, Carlo Drago and Riccardo Macchioni discusses the role of information transparency. As information becomes increasingly important to business this helps to understand the way family firms handle the information sharing process. The twelfth chapter by Bachruddin Saleh Luturleen, Ratih Hurriyati, Lili Adi Wibowo and Grisna Anggadwita discusses the role of customers intentions to re-visit hotel resorts. This is an important way organisations can gather knowledge about the success of their innovations.

3 Conclusion

Knowledge, learning and innovation are key strategic issues in the global marketplace. At the heart of these issues is entrepreneurship, which can take a variety of different forms for cross-sector collaboration. In this introductory chapter, we have discussed the importance of innovation and how it is linked to learning and knowledge. In this book, we suggest that there is a need for a more holistic understanding of cross-sector collaboration, by highlighting entrepreneurial capabilities of individuals and organizations.

References

Baregheh, A., Rowley, J., & Sambrook, S. (2009). Towards a multidisciplinary definition of innovation. *Management Decision, 47*(8), 1323–1339.

Damanpour, F. (1991). Organisational innovation: A meta-analysis of effects of determinants and moderators. *Academy of Management Journal, 34*(3), 555–590.

Ettlie, J. E., & Reza, E. M. (1992). Organizational integration and process innovation. *Academy of Management Journal, 35*(4), 795–827.

Ferreira, J. J., Fernandes, C., & Ratten, V. (2016). A co-citation bibliometric analysis of strategic management research. *Scientometrics, 109*(1), 1–32.

Gerguri-Rashiti, S., Ramadani, V., Abazi-Alili, H., Dana, L. P., & Ratten, V. (2017). ICT, innovation and firm performance: The transition economies context. *Thunderbird International Business Review, 59*(1), 93–102.

Kimberly, T. R. (1981). Management innovation. In P. C. Nystrom & W. H. Starbuck (Eds.), *Handbook of organization design*. Oxford: Oxford University Press.

Ratten, V. (2011). Ethics, entrepreneurship and the adoption of e-book devices. *International Journal of Innovation and Learning, 10*(3), 310–325.

Ratten, V. (2012). Sports entrepreneurship: Towards a conceptualisation. *International Journal of Entrepreneurial Venturing, 4*(1), 1–17.

Ratten, V. (2016). The dynamics of sport marketing: Suggestions for marketing intelligence and planning. *Marketing Intelligence and Planning, 34*(2), 162–168.

Rothwell, R. (1992). Successful industrial innovation: Critical factors for the 1990s. *R&D Management, 22*(3), 221–237.

Entrepreneurial Competencies and Firm Performance in Emerging Economies: A Study of Women Entrepreneurs in Malaysia

Noor Hazlina Ahmad, Yuliani Suseno, Pi-Shen Seet, Pattanee Susomrith, and Zaiben Rashid

Abstract This study examines the effects of the different types of entrepreneurial competencies on firm performance in ventures founded by women entrepreneurs in Malaysia. Focusing on the concept of entrepreneurial competencies incorporating competencies of analytical planning, innovation, enforcement/implementation, leadership, teamwork and networking, we tested the relationships between these different types of entrepreneurial competencies and firm performance using data collected from 117 women entrepreneurs in Malaysia. Our findings indicate that only enforcement/implementation and network competencies have significant effects on firm performance. In particular, we find that network competency firm performance. The paper sheds some light in relation to women's entrepreneurship in emerging economies, and recommends further research that could assist policymakers in implementing more effective initiatives to encourage and develop women entrepreneurs for the success of the economy.

Keywords Entrepreneurial competencies • Firm performance • Women entrepreneurs • Emerging economies

1 Introduction

Entrepreneurs have long been considered as playing an important role in facilitating economic development and growth (Acs & Audretsch, 2010; Carree & Thurik, 2010; Thurik, Carree, Stel, & Audretsch, 2008). Entrepreneurship scholars have highlighted that entrepreneurship provides opportunities for job creation (e.g., Litwin & Phan, 2013), alleviates high unemployment among youth (e.g., Baptista & Preto, 2007; Thurik et al., 2008), and even facilitates innovation and economic

N.H. Ahmad • Z. Rashid
Universiti Sains Malaysia, Penang, Malaysia
e-mail: hazlina@usm.my; zaibenrashid@yahoo.com

Y. Suseno (✉) • P.-S. Seet • P. Susomrith
Edith Cowan University, Joondalup, WA, Australia
e-mail: y.suseno@ecu.edu.au; p.seet@ecu.edu.au; p.susomrith@ecu.edu.au

V. Ratten et al. (eds.), *Knowledge, Learning and Innovation*, Contributions to Management Science, DOI 10.1007/978-3-319-59282-4_2

growth (e.g., Keilbach, Tamvada, & Audretsch, 2009). Arguably, entrepreneurship is also a crucial mechanism in the development of emerging economies as entrepreneurship contributes to increased productivity and economic growth (Acs & Virgill, 2010; Beck, 2009; OECD, 2009).

Within the entrepreneurship field, research on women's entrepreneurship is progressing steadily (e.g., Ahl, 2006; Ahl & Marlow, 2012; Baughn, Chua, & Neupert, 2006; de Bruin, Brush, & Welter, 2006, 2007; Elam, 2008; Elam & Terjesen, 2007). As Minniti, Allen, and Langowitz (2006) noted, there is "a clear picture of a gender gap in new venture creation and ownership activity". However, most of the research on women's entrepreneurship has been in the context of developed economies (Minniti & Naudė, 2010), and less in fact has been known about female participation in family businesses' entrepreneurial activities in emerging economies. For instance, while findings from the Global Entrepreneurship Monitor (GEM) studies indicate that women entrepreneurs in low/middle-income countries are less likely than male entrepreneurs to keep their business surviving beyond 42 months (Allen, Elam, Langowitz, & Dean, 2007; Minniti et al., 2006), they did not examine some of the factors that helped those women entrepreneurs to survive and succeed. Recent studies on women's entrepreneurship have thus called for greater attention to the role of women entrepreneurs (Calás, Smircich, & Bourne, 2009; Verheul, Uhlaner, & Thurik, 2005), particularly in emerging economies.

New start-ups by women entrepreneurs have accelerated significantly in the past decade, and this rate has even outpaced the rate of businesses created by male entrepreneurs (Minniti & Naudė, 2010; Weiler & Bernasek, 2001). Coupled with the fact that women entrepreneurs own a total of approximately 37% of companies globally (VanderBrug, 2013), there is a need to examine women entrepreneurs as the founders and leaders of family businesses (Pines, Lerner, & Schwartz, 2010). There is indeed still limited empirical research into understanding what these women entrepreneurs have or do to succeed in their business, especially in the resource-constrained environments of emerging economies.

Using the theory of the resource-based view (RBV) of new ventures, we focus on the concept of entrepreneurial competencies using validated measures developed by Brinckmann (2006), incorporating competencies of analytical planning, innovation, enforcement/implementation, teamwork, leadership and networking. Specifically, we examine the role of the different types of entrepreneurial competencies in an emerging economy, in this case Malaysia, and address the extent to which women entrepreneurs have these entrepreneurial competencies to help their firm performance.

The study makes the following two significant contributions. First, it provides an empirical test of the importance of entrepreneurial competencies to firm performance in entrepreneurial ventures by women entrepreneurs. Second, it provides a further understanding of women entrepreneurs in family businesses in the context of emerging economies—a focus that has not been sufficiently explored in existing research studies. Indeed, Hughes, Jennings, Brush, Carter, and Welter (2012) note that further research on women's entrepreneurship needs to be explored in new directions. This study thus provides a starting point for discussion to ensure greater involvement and success of women entrepreneurs in developing and growing their family businesses in emerging economies.

The chapter starts as follows. We first outline a section on women's entrepreneurship in the context of Malaysia as the focus of the study. We then describe the theory of the resource-based view particularly with regard to entrepreneurial competencies. Third, we outline our methodology and the findings of our study. We next outline our discussion and the limitations of the research, and conclude by recommending that further research be conducted on other aspects of the Global Entrepreneurship Monitor's (GEM's) conceptual model such as the entrepreneurial framework conditions, that could assist policymakers help grow and assist women entrepreneurs to enhance their contributions to the economy.

2 Women Entrepreneurs in Malaysia

Women entrepreneurs make significant contributions to employment, wealth creation and innovation in all economies (Ahl & Marlow, 2012; Brush, Carter, Gatewood, Greene, & Hart, 2006; Elam, 2008; Elam & Terjesen, 2007). Although entrepreneurial activities among women in many countries are growing (Minniti et al., 2006), women's entrepreneurship remains an understudied area (de Bruin et al., 2006). One of the many reasons cited for this is that studies on entrepreneurship were conducted in a "generic" manner, with an assumption that there is no need to segregate women from men entrepreneurs for they presumably would have similar characteristics (de Bruin et al., 2007). This has led to entrepreneurship theory explaining new venture creation based simply on three basic constructs of the 3Ms, i.e. "market, money and management" (Brush, de Bruin, & Welter, 2009). However, Brush et al. (2009) have argued that since all entrepreneurship is socially embedded (Davidsson, 2004; Steyaert & Katz, 2004), there is a need to extend the field of entrepreneurship research to further understand women's entrepreneurship.

Extant research findings have noted that women seem to be less entrepreneurial than their men counterpart. Women entrepreneurs were also found to display lower risk-taking approaches (Brindley, 2005) and were less likely to be successful at new venture creation than men as they were more cautious and conservative (de Bruin et al., 2006). In addition, there is a societal expectation that women's main role is to be the main care-givers for their families and that they possess less entrepreneurial capabilities. The challenges of overcoming societal perceptions have an impact on women acquiring resources for entrepreneurial ventures (Mitchelmore & Rowley, 2013). This is evident in the findings of the Diana Project indicating that <6% of equity investments over a 30-year period in the USA went to women-owned ventures (Greene, Brush, Hart, & Saparito, 2001). Subsequent research has confirmed that this could either be due to discrimination among providers of capital against women entrepreneurs or that women entrepreneurs themselves were unwilling to seek capital (Orser, Riding, & Manley, 2006).

The Malaysian economy has undergone dramatic changes in the last two decades as part of the country's move to transform itself from a labour-intensive manufacturing economy into a knowledge-based one. The role of women in Malaysia's economic transformation is significant especially in terms of increasing the pool of human capital in the country. With an increasing level of education among female workers, and with more girls than boys progressing to advanced level of education in Malaysia (UNICEF, 2005), women provide not only skilled and professional human capital to small-medium sized companies and to large corporations but also contribute as entrepreneurs to the future growth of the Malaysian economy.

Malaysian women entrepreneurs play an important role in the economic growth of the country. To promote, encourage and support women entrepreneurs in Malaysia, there are several women entrepreneur associations in Malaysia that provide a platform for them to network, for example, the Federation of Women Entrepreneurs Association Malaysia (FEM), National Association of Women Entrepreneurs of Malaysia (NAWEM), and the Persatuan Usahawan Wanita Bumiputera (USAHANITA). However, despite the role that women play in contributing to the growth of the economy, empirical studies on women's entrepreneurship is still limited. There is indeed little research into understanding what these women entrepreneurs have and do to overcome social and economic hurdles, especially in the resource-constrained environments of emerging economies.

To better inform the field of research on women's entrepreneurship, we use the resource-based theory, focusing on entrepreneurial competencies, as competencies have been found to be related to the growth of women-led businesses (Langowitz & Minniti, 2007; Mitchelmore, Rowley, & Shiu, 2014). To become successful entrepreneurs, women essentially need to look for every single opportunity, and need to have the ability to assess all these opportunities and exploit them. Women entrepreneurs also need to possess skills, knowledge and the ability to gather information and execute opportunities for success (Naser, Mohammed, & Nuseibeh, 2009). Such skills, knowledge and ability are essentially competencies, or to be more exact, entrepreneurial competencies. Alvarez and Barney (2000) have argued that entrepreneurial cognition, entrepreneurial alertness and coordinating knowledge are examples of such entrepreneurial competencies. In this study, we aim to analyse the role of the different types of entrepreneurial competencies and address the extent to which women entrepreneurs in Malaysia have these entrepreneurial competencies to help their firm performance.

3 Resource-Based View Theory and Entrepreneurial Competencies

The resource-based view (RBV) theory implies that a firm's competitive advantage is generated from its unique set of resources (Barney, 1991). These resources can be management skills, organisational processes, and knowledge (Barney, 1991). In order to sustain competitive advantage, a resource must be valuable (worth something), rare (unique), inimitable (cannot be easily sold or traded), and non-substitutable (Barney, 1991). One critical resource to gain such competitive advantage is entrepreneurial competencies (Mitchelmore et al., 2014).

In advocating a competency approach, it is necessary to have a clear understanding of the concept of "competency". Many definitions of "competency(ies)" appear in the literature, leading to considerable confusion around the exact meaning of the concept. Arguably, the most common argument is related to the difference between "competency(ies)" and "competence". These terms are often used interchangeably, despite being seen as distinct concepts. For example, Rowe (1995) defines "competence" as a skill or standard of performance, in contrast to "competency(ies)" which refers to a behaviour in which performance is achieved. Hoffmann (1999) further observes that competencies can be defined in three different ways: (i) observable performance (the output); (ii) the standard of the outcome, or result, of a person's performance; and (iii) the underlying attributes of a person, such as his/her knowledge, skills, and abilities. Most studies that attempt to understand managerial competencies adopt this definition of competency.

Clearly, the meanings given to the concept of a competency, or competencies, drawn from the management and entrepreneurship literature are applied in different ways ranging from the very broad to more specific. However, four important facets of competencies appear to be common to these definitions:

1. Competencies include the overall characteristics of an individual that are related to the his/her effective performance of a given job;
2. Competencies are manifested in the individual's behaviour, and are therefore observable and measurable;
3. Competencies facilitate the accomplishment of goals and objectives;
4. Competencies are organisational resources that can be fostered and nurtured.

Researchers have argued that there are competencies specific to managers and entrepreneurs and that these may differ, with entrepreneurial competencies being perceived to be more complex (Busenitz & Barney, 1997). Hodgetts and Kuratko (2001) concur that there is a distinction between entrepreneurial behaviours and managerial behaviours, but assert that in managing a business, each complements the other, and that the ability to blend these two areas of competencies is crucial to organisational success. Sadler-Smith, Hampson, Chaston, and Badger (2003: 48) further echo the importance of entrepreneurial competencies:

> Entrepreneurship and managerial competence represent two important and complementary strands for small firm research and practice that appear to have led largely separate existences. An exploration of both of these issues may help to further meaningfully circumscribe the areas of entrepreneurship and small business management and to shed additional light on those managerial behaviours that are associated with entrepreneurship and small firm performance.

Building on from these arguments, Muzychenko and Saee (2004) differentiate between innate and acquired aspects of competency. The former involve traits, attitudes, self-image and social roles and are sometimes referred to as "internalised elements" (Bartlett & Ghoshal, 1997), while the latter involve components acquired at work or through theoretical or practical learning (i.e., skills, knowledge, and experience) and are often referred to as "externalised elements" (Muzychenko & Saee, 2004). The internalised aspects of competencies are difficult to change, whereas the externalised elements can be acquired through proper training and education programs and need to be practised (Garavan & McGuire, 2001; Man & Lau, 2005). In the entrepreneurial context, these competencies are normally studied as characteristics of the entrepreneur who owns and actively manages the business (McGregor & Tweed, 2001).

Studies of entrepreneurial competencies and their association with new venture performance are noteworthy for there are still considerable gaps in the literature (Mitchelmore & Rowley, 2010). Snell and Lau (1994), in a qualitative study to understand the competencies important for the owners and senior managers of small businesses in Hong Kong, found several important competencies for small growing firms, including: having a clear vision and clear purpose; having the ability to formulate effective strategy; using a strategic approach to human resource management; promoting a learning culture; maintaining closeness to customers; and having a focused approach for quality.

Thompson, Stuart, and Lindsay (1997), in an investigation of 30 SMEs in Northern Ireland, further found different types of competencies that are required at the various stages of a firm's development. Competencies found to be important at the early stage of development included foresight and strategic planning, flexibility (ability to change), having a focused mind, fearlessness, tenaciousness, drive and dedication, communication skills, initiative flair, ability to create a good profit margin, global awareness, and an ability to motivate others. In all the other stages of development, competencies such as financial management skills, advertising skills, the ability to assess people and their fit with the organisation, the ability to socialise easily, the ability to understand changing external forces and customer needs, problem solving capability, and the ability to sell ideas (Bortkevičiene & Vaitkevičius, 2016), are important.

Entrepreneurial competencies are essentially viewed as competencies that are most "relevant to the exercise of successful entrepreneurship" (Mitchelmore & Rowley, 2010: 93). Bird (1995) viewed entrepreneurial competencies as the underlying characteristics of specific knowledge, motives, self-images, social roles and skills that can result in the development and growth of a new venture. Entrepreneurial competencies in essence take into account the fact that entrepreneurs need to not only deal with individuals within the organisation, they must also be able to look outside the organisation, take proactive actions and interact effectively with others. In the context of this study, entrepreneurs need to be strategic and analytical in their planning, be innovative, be able to take proactive actions and implement decisions, be competent in their leadership and teamwork skills, as well as being able to interact effectively with others (Brinckmann, 2006). As such, six entrepreneurial competencies are examined: analytical planning competency, innovation competency, enforcement/implementation competency, leadership competency, teamwork competency and networking competency.

Analytical Planning Competency

Analytical planning competency involves the ability to think analytically and be able to cope with uncertainty (Bird, 1995). According to Man and Lau (2005), this competency requires the abilities of entrepreneurs in analysing, problem solving, decision-making, and risk taking. Analytical planning competency also reflects the mental ability to coordinate all of the organisation's interests and activities (Chandler & Jansen, 1992). Entrepreneurs with analytical planning competency are able to identify patterns or situations and are also able to recognise key underpinning issues in complex, challenging situations. Entrepreneurs with analytical planning competency are thus more strategic as they consider industry trends, emerging technology and various opportunities they can capitalise on. In terms of competencies relevant to women entrepreneurs, in their study of 210 women entrepreneurs in England and Wales, Mitchelmore and Rowley (2013) found evidence of analytical thinking in two of their competency clusters as part of their Female Entrepreneur Competence (FEC) framework, namely, business and management competencies and entrepreneurial competencies. Entrepreneurs with analytical planning competency are more open to different approaches, and frequently have fresh and analytical viewpoints to solve problems. They also tend to make better decisions as their analytical thinking is more systematic and logical to address critical business issues to achieve their vision, which potentially contributes to a better firm performance. Therefore, the following hypothesis is formulated:

H_1 Women entrepreneurs' analytical planning competency has a positive relationship with their firm performance.

Innovation Competency

Innovation competency is characterised by divergent and unconventional thinking, imaginativeness, novelty and originality. Innovation competency however does not simply suggest the behaviours necessary to produce novel products, services and/or work processes (Scott & Bruce, 1994; West & Farr, 1990) but it also encompasses the need to be creative. Creativity is essentially a critical stage in the innovation process where performance gaps are recognised and ideas are generated (West, 2002). Earlier research has found evidence of innovativeness being strong among women entrepreneurs (Hisrich & Brush, 1984; Sexton & Bowman-Upton, 1990). Mitchelmore and Rowley (2013), for example, found evidence of innovation competency in the entrepreneurial competencies cluster as part of their Female Entrepreneur Competence (FEC) research. Entrepreneurs with innovation competency are ones who are more likely to identify problems, generate new ideas and be able to implement and commercialise such ideas. They have a creative mind and are often able to imagine how best to exploit opportunities or create demand. Accordingly, they are more likely to deliver new products and/or service which can better serve their customers. This consequently increases firm performance. Hence, the following hypothesis is formulated:

H_2 Women entrepreneurs' innovation competency has a positive relationship with their firm performance.

Enforcement/implementation Competency
Innovative plans in business alone will not bring business success but the implementation of such plans is important to ensure the growth of the business. Thus, enforcement or implementation competency represents another core part of entrepreneurial competencies (Brinckmann, 2006).

Enforcement competency refers to one's persistence to capitalise on opportunities and follow a certain course of actions. This competency is reflected by the "proactiveness" dimension of the entrepreneurial orientation construct. Successful entrepreneurs are ones who take initiatives and make things happen (Brinckmann, 2006). Earlier research on women entrepreneurial competencies have also indicated that women entrepreneurs have enforcement/implementation competency as part of their cluster of business and management competencies (Mitchelmore & Rowley, 2013). These entrepreneurs are proactive in ensuring that they have the critical expertise and experience to implement value-creating strategies. They are focused on implementing strategies to manage resources to achieve their vision. Entrepreneurs who possess enforcement/implementation competency are thus more likely to lead their firm to have better performance. This results in the following hypothesis:

H_3 Women entrepreneurs' enforcement/implementation competency has a positive relationship with their firm performance.

Teamwork Competency
Teamwork competency is crucial when starting a new business. Teamwork competency in entrepreneurial teams is about communication quality, conflict resolution and equal sharing of tasks within the team (Brinckmann, 2006). Teamwork competency is also important to garner cooperation from employees especially when new changes or new strategies are implemented. Teamwork also increases the productivity of the company where tasks can be carried out on time and products and services can be provided in the most effective and efficient manner to customers. Entrepreneurs with high teamwork competency are thus more likely to be able to work interdependently with others while fostering a collaborative environment. With teamwork competency, the performance of the firm is likely to be better as these entrepreneurs encourage collaboration among members, build shared core values and get team members to work towards the same direction. Research on women entrepreneurs have found that successful entrepreneurs tend to focus more on their teams' development, empowering their employees and encouraging their achievements and perseverance (Gundry, Miriam, & Posig, 2002). The teamwork competency was also found to feature and be valued more strongly in women networks than their male counterparts, with women entrepreneurs demonstrating teamwork competency as part of their personal and relationship competencies as well as human relations competencies (Mitchelmore & Rowley, 2013). Therefore, the following hypothesis applies:

H_4 Women entrepreneurs' teamwork competency has a positive relationship with their firm performance.

Leadership Competency

Leadership competency implies a capability to inspire the whole organisation to align employee behaviours to the vision, mission and objectives of the organisation. It is about creating a performance-driven culture, where leaders provide consultation, joint decision making and delegation (Yukl, 2013). Leadership competency facilitates everyone to work towards a common goal despite dealing with adversity in order to produce a beneficial outcome (de Jong & Den Hartog, 2007). Leadership competency, especially in women, was found to feature and be valued more strongly than their male counterparts (Mitchelmore & Rowley, 2013), and this had a significant link to their leadership styles (Bamiatzi, Jones, Mitchelmore, & Nikolopoulos, 2015). Entrepreneurs with leadership competency are capable of directing their followers towards specific goals (Shane, 2003). They are more likely to be committed (Erikson, 2002), and are also driven to use their capability to create a positive culture for the growth of the company. In addition, they are able to influence others to achieve value-added results. As such, we argue that entrepreneurs with leadership competency can potentially able to drive their firm to achieve better performance. Hence, the following hypothesis is formulated:

H_5 Women entrepreneurs' leadership competency has a positive relationship with their firm performance.

Network Competency

Network competency has been defined as the ability to build social interactions that enable the execution of tasks such as planning, coordination and control (Ritter, Wilkinson, & Johnston, 2002). In addition, network competency is also about the ability to build and utilise networks with partners like investors, technology and marketing partners, and other stakeholders (Brinckmann, 2006). Such networks facilitate social interactions that enable resources to be exchanged and benefits to be created.

Earlier research has suggested that one of the areas in which women entrepreneurs may outshine men is in their abilities to build strong inter-personal relationships (Daniel, 2004; Fuller-Love, Lim, & Akehurst, 2006). Women entrepreneurs have also been found to be effective at using networking as part of their strategic planning (Lerner, Brush, & Hisrich, 1997; Morris, Miyasaki, Watters, & Coombes, 2006). Previous studies have further indicated that individuals with good networking skills are better placed in achieving beneficial outcomes than those who lack the same (Baron & Markman, 2003).

Entrepreneurs need to do a lot of negotiations, and they are continuously meeting and interacting with individuals within and outside their business. Therefore, networking competency is important to help entrepreneurs accomplish the goals which would enhance their ventures' success. In a study by Ahmad, Ramayah, Wilson, and Kummerow (2010), it was found that Malaysian entrepreneurs rated relationship competency (as reflected in their good networking skill) as one of the important skills that entrepreneurs need to be equipped with. Entrepreneurs need to not only be connected with others, but more importantly, they must be able to use their connections with others in order for them to move their ventures forward (Baron & Markman, 2003). Entrepreneurs with better networking competencies are thus more likely to achieve better firm performance. Therefore, this results in the following hypothesis:

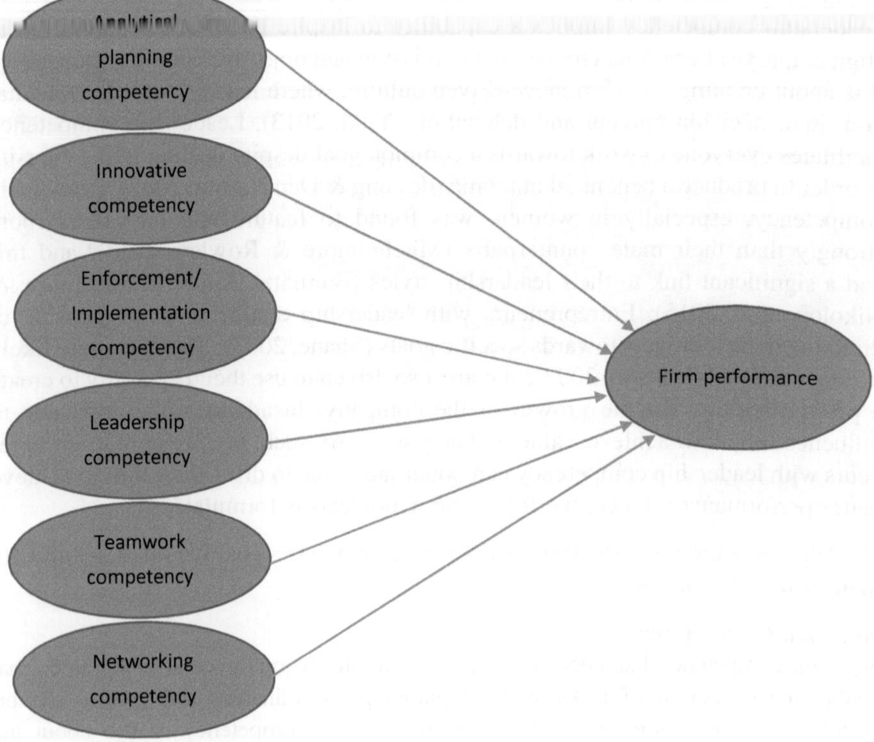

Fig. 1 Theoretical framework for the study

Figure 1 depicts the theoretical framework and the hypotheses.

H_6 Women entrepreneurs' network competency has a positive relationship with their firm performance.

4 Methodology

We adopted a quantitative method to collect data using established items and scales from earlier studies. Participants were selected using convenience sampling from women entrepreneurs in Malaysia. Our questionnaire was pre-tested using a group of 20 women entrepreneurs from the service industry such as laundry service, education (tuition centre and pre-school), computer centres, travel agencies and wedding planners. Feedback from these participants indicated that the questionnaire items were clear and easy to understand. Minor changes were implemented as a result of the feedback.

A total of 300 questionnaires were then distributed to women entrepreneurs and 117 questionnaires were returned as completed questionnaires, representing a response rate of 39%. A total of 23 items were used to measure the study's independent variable (firm performance) and entrepreneurial competencies, incorporating six main dimensions: analytical planning competency, innovation competency, enforcement/implementation competency, teamwork competency, leadership competency and networking competency. The construct of entrepreneurial competencies and their dimensions were adapted from the study by Brinckmann, Salomo, and Gemuenden (2005). To measure the construct of firm performance, the scale developed by Gupta and Govindarajan (1984) was adopted. All items were based on a 5-point Likert scale ranging from very low (1) to very high (5). The reliability test was used to ensure the consistency or stability of the items (Sekaran & Bougie, 2006). All measures showed good levels of internal consistency with Cronbach's alpha values above 0.70 (Nunnally & Bernstein, 1994).

The data was checked for model assumptions of normality, linearity, independence of error, and homogeneity of variance. The histogram of the standardised residual values showed a normal bell curve, indicating a normal distribution. In addition, the standardised residuals in the P–P plot were close to the diagonal line when this was regressed with the dependent variable. The Durbin–Watson statistic was computed to evaluate independence of the errors and the value was 1.952, which was between the acceptable levels of 1.50–2.50 (Coakes, Steed, & Ong, 2010). This indicates that the assumption of independent errors has been met. To test the homoscedasticity assumption, the scatter plot between standardised residuals against predicted criterion value was examined (Hair, Black, Babin, Anderson, & Tatham, 2006). The spread of residuals appeared relatively constant over the range of values of the independent variables, indicating homoscedasticity of variance. The tolerance value of more than 0.10 and variance inflation factor (VIF) value of <10 further indicated that multicollinearity did not pose as an issue (Hair et al., 2006) (Table 1).

5 Results

Table 2 illustrates the profile of the respondents with Malays representing almost 42%. Many of the respondents were in the age categories of 31–35 years old and over 41 years old age groups (29.1% for each of these age groups), with the majority (60.7%) being married and holding a diploma (36.8%). Just over half the respondents (54.7%) held the position of partner and did not have previous work experience in the area of the current business. The respondents generally had worked 3–5 years prior to starting the business (28.2%), with only 11% having had no experience. The majority of businesses have 5–20 employees (79.4%).

A factor analysis with varimax rotation was carried out to validate whether the respondents perceived the six constructs of entrepreneurs' competencies to be distinct. The retention decision of each item was based on factor loadings that were greater than or equal to 0.50 and cross-loadings with the other factors were

Table 1 Regression analysis—coefficients[a]

Model		Unstandardised coefficients		Standardised coefficients			95.0% confidence interval for B		Correlations			Collinearity statistics	
		B	Std. Error	Beta	t	Sig.	Lower bound	Upper bound	Zero-order	Partial	Part	Tolerance	VIF
1	(Constant)	−0.145	0.421		−0.344	0.731	−0.981	0.690					
	APC	0.209	0.086	0.207	2.422	0.017	0.038	0.381	0.500	0.226	0.169	0.669	1.[illegible]94
	IC	0.059	0.084	0.055	0.703	0.483	−0.108	0.226	0.340	0.067	0.049	0.791	1.[illegible]64
	EC	0.259	0.086	0.259	3.009	0.003	0.089	0.430	0.445	0.277	0.210	0.658	1.[illegible]19
	TC	−0.051	0.099	−0.052	−0.521	0.603	−0.247	0.144	0.433	−0.050	−0.036	0.494	2.[illegible]26
	LC	0.052	0.111	0.045	0.468	0.641	−0.168	0.272	0.414	0.045	0.033	0.517	1.[illegible]34
	NC	0.374	0.101	0.366	3.708	0.000	0.174	0.574	0.542	0.335	0.259	0.500	2.[illegible]00
	FS	0.098	0.085	0.100	1.163	0.248	−0.069	0.266	0.375	0.111	0.081	0.652	1.[illegible]35

[a]Dependent variable: FP

Table 2 Profile of the respondents

		Frequency	Percent
Ethnicity	Malay	49	41.9
	Chinese	37	31.6
	Indian	22	18.8
	Other	9	7.7
Age	20–25 years old	12	10.3
	26–30 years old	16	13.7
	31–35 years old	34	29.1
	36–40 years old	21	17.9
	>41 years old	34	29.1
Status	Single	38	32.5
	Married	71	60.7
	Separated	8	6.8
Education	Diploma	43	36.8
	Degree	30	25.6
	Master	9	7.7
	Other	35	29.9
Experience	Yes	104	88.9
	No	13	11.1
Work before starting current business	2 years or less	20	17.1
	3–5 years	33	28.2
	6–10 years	27	23.1
	>10 years	24	20.5
Work experience relevant to current business	Yes	49	41.9
	No	64	54.7
Position	Owner	53	45.3
	Partner	64	54.7
Number of employees	5–20 employees	93	79.4
	21–50 employees	24	20.6

generally smaller than 0.35 (Igbaria, Iivari, & Maragahh, 1995). Five factors explained 75.7% of the variance in the questionnaire data (Table 3).

To test the research hypotheses, multiple regression analysis was conducted and results are presented in Table 4. The R^2 was 0.439 indicating that 43.9% of the variation in firm performance among women entrepreneurs can be explained by the five types of entrepreneurial competencies. Implementation/enforcement competency was positively related to firm performance ($\beta = 0.338$, $p < 0.001$) and so was network competency ($\beta = 0.372$, $p < 0.001$). Thus, H_3 and H_6 of this study are fully supported while H_1, H_2, H_4 and H_5 are rejected. The findings also indicate that women entrepreneurs' network competency was a more influential predictor of their firm performance.

Table 3 Factor analysis for entrepreneurial competencies

		Factor***				
		F1	F2	F3	F4	F5
F5: Analytical planning competencies						
Ability to develop solutions analytically for my business	APC2	0.122	0.173	0.298	0.051	**0.816**
Aware of the importance of systematic approach as compared to intuition	APC4	0.205	0.057	−0.063	0.137	**0.802**
Ability to perform an extensive information gathering for my business development	APC1	0.195	0.181	0.132	0.088	**0.796**
Ability to consider several alternatives for my business development	APC3	0.058	0.173	0.265	0.194	**0.681**
F4: Innovation competencies						
Introduce new or substantially modified products or processes for my business growth	IC2	0.072	0.107	0.023	**0.849**	0.111
Ability to develop unconventional solutions for my business	IC5	0.129	0.051	0.144	**0.847**	0.146
Introduce product innovation to help my business growth	IC1	0.155	0.130	0.207	**0.825**	0.015
Seek innovative solutions for existing problems in my business	IC3	0.173	0.095	0.146	**0.800**	0.165
F3: Enforcement/implementation competencies						
Make quick decisions for my business	EC4	0.095	0.004	**0.883**	0.168	0.095
Willing to make big personal sacrifices for my business	EC1	0.202	−0.032	**0.878**	0.102	0.093
Willing to try for anything to be successful	EC3	0.142	0.097	**0.832**	0.110	0.166
Strive for goals in spite of setbacks	EC2	0.150	0.086	**0.816**	0.124	0.160
F1: Teamwork competencies						
My business has mutual support among employees	TC5	**0.867**	0.202	0.136	0.146	0.180
My business has specific team goal setting	TC1	**0.850**	0.256	0.233	0.020	0.071
My business has a formal evaluation on team performance	TC2	**0.817**	0.240	0.263	0.045	0.124
My business has an atmosphere of cooperation among employees	TC6	**0.805**	0.254	0.142	0.113	0.076
My business has coordination of tasks	TC4	**0.781**	0.231	0.024	0.245	0.200
My business has team selection and training	TC3	**0.767**	0.195	0.045	0.179	0.144

(continued)

Table 3 (continued)

		Factor***				
		F1	F2	F3	F4	F5
F2: Leadership competencies						
Be an example of innovative behaviour, exploring opportunities, generating ideas, championing and putting efforts in development of my business	LC2	0.176	**0.827**	0.053	0.078	0.081
Check with people before initiating changes that may affect them, incorporating their ideas and suggestions in decisions	LC5	0.296	**0.823**	−0.020	0.161	0.053
Encourage employees to come up with ideas and to evaluate current practice in my business	LC3	0.211	**0.813**	0.038	−0.029	0.142
Stimulate open and transparent communication, introducing supportive communication structures like informal work meetings in my business	LC4	0.317	**0.762**	0.045	0.051	0.188
Give subordinates sufficient autonomy to determine relatively independently how to do a job	LC6	0.213	**0.742**	0.083	0.253	0.193
Percentage variance (75.74%)		19.831	15.764	14.581	13.569	12.000

Note: ***$p < 0.001$
Factor loadings over 0.50 appear in bold.

Table 4 Result of regression analysis for entrepreneurial competencies variables predicting firm performance

Variable	Standardised B
Predictor (s)	
Analytical planning competency	0.108
Innovation competency	0.034
Enforcement/implementation competency	0.338***
Teamwork competency	0.015
Leadership competency	0.054
Network competency	0.372***
R^2	0.439
Adjusted R^2	0.420

Note: ***$p < 0.001$

6 Discussion

The results of the study were equivocal. Two of the competency areas i.e. implementation/enforcement competency and network competency had significant positive relationships with firm performance. However, the other four competencies i.e. analytical planning competency, innovation competency, teamwork competency and leadership competency had no significant positive relationships with performance. The results contradict the research conducted by Brinckmann et al. (2005) on young high-technology firms which found that all the different competency domains relate positively and significantly to firm success and we discuss some of the similarities and differences below.

Even among the competency areas that were significantly related to performance, our study differed to some extent. While Brinckmann et al. (2005) found that analytical planning had the strongest relationship and that this was stronger than enforcement and network competencies, we however find that network competency was stronger (with $\beta = 0.372$) than enforcement/implementation ($\beta = 0.338$) competency.

One possible reason, as noted by Lee, Lee, and Pennings (2001) is that the importance of building and maintaining networks is especially important in environments of extreme uncertainty whereby potential partners are usually very reluctant to share risks with a business with uncertain financial situation. This is relevant in the context of entrepreneurial ventures. We go further and argue that there is likely to be a gender effect at work here in terms of entrepreneurial decision-making. While it is acknowledged that knowledge and analytical skills are important in new venture creation (Greve, 1995), men and women make decisions differently (Ndemo & Maina, 2007). Even Brinckmann et al. (2005) classify network competencies as softer, "social" competencies as compared to the harder competencies of analytical planning and enforcement and women in general tend to use these social competencies more effectively than their male counterparts (Godwin, Stevens, & Brenner, 2006). As noted by Ndemo and Maina (2007), men tend to make decisions based on facts, analysis and also reliable information while women make decisions based on less tangible elements. This reinforces earlier research that found that women entrepreneurs outshine men in their abilities to build strong inter-personal relationships (Daniel, 2004; Fuller-Love et al., 2006) and are indeed better at networking (Lerner et al., 1997; Morris et al., 2006).

As to enforcement/implementation competency being significantly related to firm performance, a possible explanation can be found in previous research done where females were found to be more anxious and hence more likely to try anything to be successful than males (Brindley, 2005). This also reinforces other research that find that women make bigger personal sacrifices and hence are more committed to striving for goals in spite of setbacks (Brindley, 2005; Brush et al., 2006).

The competency areas that did not have a significant positive relationship with firm performance were analytical planning competency (0.108), innovation competency (0.034), teamwork competency (0.015) and leadership competency

(0.054). In a way, this corroborates Mitchelmore and Rowley (2013)'s research that found that among women, the categories of business and management competencies and entrepreneurial competencies, of which evidence of analytical thinking, innovation, teamwork and leadership were less significant than the category of personal and relationship competencies, of which network competencies fall under. In terms of innovation, there may be an added industry effect in that the sample consisted of women who all ran service-based ventures where there is less of a need for innovation. This corroborates the relatively weak contribution for innovation competency that Brinckmann et al. (2005) found in young high-technology ventures. In addition, the finding also reinforces Reid and Smith's (2000) research that also found a negative effect on the firm innovativeness in new venture business success (as measured by the combination of employment growth, firm's productivity and also the rate of return). In terms of leadership, this may be due to the small size of the businesses owned by the respondents.

In this present study, 79.4% of the respondents have a business with <20 employees. This also supports Brinckmann et al.'s (2005) findings that leadership competence gives a smaller long term growth effect. What is interesting is that there is an almost negligible relationship between teamwork competence and firm performance ($\beta = 0.015$). This lends support to Brinckmann et al.'s (2005) findings of a weak but positive relationship. One reason may be due to firm size effects as noted above. However, there may be a strong gender-specific effect at work here. In Asia, there is evidence that 66% of the women entrepreneurs doing business are primarily motivated by the desire for autonomy as well as the freedom and flexibility offered in running one's own business. The remaining 34% are motivated by personal crises, social considerations and family loyalty (Deng, Hassan, & Jivan, 1995). It may not be just an Asian women phenomenon as another study conducted in Norway reported that the independence factor was emphasised by female entrepreneurs more than males (Greene et al., 2003). Hence, it may be concluded that the majority of the Malaysian women entrepreneurs who start their own ventures may not value or develop their teamwork competencies and this would not affect their firm performance positively.

In terms of entrepreneurial competencies, the study therefore finds evidence that, based on the non-significant effects of the three competencies, context matters and that these competencies affect performance in a different way for entrepreneurs operating in Asian emerging economies as compared to traditional research conducted in developed economies. More significantly, as the study focuses on women entrepreneurs, it raises the issue that since past studies in entrepreneurial competencies were mainly conducted on male entrepreneurs, there could be significant gender effects at work. This reinforces research that show that there are significant gender differences between male and female entrepreneurs between countries.

This study is not without limitations. The first limitation is that due to access difficulty, the sample was a convenient one. Future studies could incorporate random/theoretical sampling approach for the findings to be generalisable. In addition, our study is predominantly based on service sector ventures and as such, future research should include other types of ventures e.g., manufacturing and agriculture. A second limitation is concerned with translation issues in that the survey was translated into Bahasa Malay for those who did not have strong command of the English language. This research needs to be replicated in other emerging economies and should also incorporate other contextual variables in order to confirm that these findings were not unique to just the Malaysian context.

7 Conclusion

An important conclusion from the 2012 Global Entrepreneurship Monitor study of women entrepreneurs is that if women perceive that they have the capabilities or competencies for entrepreneurship, they are more likely to believe that entrepreneurial opportunities exist (Kelley, Brush, Greene, & Litovsky, 2013). In addition, women are the backbone of economic development in many emerging economies (Ndemo & Maina, 2007). With Malaysia's economy undergoing dramatic changes in the last two decades, a dramatic shift in the economy is evident to transform the economy to one that is based on knowledge-based industries. The role of women in the economic transformation is significant especially in terms of enhancing the pool of human capital in terms of providing skilled and professional human capital to contributing as entrepreneurs to support the future growth of the Malaysian economy.

In our research, as compared to existing studies which are conducted largely in the context of male-founded ventures in the developed world, we find differences in the effect of entrepreneurial competencies of analytical planning, innovation, enforcement/implementation, leadership, teamwork and networking on firm performance among women entrepreneurs in Malaysia, an emerging Asian economy. We find that among Malaysian women entrepreneurs, only enforcement/implementation and network competencies have significant effects on firm performance. In particular, we find that network competency has a stronger significant relationship with firm performance. Hence, our research makes two significant contributions: (1) it provides an empirical test of the importance of entrepreneurial competencies to business performance in entrepreneurial ventures started by women; and (2) it provides a further understanding of how and why this may be different in the context of emerging economies. In so doing, our research reinforces the ongoing call for more research into women entrepreneurs in different countries and contexts. Gender effects on entrepreneurship, far from being a simple, convergent phenomenon, is actually a complex issue with widely varying dimensions and characteristics. This essentially calls for more research, especially in different countries and contexts, to understand the underlying drivers for the gender gap in entrepreneurship.

References

Acs, Z. J., & Audretsch, D. B. (2010). Introduction to the 2nd edition of the Handbook of entrepreneurship research. In Z. J. Acs & D. B. Audretsch (Eds.), *Handbook of entrepreneurship research: An interdisciplinary survey and introduction* (2nd ed., pp. 1–19). New York: Springer.

Acs, Z. J., & Virgill, N. (2010). Entrepreneurship in developing countries. In Z. J. Acs & D. B. Audretsch (Eds.), *Handbook of entrepreneurship research: An interdisciplinary survey and introduction* (2nd ed., pp. 485–515). New York: Springer.

Ahl, H. J. (2006). Why research on women entrepreneurs needs new directions. *Entrepreneurship Theory and Practice, 30*(5), 595–621.

Ahl, H. J., & Marlow, S. (2012). Exploring the dynamics of gender, feminism and entrepreneurship: Advancing debate to escape a dead end? *Organization, 19*(5), 543–562.

Ahmad, N. H., Ramayah, T., Wilson, C., & Kummerow, L. (2010). Is entrepreneurial competency and business success relationship contingent upon business environment? A study of Malaysian SMEs. *International Journal of Entrepreneurial Behaviour & Research, 16*(3), 182–204.

Allen, I. E., Elam, N., Langowitz, N., & Dean, M. (2007). *Global entrepreneurship monitor report on women and entrepreneurship*. Babson Park, MA and London: Babson College and London Business School.

Alvarez, S. A., & Barney, J. B. (2000). Entrepreneurial capabilities: A resource-based view. In G. D. Meyer & K. A. Heppard (Eds.), *Entrepreneurship as strategy: Competing on the entrepreneurial edge* (pp. 63–81). London: Sage.

Bamiatzi, V., Jones, S., Mitchelmore, S., & Nikolopoulos, K. (2015). The role of competencies in shaping the leadership style of female entrepreneurs: The case of North West of England, Yorkshire, and North Wales. *Journal of Small Business Management, 53*(3), 627–644.

Baptista, R., & Preto, M. (2007). The dynamics of causality between entrepreneurship and unemployment. *International Journal of Technology, Policy and Management, 7*(3), 215–224.

Barney, J. (1991). Firm resources and sustained competitive advantage. *Journal of Management, 17*(1), 99–121.

Baron, R. A., & Markman, G. D. (2003). Beyond social capital: The role of entrepreneurs' social competence in their financial success. *Journal of Business Venturing, 18*(1), 41–60.

Bartlett, C. A., & Ghoshal, S. (1997). The myth of the generic manager: New personal competencies for new management roles. *California Management Review, 40*(1), 92–116.

Baughn, C., Chua, B. L., & Neupert, K. (2006). The normative context for women's participation in entrepreneurship: A multi-country study. *Entrepreneurship Theory and Practice, 30*(5), 687–708.

Beck, T. (2009). *The international library of entrepreneurship series: Entrepreneurship in developing countries*. Cheltenham: Edward Elgar.

Bird, B. (1995). Towards a theory of entrepreneurial competency. *Advances in Entrepreneurship, Firm Emergence and Growth, 2*, 51–72.

Bortkevičiene, V., & Vaitkevičius, R. (2016). The development of adults' entrepreneurial competence for their successful career. *International Journal of Learning and Intellectual Capital, 13*(2–3), 238–249.

Brinckmann, J. (2006). *Competence of top management teams and success of new technology-based firms*. Berlin: Deutscher Universitätsverlag.

Brinckmann, J., Salomo, S., & Gemuenden, H. (2005). Entrepreneurial management competence and the development of young high-technology companies. *Frontiers of Entrepreneurship Research, 25*(5).

Brindley, C. (2005). Barriers to women achieving their entrepreneurial potential: Women and risk. *International Journal of Entrepreneurial Behaviour and Research, 11*(2), 144–161.

Brush, C. G., Carter, N. M., Gatewood, E. J., Greene, P., & Hart, M. M. (2006). *Growth-oriented women entrepreneurs and their businesses: A global research perspective*. Cheltenham: Edward Elgar Publishing.

Brush, C., de Bruin, A., & Welter, F. (2009). A gender-aware framework for women's entrepreneurship. *International Journal of Gender and Entrepreneurship, 1*(1), 8–24.

Busenitz, L. W., & Barney, J. B. (1997). Differences between entrepreneurs and managers in large organizations: Biases and heuristics in strategic decision-making. *Journal of Business Venturing, 12*(1), 9–30.

Calás, M., Smircich, L., & Bourne, K. (2009). Extending the boundaries: Reframing "entrepreneurship as social change" through feminist perspectives. *Academy of Management Review, 34* (3), 552–569.

Carree, M. A., & Thurik, A. R. (2010). The impact of entrepreneurship on economic growth. In Z. J. Acs & D. B. Audretsch (Eds.), *Handbook of entrepreneurship research: An interdisciplinary survey and introduction* (2nd ed., pp. 557–594). New York: Springer.

Chandler, G. N., & Jansen, E. (1992). The founder's self-assessed competence and venture performance. *Journal of Business Venturing, 7*(3), 223–236.

Coakes, S., Steed, L., & Ong, C. (2010). *SPSS without anguish*. Milton, QLD: Wiley.

Daniel, T. A. (2004). The exodus of women from the corporate workplace to self-owned businesses. *Employment Relations Today, 30*(4), 55–61.

Davidsson, P. (2004). *Researching entrepreneurship*. New York: Springer.

de Bruin, A., Brush, C. G., & Welter, F. (2006). Introduction to the special issue: Towards building cumulative knowledge on women's entrepreneurship. *Entrepreneurship Theory and Practice, 30*(5), 585–593.

de Bruin, A., Brush, C. G., & Welter, F. (2007). Advancing a framework for coherent research on women's entrepreneurship. *Entrepreneurship Theory and Practice, 31*(3), 323–339.

de Jong, J., & Den Hartog, D. (2007). How leaders influence employees' innovative behaviour. *European Journal of Innovation Management, 10*(1), 41–64.

Deng, S., Hassan, L., & Jivan, S. (1995). Female entrepreneurs doing business in Asia: A special investigation. *Journal of Small Business and Enterprise, 12*(2), 60–80.

Elam, A. B. (2008). *Gender and entrepreneurship: A multilevel theory and analysis*. Cheltenham: Edward Elgar.

Elam, A., & Terjesen, S. (2007). Institutional logics: Gender and business creation across GEM countries. *Frontiers of Entrepreneurship Research, 27*(8). Accessed on January 6, 2017, from http://digitalknowledge.babson.edu/fer/vol27/iss8/1

Erikson, T. (2002). Entrepreneurial capital: The emerging venture's most important asset and competitive advantage. *Journal of Business Venturing, 17*(3), 275–290.

Fuller-Love, N., Lim, L., & Akehurst, G. (2006). Guest editorial: Female and ethnic minority entrepreneurship. *The International Entrepreneurship and Management Journal, 2*(4), 429–439.

Garavan, T. N., & McGuire, D. (2001). Competencies and workplace learning: Some reflections on the rhetoric and the reality. *Journal of Workplace Learning, 13*(4), 144–164.

Godwin, L. N., Stevens, C. E., & Brenner, N. L. (2006). Forced to play by the rules? Theorizing how mixed-sex founding teams benefit women entrepreneurs in male-dominated contexts. *Entrepreneurship Theory and Practice, 30*(5), 623–642.

Greene, P., Brush, C., Hart, M., & Saparito, P. (2001). Patterns of venture capital funding: Is gender a factor? *Venture Capital, 3*(1), 63–83.

Greene, P., Hart, M., Gatewood, E., Brush, C., & Carter, N. (2003). Women entrepreneurs: Moving front and center: An overview of research and theory. *Coleman White Paper Series, 3*, 1–47.

Greve, A. (1995). Networks and entrepreneurship—An analysis of social relations, occupational background, and use of contacts during the establishment process. *Scandinavian Journal of Management, 11*(1), 1–24.

Gundry, L. K., Miriam, B.-Y., & Posig, M. (2002). Contemporary perspectives on women's entrepreneurship: A review and strategic recommendations. *Journal of Enterprising Culture, 10*(01), 67–86.

Gupta, A., & Govindarajan, V. (1984). Business unit strategy, managerial characteristics, and business unit effectiveness at strategy implementation. *Academy of Management Journal, 27* (1), 25–41.

Hair, J., Jr., Black, W., Babin, B., Anderson, R., & Tatham, R. (2006). *Multivariate data analysis*. New Jersey: Prentice Hall.

Hisrich, R., & Brush, C. (1984). The woman entrepreneur: Management skills and business problems. *Journal of Small Business Management, 22*(1), 30–37.

Hodgetts, R. M., & Kuratko, D. F. (2001). *Effective small business management*. Orlando, FL: Hartcourt College Publishers.

Hoffmann, T. (1999). The meanings of competency. *Journal of European Industrial Training, 23* (6), 275–285.

Hughes, K. D., Jennings, J. E., Brush, C., Carter, S., & Welter, F. (2012). Extending women's entrepreneurship research in new directions. *Entrepreneurship Theory and Practice, 36*(3), 429–442.

Igbaria, M., Iivari, J., & Maragahh, H. (1995). Why do individuals use computer technology? A Finnish case study. *Information and Management, 29*(5), 227–238.

Keilbach, M. C., Tamvada, J. P., & Audretsch, D. B. (2009). *Sustaining entrepreneurship and economic growth: Lessons in policy and industry innovations from Germany and India*. New York: Springer.

Kelley, D. J., Brush, C. G., Greene, P. G., & Litovsky, Y. (2013). *Global entrepreneurship monitor 2012 report: Women's entrepreneurship worldwide*. London: Global Entrepreneurship Research Association (GERA).

Langowitz, N., & Minniti, M. (2007). The entrepreneurial propensity of women. *Entrepreneurship Theory and Practice, 31*(3), 341–364.

Lee, C., Lee, K., & Pennings, J. (2001). Internal capabilities, external networks, and performance: A study on technology based ventures. *Strategic Management Journal, 22*(6/7), 615–640.

Lerner, M., Brush, C., & Hisrich, R. (1997). Israeli women entrepreneurs: An examination of factors affecting performance. *Journal of Business Venturing, 12*(4), 315–339.

Litwin, A. S., & Phan, P. H. (2013). Quality over quantity: Re-examining the link between entrepreneurship and job creation. *Industrial and Labor Relations Review, 66*(4), 833–873.

Man, T. W. Y., & Lau, T. (2005). The context of entrepreneurship in Hong Kong: An investigation through the patterns of entrepreneurial competencies in contrasting industrial environments. *Journal of Small Business and Enterprise Development, 12*(4), 464–481.

McGregor, J., & Tweed, D. (2001). Gender and managerial competence: Support for theories of androgyny? *Women in Management Review, 16*(6), 279–287.

Minniti, M., & Naudė, W. (2010). *Female entrepreneurship in developing countries*. United Nations University World Institute for Development (UNU-WIDER). Accessed January 6, 2016, from https://www.wider.unu.edu/publication/female-entrepreneurship-developing-countries

Minniti, M., Allen, I. E., & Langowitz, N. (2006). *Global entrepreneurship monitor 2005 report on women and entrepreneurship*. London: Babson College, London Business School.

Mitchelmore, S., & Rowley, J. (2010). Entrepreneurial competencies: A literature review and development agenda. *International Journal of Entrepreneurial Behavior and Research, 16*(2), 92–111.

Mitchelmore, S., & Rowley, J. (2013). Growth and planning strategies within women-led SMEs. *Management Decision, 51*(1), 83–96.

Mitchelmore, S., Rowley, J., & Shiu, E. (2014). Competencies associated with growth of women-led SMEs. *Journal of Small Business and Enterprise Development, 21*(4), 588–601.

Morris, M. H., Miyasaki, N. N., Watters, C. E., & Coombes, S. M. (2006). The dilemma of growth: Understanding venture size choices of women entrepreneurs. *Journal of Small Business Management, 44*(2), 221–244.

Muzychenko, O., & Saee, J. (2004). Cross cultural professional competence in higher education. *Journal of Management Systems, 16*(4), 1–19.

Naser, K., Mohammed, W., & Nuseibeh, R. (2009). Factors that affect women entrepreneurs: Evidence from an emerging economy. *International Journal of Organizational Analysis, 17*(3), 225–247.

Ndemo, B., & Maina, F. (2007). Women entrepreneurs and strategic decision making. *Management Decision, 45*(1), 118–130.

Nunnally, J., & Bernstein, I. (1994). *Psychometric theory* (3rd ed.). New York: McGraw-Hill.

OECD (Organisation for Economic Co-operation and Development). (2009). *Strengthening entrepreneurship and economic development in East Germany: Lessons from local approaches.* Accessed on January 7, 2017, from http://www.oecd.org/site/cfecpr/42367462.pdf

Orser, B., Riding, A., & Manley, K. (2006). Women entrepreneurs and financial capital. *Entrepreneurship Theory and Practice, 30*(5), 643–665.

Pines, A. M., Lerner, M., & Schwartz, D. (2010). Gender differences in entrepreneurship: Equality, diversity and inclusion in times of global crisis. *Equality, Diversity and Inclusion: An International Journal, 29*(2), 186–198.

Reid, G., & Smith, J. (2000). What makes a new business start-up successful? *Small Business Economics, 14*(3), 165–182.

Ritter, T., Wilkinson, I., & Johnston, W. (2002). Measuring network competence: Some international evidence. *Journal of Business and Industrial Marketing, 17*(2/3), 119–138.

Rowe, C. (1995). Clarifying the use of competence and competency models in recruitment, assessment and staff development. *Industrial and Commercial Training, 27*, 12–17.

Sadler-Smith, E., Hampson, Y., Chaston, I., & Badger, B. (2003). Managerial behavior, entrepreneurial style, and small firm performance. *Journal of Small Business Management, 41*, 47–67.

Scott, S., & Bruce, R. (1994). Determinants of innovative behavior: A path model of individual innovation in the workplace. *Academy of Management Journal, 37*(3), 580–607.

Sekaran, U., & Bougie, R. J. (2006). *Research methods for business: A skill building approach* (7th ed.). Milton, QLD: Wiley.

Sexton, D. L., & Bowman-Upton, N. (1990). Female and male entrepreneurs: Psychological characteristics and their role in gender-related discrimination. *Journal of Business Venturing, 5*(1), 29–36.

Shane, S. A. (2003). *A general theory of entrepreneurship: The individual-opportunity nexus.* Northampton, MA: Edward Elgar.

Snell, R., & Lau, A. (1994). Exploring local competences salient for expanding small businesses. *Journal of Management, 13*(4), 4–15.

Steyaert, C., & Katz, J. (2004). Reclaiming the space of entrepreneurship in society: Geographical, discursive and social dimensions. *Entrepreneurship and Regional Development, 16*(3), 179–196.

Thompson, J., Stuart, R., & Lindsay, P. (1997). The competence of top team members: A framework for successful performance. *Team Performance Management, 3*(2), 57–75.

Thurik, R., Carree, M., Stel, A., & Audretsch, D. (2008). Does self-employment reduce unemployment? *Journal of Business Venturing, 23*(6), 687–698.

UNICEF. (2005). *Malaysia: More girls than boys stay in education to advanced level.* Accessed on January 7, 2017, from https://www.unicef.org/malaysia/gift_6069.html

VanderBrug, J. (2013). The global rise of female entrepreneurs. *Harvard Business Review.* Accessed January 7, 2017, from https://hbr.org/2013/09/global-rise-of-female-entrepreneurs

Verheul, I., Uhlaner, L., & Thurik, R. (2005). Business accomplishments, gender and entrepreneurial self-image. *Journal of Business Venturing, 20*(4), 483–518.

Weiler, A. S., & Bernasek, A. (2001). Dodging the glass ceiling? Networks and the new wave of women entrepreneurs. *Social Science Journal, 38*(1), 85–103.

West, M. (2002). Sparkling fountains or stagnant ponds: An integrative model of creativity and innovation implementation in work groups. *Applied Psychology, 51*(3), 355–387.

West, M., & Farr, J. (1990). *Innovation and creativity at work: Psychological and organizational strategies.* Milton, QLD: Wiley.

Yukl, G. A. (2013). *Leadership in organisations* (8th ed.). New York: Pearson.

Can Online Co-creation Influence Lead Users' and Opinion Leaders' Behaviors?

Mathilde Bru and Laurent Scaringella

Abstract This article aims to study the effects of online co-creation on consumer behavior in terms of customer loyalty and purchase intention. In contrast to the existing literature that focuses on the results of co-creation or on participants' perceptions of companies using co-creation, we focus on lead userness and opinion leadership of consumers during new product and service development. The empirical study is based on 303 consumers from the fast-moving consumer goods industry. Our findings suggest that online co-creation has significant effects on lead userness, opinion leadership, and consumer behavior. Our findings further indicate that lead userness is a full mediator between online co-creation and opinion leadership. Our study contributes to the research gap about the effect of co-creation on consumer behavior of lead users—the most innovative of consumers—and opinion leaders, who have the capacity to influence other consumers.

Keywords Co-creation • Lead users • Opinion leaders • Brand experience • Customer loyalty • Purchase intention

1 Introduction

Co-creation is considered one of the most effective ways to innovate, thanks to consumer participation. This necessary collaboration comes from service-dominant logic (Vargo & Lusch, 2004), which incites companies to offer more complex products and services than before. To meet these expectations, the relationships between consumers and companies can become a source of value creation (Prahalad & Ramaswamy, 2004). In that sense, consumers take part in innovation development as a result of growing internet use (Franke, von Hippel, & Schreier, 2006) as a tool for connecting with consumers through brand communities, fan pages, social media, or specific platforms (Fuchs & Schreier, 2011; Gebauer, Füller, & Pezzei, 2013; Nysveen & Pedersen, 2014; Ramaswamy & Ozcan, 2015).

M. Bru • L. Scaringella (✉)
Rennes School of Business, Rennes, France
e-mail: Mathilde.bru@esc-rennes.fr; laurent.scaringella@esc-rennes.fr

V. Ratten et al. (eds.), *Knowledge, Learning and Innovation*, Contributions to Management Science, DOI 10.1007/978-3-319-59282-4_3

As a consequence of this digital revolution, large firms such as Nike, Décathlon, or Starbucks have succeeded in developing online co-creations (Vernette & Hamdi-Kidar, 2013). Co-creation outcomes have been investigated in numerous spheres: consumer satisfaction and loyalty (Cossío-Silva, Revilla-Camacho, Vega-Vazquez, & Palacios, 2015), consumers' perception of companies using co-creation (Kunz, Schmitt, & Meyer, 2011), marketing results (Fidel, Schlesinger, & Cervera, 2015), etc. Antecedents of co-creation involving customers also raised the attention of scholars who found that in particular, the participants have specific motivations and competences (Prahalad & Ramaswamy, 2000). In the context of concept development, the behavior and capacities of consumers to innovate have been focused upon (Hoffman, Kopalle, & Novak, 2010).

On that specific topic, we look to von Hippel (1986), the initiator of the major stream of research dedicated to lead users. Von Hippel revealed lead users are considered as the most innovative and powerful consumers in new product development. Different from regular consumers, lead users advance more successful ideas than those developed within companies. Furthermore, lead users are considered as breakthrough ideas sources (Schreier, Oberhauser, & Prügl, 2007), and Schreier et al. (2007) argued that lead users could also be related to opinion leaders who, in that respect, play a significant role in the co-creation process. Additionally, opinion leaders are recognized as powerful promoters of new products or services. Consequently, both lead users and opinion leaders can influence other consumers looking for information, and therefore, a consumer can concurrently be identified as a lead user and as an opinion leader.

Nevertheless, the relationship between lead users and opinion leaders has been understudied (Schreier et al., 2007) because only a few empirical studies have investigated co-creation while considering both lead users and opinion leaders as important stakeholders in the process of new product and service development. For instance, Béji-Bécheur and Gollety (2007) discussed the way consumers gather lead users' and opinion leaders' competences and argued that lead users and opinion leaders are very different. They also found companies that successfully collaborate with both of them benefit from a competitive advantage.

We agree with Schreier et al. (2007) that the current literature suffers from a lack of understanding of co-creation in relation with both lead users, who are the most innovative consumers, and opinion leaders, those with the capacity to influence other consumers. The existing literature remains unclear about whether co-creation positively influences customer loyalty and purchase intention through lead userness and opinion leadership. Therefore, our study asks the following research question: What are the effects of online co-creation on consumer behavior through lead userness and opinion leadership?

This article brings three contributions to the literature. First, our research targets better understanding of the effects of co-creation on consumers' ability to innovate and to spread their influence on other consumers. This will contribute to Béji-Bécheur and Gollety's (2007) and Schreier et al.'s (2007) previous studies. Second, we focus on the influence of co-creation on customer loyalty and brand experience, which intends to fill the gap identified by Nysveen and Pedersen

(2014) and Cossío-Silva et al. (2015). Third, we concentrate on the impacts of lead userness and opinion leadership on the brand experience and consumer intentions towards brands, such as loyalty and purchase intention. This last contribution is important because the existing literature tends to separately study lead userness and opinion leadership; our intent is to study the role of lead userness in the relationship between online co-creation and opinion leadership.

First, we will discuss the theoretical background on co-creation, lead users, opinion leaders, and purchase intention. Then, we will present the research methodology used. Based on our empirical study, we will discuss our study's findings and limitations and the paths for further studies.

2 Theoretical Background

2.1 Building Relationships with Consumers Through the Internet

2.1.1 Co-creation and Virtual Environment

The role of consumers in the value-creation process has evolved with the improvement of technology, and consumers have moved from "recipients of offerings" to co-creators in this process (Ramaswamy & Ozcan, 2015). Such co-creation is defined as every contact between companies and consumers that aims to create, develop, or improve actual offers or the image of a company (Gebauer et al., 2013; Prahalad & Ramaswamy, 2000).

In supporting co-creation, the web permits the creation of new connections between firms and consumers (Sawhney, Verona, & Prandelli, 2005). Indeed, the Internet enables the creation of new activities for companies (Frambach, Roest, & Krishnan, 2007). The Internet also allows consumers to be informed and to create closer relationships with firms and other consumers (Nysveen & Pedersen, 2014; Sashi, 2012; Vernette & Hamdi-Kidar, 2013), and these relationships are facilitated by online media, especially via brand communities or platforms (Nysveen & Pedersen, 2014). However, few studies have investigated co-creation in online contexts (Baldus, Voorhees, & Calantone, 2015; Gebauer et al., 2013; Ramaswamy & Ozcan, 2015; Sawhney et al., 2005, van der Merwe & van Heerden, 2009), and this prompts our further study on online co-creation.

2.1.2 Co-creation Through Brand Communities

Hagel and Armstrong (1997) were the first to recognize the benefits of online brand communities for business applications. However, there are some potential drawbacks in using such collaborative platforms. For instance, conflicts between participants, dissatisfaction with the outcomes of co-creation, and negative behaviors may occur (Gebauer et al., 2013). In spite of this, the benefits seem to outweigh the drawbacks, causing firms to continue to develop relationships with consumers to improve consumers' shopping experiences and earn consumer loyalty and to grow their businesses (Grewal, Levy, & Kumar, 2009). According to Rafiq, Fulford, and Lu (2013) and Srinivasan, Anderson, and Ponnavolu (2002), customer loyalty is essential for online companies because of exceedingly intense competition.

Therefore, firms develop their business both offline and online to reach more consumers. However, consumers may react differently to these different channels depending on their ability to use them and their comfort levels with the Internet. Thus, companies must identify the most relevant and most efficient channel (Frambach et al., 2007) to maximize their chances of reaching new customers (Payne & Frow, 2005), and this has led companies to offer various co-creation activities, such as discussions, idea reviews, or evaluations, to different customers.

Online brand communities offer many benefits to co-creational companies in terms of visibility and knowledge (Baldus et al., 2015; Morgan-Thomas & Veloutsou, 2013). Indeed, by fostering relationships with consumers, firms can improve their offers and better meet customers' needs (Adjei, Griffith, & Noble, 2009). Currently, companies invest in community development because this activity has turned out to be profitable (Ramaswamy & Ozcan, 2015). When these interactions between companies and consumers are long lasting and rich, it creates emotional relationships between consumers and the brand, which is also named "the brand experience" (Morgan-Thomas & Veloutsou, 2013). Such brand experiences are defined as "subjective, internal consumer responses (sensations, feelings, and cognitions) and behavioral responses evoked by brand-related stimuli" (Brakus, Schmitt, & Zarantonello, 2009, p. 53). Furthermore, the brand experience cannot be copied as easily as product or services can be copied. In Nysveen and Pedersen's (2014) empirical study on the banking sector, they argued that when consumers engage in co-creation, the brand experience is strengthened, and overall, the literature supports the following hypothesis, H_1:

H_1 Online co-creation has a positive impact on brand experience.

2.1.3 Customer Loyalty

Currently, most co-creation activities are conducted online and require companies to develop online community management associated with a novel means of communication between consumers and companies because the brand experience and the relationship with the firm influence customer loyalty (Brodie, Illic, Juric, & Hollebeek, 2013; Ramaswamy & Ozcan, 2015). In that sense, customer loyalty can be considered as a consequence of the quality of the relationship between the consumer and the firm (Palmatier, Dant, Grewal, & Evans, 2006) or as a consequence of past shopping experiences (Brakus et al., 2009; Payne & Frow, 2005). In the online co-creation context, it has been argued that customer loyalty is the consequence of activities via brand communities (Hsieh & Hsieh, 2015; Morgan-Thomas & Veloutsou, 2013). Consequently, we introduce hypothesis H_2:

H_2 Brand experience is positively related to customer loyalty.

By considering consumers as co-producers, companies may procure useful information concerning consumers' expectations (Baldus et al., 2015; von Hippel, 1986), which enables them to successfully fulfill their needs (Wikström, 1996). By interacting with brands to develop new offers (Franke et al., 2006; Nambisan & Baron, 2007), consumers can be rewarded with access to the products or services they need. Finally, by finding an answer to their problems, consumers will adopt the positive behavior of loyalty towards co-creational companies (Brodie et al., 2013; Fuchs & Schreier, 2011; Jaakkola, 2014). Consequently, co-creation is recognized as positively influencing customer loyalty (Auh, Bell, McLeod, & Shih, 2007; Bharti, Agrawal, & Sharma, 2015). It makes us consider hypothesis H_3:

H_3 Online co-creation is positively related to customer loyalty.

According to Keller (1993), customer loyalty is defined by a favorable attitude toward a brand that will positively profit companies. Indeed, loyal customers are ready to pay more for extra services (Rafiq et al., 2013; Reinartz & Kumar, 2000) and tend to "buy more often and attract new customers thanks to advocacy, positive comments and positive word-of-mouth" (Cossío-Silva et al., 2015, p. 4). Therefore, as Wa and Yiyan (2010) explained, the members of brand communities may look to develop bonds with companies that might make them loyal and increase their willingness to purchase. As a consequence, we consider the following hypothesis, H_4:

H_4 Customer loyalty is positively related to purchase intention.

2.2 *Value Co-creation: Collaborating with Different Types of Consumers*

2.2.1 Involving Stakeholders in Co-creation

Griffin and Hauser (1993) argued that companies are traditionally responsible for new product development, but this model was challenged under the influence of lead users who are progressively more involved in the democratization of innovations (von Hippel, 2005). As a consequence, consumers are increasingly active in the development of new products or services by expressing their points of view and by becoming involved in creation. Companies enable lead users to participate in co-creation by creating platforms with the intent to improve lead users' brand experiences and to maximize the outcome of such collaborations (Ramaswamy & Ozcan, 2015). As an example, Vernette and Hamdi-Kidar (2013) argued that some brands, such as Starbucks, encourage lead users to offer feedback based on their brand experience toward the goal of improving it. Similarly, Nysveen and Pedersen (2014) also contended that engaging consumers in the innovation process may positively influence their brand experiences (Hollebeek, 2011). Based on the support of the literature, we consider hypothesis H_5.

H_5 Lead userness is positively related to brand experience.

2.2.2 Lead Users in the Co-creation Process

During co-creation, consumers take part in the innovation process, which may require some specific skills and competences. According to Vernette and Hamdi-Kidar (2013), there are two kinds of co-creation: the upstream co-creation that corresponds to idea generation and conception and the downstream co-creation that consists of giving feedback that does not require any specific skills. Von Hippel (1986) defined lead users as more suitable for upstream co-creation because lead users are considered as being ahead of trends and expecting high benefits from a solution to fulfill their needs. In that sense, co-creation enables consumers to develop their innovativeness abilities by considering them as co-producers of new products or services (Franke et al., 2006; von Hippel, 1986). In contradiction with von Hippel (1986), Vernette and Hamdi-Kidar (2013) argued that lead users are appropriate for both up-stream and down-stream co-creation and considered co-creation communities as heterogeneous and mainly composed of regular and passive consumers and only a minority of lead users. Overall, we make the hypothesis, H_6.

H_6 The online co-creation situation is positively related to lead userness.

2.2.3 Opinion Leaders as Promoters of Innovations

We consider two categories of consumers: those who provide information and influence the other consumers (opinion leaders) and those who look for information to make decisions (opinion seekers) (Schreier et al., 2007). Lead users are seen as opinion leaders because of their knowledge and competences and are also considered experts because of their experiences (Béji-Bécheur & Gollety, 2007; Sashi, 2012; Schreier et al., 2007).

However, lead users are not seen as opinion seekers because they are less dependent on others when making the decision to purchase something new (Schreier et al., 2007). Opinion leaders influence other consumers' consumption choices; therefore, they have an impact on the success of a new product on the market (Béji-Bécheur & Gollety, 2007). Opinion leaders also quickly spread ideas and innovations (van der Merwe & van Heerden, 2009), but depending on the context, they can also be influenced by other opinion leaders and tend to better receive such information in comparison to non-leaders (Reynolds & Darden, 1971).

Only a few empirical studies have emphasized the role of lead users as opinion leaders (Béji-Bécheur & Gollety, 2007; Schreier et al., 2007; Urban & von Hippel, 1988). For instance, Schreier et al. (2007) and Urban and von Hippel (1988) explained that lead users are considered valuable resources for marketers in terms of not only the development and adoption but also the diffusion of new products. Béji-Bécheur and Gollety (2007) further argued that there is an urge to associate both lead users and opinion leaders because their functions are complementary during the development and the diffusion of innovation. Overall, we consider the following hypothesis, H_7.

H_7 Lead userness is positively related to opinion leadership.

Co-creation is conducted through brand communities with a wide range of activities (Ramaswamy & Ozcan, 2015) and a diversity of participants (Vernette & Hamdi-Kidar, 2013). Indeed, co-creation involves lead users or opinion leaders or both of them (Béji-Bécheur & Gollety, 2007). We consider opinion leaders to be the consumers "who generate a higher proportion of word-of-mouth in a certain category" (Shi & Wojnicki, 2014, p. 83). In their empirical study conducted among a wide range of products retailers, Martin and Lueg (2013) argued that the opinion leaders influence regular consumers who will develop a positive attitude towards the product and the brand, such as spreading a positive word-of-mouth opinion. Based on the existing literature, we consider the next hypothesis, H_8:

H_8 The online co-creation situation is positively related to opinion leadership.

These opinion leaders create specific bonds with companies through a two-way dialogue with the brand (Morgan-Thomas & Veloutsou, 2013). By influencing information seekers, opinion leaders may impact the diffusion process, and this phenomenon matters to firms aiming to develop relationships with opinion leaders by providing them with rewards. With this, they hope to increase opinion leaders' brand experiences and reap possible positive recommendations afterwards (Kozinets, de Valck, Wojnicki, & Wilner, 2010; Shi & Wojnicki, 2014). Consequently, our research considers the next hypothesis, H_9:

H_9 Opinion leadership is positively related to brand experience.

2.3 *Benefits of Online Co-creation*

Consumer collaboration in the innovation process has a positive influence not only on customer loyalty but also on business performance (Fidel et al., 2015). Indeed, co-creation positively influences customer loyalty, when keeping in mind that loyal customers are likely to spend more money than regular customers (Keller, 1993). In the empirical study conducted in the Spanish personal care sector, Cossío-Silva et al. (2015) argued that loyal customers may play the role of opinion leaders by taking part in the promotion of the brand and the products, by making recommendations to other consumers, and by spreading a positive word-of-mouth. We consider the following hypothesis, H_{10}:

H_{10} Customer loyalty is positively related to opinion leadership.

Lead users can competently provide innovative and attractive ideas during co-creation (Franke et al., 2006). Moreover, lead users are interested in purchasing new products or services when they have enjoyed co-creation (Moreau & Herd, 2010; von Hippel, 1986). Therefore, consumers are likely to develop favorable behavioral intentions, such as a positive word-of-mouth or a greater interest and a stronger purchase intention for user-designed products (Brady & Cronin, 2001; Brown & Dacin, 1997; Franke et al., 2006; Schreier, Fuchs, & Dahl, 2012). Benefiting from a very high degree of opinion leadership and from competences to innovate, lead users could be ready to purchase new products or services if their needs can be fulfilled (Franke et al., 2006). This leads to stating the following hypothesis, H_{11}:

H_{11} Lead userness is positively related to purchase intention.

As part of co-creation, consumers can either be creators or influencers, which are two dimensions critical to the success of the innovation (Béji-Bécheur & Gollety, 2007). In particular, the status of the co-creator has an impact on the advertising of the innovation which, in fine, impacts the purchase intention. This finding has been supported by Liljddal (2016) in an empirical study of luxury goods in which it was argued that celebrities who are co-producers are effective in the product's promotion in comparison to regular consumers. Indeed, celebrities can be considered as opinion leaders because of their expertise, their attractiveness to consumers, and their number of followers; thus, they have a positive influence on purchase intention for the brand product (Jin & Phua, 2014; Tripp, Jensen, & Carlson, 1997). We consequently develop the next hypothesis, H_{12}:

H_{12} Opinion leadership is positively related to purchase intention.

We developed the following research model (Fig. 1) composed of 12 hypotheses to further investigate our research question: What are the effects of online co-creation on consumer behavior through lead userness and opinion leadership?

3 Method

3.1 Measures

The questionnaire to measure the effects of online co-creation on consumer behavior through lead userness and opinion leadership was developed through a multi-stage process (Anderson & Gerbing, 1988; Churchill, 1979; Hazan & Shaver, 1994; Hazan & Zeifman, 1999). To operationalize our theoretical framework, we measured six

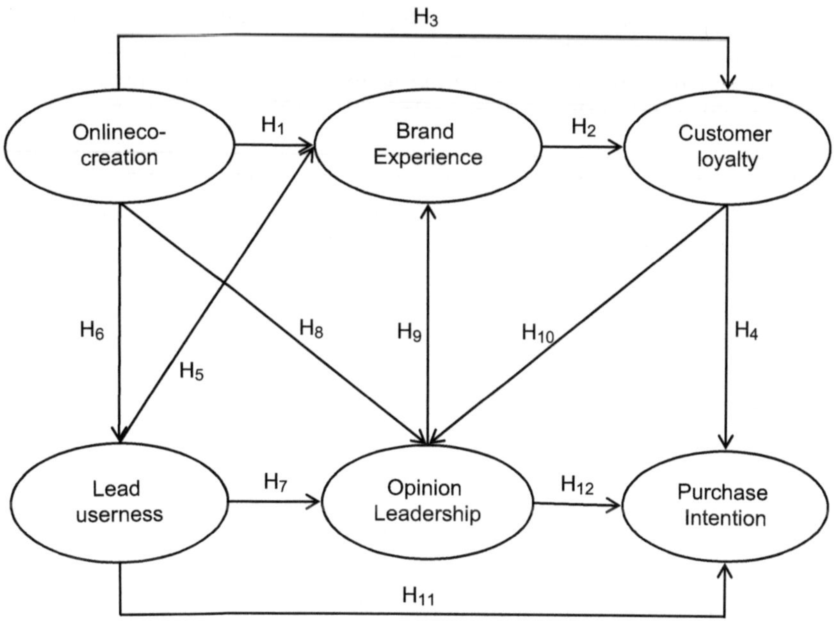

Fig. 1 Research model

constructs composed of 52 items in total. Online co-creation was measured using the scale from Nysveen and Pedersen (2014) composed of six items. We adapted the items according to the sector of activity and to the topic. Lead Userness was measured by 13 items adopted by Hoffman et al. (2010). A further 12-item scale from Brakus et al. (2009) was adopted to measure Brand Experience. A subsequent 13-item scale from Zeithaml, Berry, and Parasuraman (1996) was applied to measure Customer Loyalty. Five items derived from Reynolds and Darden (1971) served to measure Opinion Leadership. To investigate the Purchase Intention of Consumers to buy products and services from the co-creation process, we used the three-item scale from Putrevu and Lord (1994). A 7-point Likert-scale from (1) "strongly disagree" to (7) "strongly agree" was used to measure all items except for Opinion Leadership, for which a 5-point Likert scale was used. We also measured the following control variables: age, gender, educational level, communication form, personal situation, and intention of participation. The questionnaire was translated into French by an English teacher. Then, it was translated back into English by a different English teacher.

3.2 *Pre-test*

A sample of 34 master students participated in a questionnaire pre-test. The Cronbach's alpha (α) of each construct was above 0.80. The validity of the measurements was examined in a two-step approach that was recommended by Anderson and Gerbing (1988). Through exploratory factor analysis, we reduced the 6-item scale of the Co-creation situation to five items; the 5-item scale of Lead Userness to three items; the 12-item scale of Brand Experience to four items; the 13-item scale of Customer Loyalty to three items; and the 5-item scale of Opinion Leadership to four items. The scale purification was needed to insure the validity of the measurement instruments. The final questionnaire was structured as follows: Co-creation Awareness, Co-creation, Lead Userness, Brand Experience, Customer Loyalty, Opinion Leadership, and Demographic Information.

3.3 Data Collection and Sample

We targeted members of various brand communities, such as the Legocommunity or the Décathlon Création community, and the consumers of the five following brands involved in co-creation: Décathlon, Starbucks, Nike, Adidas, and Lego. The members of the communities and the consumers were accessed through websites, co-creation pages, and social media. Online communities are relevant because they can be considered the simplest ways for consumers to connect with the brands.

The 623 persons who were contacted as possible respondents to complete the online questionnaire received a letter from the different contacts associated with the questionnaire to explain the aim of the survey and to maximize the response rate. A follow-up e-mail was sent two weeks later, and in total, 303 answers (48.6% response rate) were collected in France over 4 months from March 2016 to June 2016. We did not delete any non-usable responses from our data collection, and there was not a significant difference between early and late respondents. The median respondent's age is between 25 and 29; 59.7% of the respondents are female, and the majority of respondents are employed at a job. Sample characteristics are presented in Table 1.

4 Analysis

4.1 Measurement Model

The Alpha Cronbach of all constructs was >0.70 (Nunnally & Bernstein, 1994), which insures a good convergence. None of the estimated pairwise correlations across items from different constructs was >0.49, indicating discriminant validity. Table 2 shows inter-construct correlations.

We conducted a Confirmatory Factor Analysis (CFA) to assess reliability, convergent validity, and discriminant validity of the measurement model. CFA of the measurement model showed a good fit (CMIN/Df = 1.424, CFI = 0.981,

Table 1 Sample characteristics

Characteristics	Frequency	Valid percent (%)
Gender		
Male	122	40.3
Female	181	59.7
Age		
Under 18	8	2.6
18–24	112	37.0
25–29	76	25.7
30–34	33	10.9
35–39	17	5.6
40–44	19	6.3
45–49	13	4.3
50–54	14	4.6
55–59	8	2.6
Personal situation		
Student	114	37.5
Part-time worker	17	5.6
Full-time worker	147	48.5
Retired	9	3.0
Homemaker	6	3.3
Unemployed	10	3.3
Education level		
Bachelor's degree	55	18.2
College	16	5.3
Doctoral degree	16	5.3
High school or equivalent	20	6.6
Master's degree	176	58.1
Professional degree	20	6.6

IFI = 0.982, NFI = 0.941, RMSEA = 0.037). All standardized factor loadings were over 0.5 and highly significant at p-value < 0.001, which indicates good convergent validity among the instruments of each construct (Bagozzi & Yi, 1988). Overall, our results indicate a good discriminant validity (Kline, 1998).

Composite Reliabilities of all constructs are greater than the 0.60 threshold (Bagozzi & Yi, 1988), which ensure the reliability of our constructs. In light of the CFA results, we assessed validity and reliability based on the recommendations from Fornell and Larcker (1981). To limit risk of common methods variance, our work refers to Podsakoff and Organ (1986) and Podsakoff, MacKenzie, and Lee (2003). The Harman's single factor test was employed (Podsakoff et al., 2003), and the factor explains <50% of the variance. Consequently, there is no serious problem with Common Method Variance. Table 3 presents the constructs, items measured, factor loadings, Average Variance Extracted, Composite Reliability, and Cronbach's Alpha.

Table 2 Correlation matrix

		Mean	Stand. Dev	1	2	3	4	5
1	Purchase intention	5.118	1.440					
2	Opinion leadership	3.113	1.211	0.587***				
3	Customer loyalty	5.406	1.189	0.730***	0.464***			
4	Brand experience	4.017	1.766	0.566***	0.531***	0.586***		
5	Lead userness	2.638	1.707	0.189$^{n.s}$	0.412***	0.168$^{n.s}$	0.416***	
6	Online co-creation	4.140	1.671	0.319***	0.250***	0.316***	0.305***	0.268***

ns not significant
Note: ***$p < 0.001$

Table 3 Construct, items, validity and reliability

Construct items	Factor loadings	AVE	CR	Cronbach's Alpha
Online co-creation		0.606	0.885	0.892
I often express my personal needs to the brand	0.74			
I often suggest how the brand can improve its services	0.73			
I participate in decisions about how the brand offers its services	0.80			
I often find solutions to my problems together with the brand	0.83			
I am actively involved when the brand develops new solutions for me	0.79			
Lead userness		0.678	0.859	0.832
I have suggested to stores and delivery services some new and different ways to deliver goods at home	0.92			
I have participated in offers by stores to deliver goods to my home in new and different ways	0.58			
I have come up with some new and different solutions to meet my needs for the home delivery of goods	0.93			
Brand experience		0.832	0.556	0.847
This brand induces feelings and sentiments	0.75			
This brand is an emotional brand	0.63			
I engage in physical actions and behaviors when I use this brand	0.78			
This brand results in bodily experiences	0.61			

(continued)

Table 3 (continued)

Construct items	Factor loadings	AVE	CR	Cronbach's Alpha
Opinion leadership		0.688	0.682	0.894
My friends and neighbors often ask my advice about sport articles	0.82			
I sometimes influence the types of sport articles my friends buy	0.72			
My friends come to me more often than I go to them for information about sport articles	0.86			
I feel that I am generally regarded by my friends and neighbors as a good source of advice about sport articles	0.89			
Customer loyalty		0.831	0.831	0.924
Encourage friends and relatives to buy the brand's products	0.90			
Recommend the brand to someone who seeks your advice	0.92			
Say positive things about the brand to other people	0.92			
Purchase intention		0.688	0.688	0.849
It is very likely that I will buy (brand)	0.90			
I will purchase (brand) the next time I need a (product)	0.81			
I will definitely try (brand)	0.76			

AVE average variance extracted; *CR* composite reliability
Note: RMSEA = 0.0037; CFI = 0.981; GFI = 0.925

5 Structural Model

In our structural model, there is one exogenous latent multi-item construct that can be considered as the independent variable: CCSIT. There are five endogenous multi-item latent constructs that can be considered as the dependent variables: BE, OP, LU, CLOY, and PU. There are 61 regression weights, 33 of which are fixed and 28 of which are estimated. There are six covariance and 28 variances, all of which are estimated. In total, there are 95 parameters, 62 of which are to be estimated.

Maximum Likelihood estimation is applicable because the model is over identified ($\chi^2 = 275{,}984$; df = 191; p = 0.000). The overall model fit was good (CMIN/Df = 1.445; CFI = 0.980; IFI = 0.980; NFI = 0.939; GFI = 0.924; TLI = 0.976; RMSEA = 0.038). All standardized factor loadings were over 0.5 and highly significant at p-value < 0.001, which indicates good convergent validity among the instruments of each construct (Bagozzi & Yi, 1988). All the results support the overall validity of constructs measured in the study.

Table 4 Results from the structural model

Hyp.	Variables	S.E.	Hypotheses testing	Hypotheses status
1	CCSIT → BE	0.144**	Online co-creation situation is positively related to brand experience	Supported
2	BE → CLOY	0.131***	Brand experience is positively related to customer loyalty	Supported
3	CCSIT → CLOY	0.108**	Online co-creation situation is positively related to customer loyalty	Supported
4	CLOY →PU	0.121***	Customer loyalty is positively related to purchase intention	Supported
5	LU → BE	0.159***	Lead userness is positively related to brand experience	Supported
6	CCSIT → LU	0.141***	Online co-creation situation is positively related to lead userness	Supported
7	LU → OP	0.119***	Lead userness is positively related to opinion leadership	Supported
8	CCSIT → OP	0.106n.s	Online co-creation situation is positively related to opinion leadership	Not supported
9	OP → BE	0.127***	Opinion leadership is positively related to brand experience	Supported
10	CLOY → OP	0.091***	Customer loyalty is positively related to opinion leadership	Supported
11	LU → PU	0.128n.s	Lead userness is positively related to purchase intention	Not supported
12	OP → PU	0.112***	Opinion leadership is positively related to purchase	Supported

S.E. standardized estimate; *ns* not significant
Note: CMIN/df = 1.445; CFI = 0.980; GFI = 0.924; NFI = 0.939; TLI = 0.976; RMSEA = 0.038
*p < 0.05, **p < 0.01, ***p < 0.001

6 Results

In the results of our analysis, we find support for H_1, H_2, H_3, H_4, H_5, H_6, H_7, H_9, H_{10}, and H_{12}; however, our data does not support H_8 and H_{11}. All the control variables did not significantly impact purchase intention. Table 4 provides a summary of the results from our structural model.

6.1 Mediation

The Baron and Kenny (1986) procedure was used to test the mediation effects of lead userness on the effect of online co-creation on opinion leadership. In a first step, we checked that online co-creation is related to the opinion leadership. The relationship was positive (S.E. = 0.059) and significant (p-value = 0.007). In a second step, we assessed that the relationship between online co-creation and the mediator lead userness was significant (Preacher & Hayes, 2008). The relationship was positive (S.E. 0.078) and significant (p-value < 0.001). In a third step, we assessed that the relationship between the mediator lead userness and opinion leadership is significant (Preacher & Hayes, 2008). The relationship was positive (S.E. 0.043) and significant (p-value < 0.001).

In a fourth step, we assessed that lead userness mediates the effect of online co-creation on opinion leadership. The full mediation implies that the addition of the direct paths between online co-creation and opinion leadership is insignificant, the indirect path is significant, and the model fit did not improve (Baron & Kenny, 1986; Holmbeck, 1997; Zhao, Lynch, & Chen, 2010). We observed that the direct effects between online co-creation and opinion leadership were significant (p-value < 0.01) prior to adding the mediator, lead userness. By adding the moderator, lead userness, the direct effect between online co-creation and opinion leadership became not significant (p-value $= 0.231$), while the indirect effect is significant (p-value $= 0.001$). From our empirical study, we argue that leader userness is a full mediator on the effect of online co-creation on opinion leadership.

In addition to the Baron and Kenny (1986) approach, we used the bootstrap mediation test to analyze the mediation effect (Hayes, 2013; Preacher & Hayes, 2008) and to avoid problems of non-normality, which is frequent when analyzing interaction effect composed of the two parameters because the indirect effect is the product of those two parameters (Zhao et al., 2010; Preacher & Hayes, 2008). As a non-parametric method based on resampling, bootstrapping for testing the indirect effect is very common (Bollen & Stine, 1990; Shrout & Bolger, 2002). Overall, we obtained the total effect as the following: Total effect (online co-creation → opinion leadership) = direct effect 0.179 + indirect effect (0.141 * 0.119) = 0.196.

7 Discussion and Conclusion

7.1 Theoretical Contribution

To carry innovation processes, firms frequently mobilize customers and other stakeholders through online co-creational activities. Such activities provide both functional and emotional value not only for the customers but also for the firms. Indeed, in most cases, co-creational firms benefit from positive consumer behavior. Most research concerning co-creation examines the different types of co-creation (Fuchs & Schreier, 2011; Vernette & Hamdi-Kidar, 2013) and the characteristics of consumers who are the most powerful (Béji-Bécheur & Gollety, 2007; Franke et al., 2006; von Hippel, 1986). The findings of existing works posit lead users' and opinion leaders' attitudes towards co-creational firms. However, the existing literature lacked understanding of the co-creation effect on the consumer behavior of lead users, who are the most innovative consumers, and opinion leaders, who are those with the capacity to influence other consumers.

Our study filled this gap by further studying the effects of online co-creation on consumer attitudes towards brands according to their brand experience, their lead userness, and their level of opinion leadership. Our article further highlights the impact of co-creation on brand experience, lead userness, opinion leadership, and customer loyalty. These findings indicate that participants in co-creation may have a better brand experience as long as they develop specific relationships with brands and communicate with companies and other members of the community.

The impact of online co-creation on opinion leadership is only significant in the absence of lead userness. Complementing what Béji-Bécheur and Gollety (2007) found about the direct effect of online co-creation on opinion leadership during the innovation development process, we further argue that lead userness plays the role of full mediator between online co-creation and opinion leadership.

Furthermore, consumers who enjoy a brand experience are more likely to be loyal to the brand, and this confirms Brakus et al.'s (2009) argument. In our model, we also measured a direct effect between online co-creation and customer loyalty.

Our empirical study also supports the direct effect of lead userness on opinion leadership, customer loyalty on opinion leadership, opinion leadership on purchase intentions, and opinion leadership on brand experience. However, contrary to what Fuchs and Schreier (2011) posited, our study does not support the direct effect of lead userness on purchase intention.

Moreover, both customer loyalty and opinion leadership directly influence the purchase intention in line with the existing literature (Cossío-Silva et al., 2015; Jin & Phua, 2014; Reinartz & Kumar, 2000). Indeed, loyal consumers are more likely to make positive recommendations and influence other consumers in their purchases. Furthermore, loyal customers are more willing to purchase and make repeat purchases if they enjoy a brand experience or co-creation situation.

This article provides some insights on bridging the gaps in the understanding of the effects of co-creation on brand experience and consumers' behaviors. Indeed, we demonstrate that online co-creation has a significant impact on customer loyalty and brand experience and stressed the influence of lead userness and opinion leadership on brand experience and on consumer intentions towards brands with loyalty and purchase intention.

7.2 *Managerial Implications and Recommendations*

From our findings, we can formulate the following managerial implications and recommendations. Online co-creation that consists of developing new products and services thanks to consumer collaboration should focus on a careful selection of participants and then on building brand experiences with them. Companies should focus on building online brand communities or creating specific platforms dedicated to co-creation to appeal to consumers. This may include developing activities and functionalities that give communities the opportunity to create through chat interactions between participants, and this practice would enable participants to co-create in their discussions with peers, such as the example of Lego's success in engaging participants in dialogue, which led to the development of a brand community.

Co-creation affects brand experience, which, in turn, influences customer loyalty. In particular, it appears as relevant for firms to develop new products based on participants' ideas and to be perceived as more customer oriented. Therefore, customer loyalty may bring different benefits to firms: first, because loyal customers may be ready to pay for access to firm's products and services and second, because loyal customers with opinion leadership may be powerful in the diffusion innovation process and in their recommendations to their friends and relatives.

We finally suggest firms hire community managers to detect and manage both lead users and opinion leaders within brand communities. Indeed, focusing and exploiting those consumers' abilities may lead to greater success in the commercialization of new products and services.

7.3 Limitations

In our research's focus on online co-creation through brand communities, we identified several limitations. First, the study examines the effects of co-creation on consumers in the specific case of the following five brands: Décathlon, Starbucks, Nike, Adidas, and Lego. Therefore, results cannot be generalized. Second, we did not distinguish the type of creation, whether upstream (idea contribution for new product development) or downstream (voting on or reviewing ideas), and this limits our interpretation of consumer impact in the creation process. Third, purchase intension was studied as a subjective measurement, which may differ from the objective measurement of company sales.

8 Paths for Further Studies

Because of our work's limitations, we encourage further studies (1) to examine the effects of co-creation on consumers comparing an example of a co-creational company with a more traditional company, (2) to consider not only famous co-creation brands but also lesser known brands, (3) to investigate which kind of co-creation is the most profitable in terms of customer loyalty and purchase intention, (4) to further research which kind of active consumer, either lead userness or opinion leadership, is the most efficient for downstream or upstream co-creation, and (5) to not only examine subjective measurement of purchase intent but also objective measurement of purchase intent, such as company's revenues or market shares, to investigate the difference between companies that may have implemented or not a co-creation model.

References

Adjei, T., Griffith, A., & Noble, M. (2009). When do relationships pay off for small retailers? Exploring targets and contexts to understand the value of relationship marketing. *Journal of Retailing, 85*(4), 493–501.

Anderson, J. C., & Gerbing, D. W. (1988). Structural equation modeling in practice: A review and recommended two-step approach. *Psychological Bulletin, 103*(3), 411–423.

Auh, S., Bell, S. J., McLeod, C. S., & Shih, E. (2007). Co-production and customer loyalty in financial services. *Journal of Retailing, 83*(3), 359–370.

Bagozzi, R., & Yi, Y. (1988). On the evaluation of structural equation models. *Journal of the Academy of Marketing Science, 16*(1), 74–94.

Baldus, B. J., Voorhees, C., & Calantone, R. (2015). Online brand community engagement: Scale development and validation. *Journal of Business Research, 68*(5), 978–985.

Baron, R. M., & Kenny, D. A. (1986). The moderator-mediator variable distinction in social psychological research: Conceptual, strategic and statistical considerations. *Journal of Personality and Social Psychology, 51*(6), 1173–1182.

Béji-Bécheur, A., & Gollety, M. (2007). Lead user et leader d'opinion: Deux cibles majeures au service de l'innovation. *Décisions Marketing, 48*, 21–35.

Bharti, K., Agrawal, R., & Sharma, V. (2015). Value co-creation literature review and proposed conceptual framework. *International Journal of Market Research, 57*(4), 571–603.

Bollen, K. A., & Stine, R. (1990). Direct and indirect effects: Classical and bootstrap estimates of variability. *Sociological Methodology, 20*, 115–140.

Brady, M. K., & Cronin, J. J. (2001). Customer orientation: Effects on customer service perceptions and outcome behaviors. *Journal of Service Research, 3*(3), 241–251.

Brakus, J. J., Schmitt, B. H., & Zarantonello, L. (2009). Brand experience: What is it? How is it measured? Does it affect loyalty? *Journal of Marketing, 73*(3), 52–68.

Brodie, R. J., Illic, A., Juric, B., & Hollebeek, L. D. (2013). Consumer engagement in a virtual brand community: An exploratory analysis. *Journal of Business Research, 66*(1), 105–114.

Brown, T. J., & Dacin, P. A. (1997). The company and the product: Corporate associations and consumer product responses. *Journal of Marketing, 61*(1), 68–84.

Churchill, G. A. J. (1979). A paradigm for developing better measures of marketing constructs. *Journal of Marketing Research, 16*(1), 64–73.

Cossío-Silva, F.-J., Revilla-Camacho, M.-A., Vega-Vazquez, M., & Palacios, B. (2015). Value co-creation and customer loyalty. *Journal of Business Research, 69*(5), 1621–1625.

Fidel, P., Schlesinger, W., & Cervera, A. (2015). Collaborating to innovate: Effects on customer knowledge management and performance. *Journal of Business Research, 68*(7), 1426–1428.

Fornell, C., & Larcker, D. F. (1981). Evaluating structural equation models with unobservable variables and measurement error. *Journal of Marketing Research, 18*(1), 39–50.

Frambach, R. T., Roest, H. C., & Krishnan, T. V. (2007). The impact of consumer internet experience on channel preference and usage intentions across the different stages of the buying process. *Journal of Interactive Marketing, 21*(2), 26–41.

Franke, N., von Hippel, E., & Schreier, M. (2006). Finding commercially attractive user innovation: A test of lead-user theory. *Journal of Product Innovation Management, 23*(4), 301–315.

Fuchs, C., & Schreier, M. (2011). Customer empowerment in new product development. *Journal of Product Innovation Management, 28*(1), 17–32.

Gebauer, J., Füller, J., & Pezzei, R. (2013). The dark and the bright side of co-creation: Triggers of member behavior in online innovation communities. *Journal of Business Research, 66*(9), 1516–1527.

Grewal, D., Levy, M., & Kumar, V. (2009). Customer experience management in retailing: Anorganizingframework. *Journal of Retailing, 85*(1), 1–14.

Griffin, A., & Hauser, J. R. (1993). The voice of the customer. *Marketing Science, 12*(1), 1–27.

Hagel, J., III, & Armstrong, A. G. (1997). Net Gain: Expanding markets through virtual communities. *McKinsey Quarterly, 1*, 140–153.

Hayes, A. F. (2013). *Introduction to mediation, moderation, and conditional process analysis: A regression-based approach.* New York: Guilford Press.

Hazan, C., & Shaver, P. (1994). Attachment as an organizational framework for research on close relationships. *Psychological Inquiry: An International Journal for the Advancement of Psychological Theory, 5*(1), 1–22.

Hazan, C., & Zeifman, D. (1999). Pair bonds as attachments: Evaluating the evidence. In J. Shaver & P. R. Cassidy (Eds.), *Handbook of attachment: Theory, research, and clinical applications* (pp. 336–354). New York: Guilford Press.

Hoffman, D. L., Kopalle, P. K., & Novak, T. P. (2010). The "right" consumers for better concepts: Identifying consumers high in emergent nature to develop new product concepts. *Journal of Marketing Research, 47*(5), 854–865.

Hollebeek, L. D. (2011). Demystifying customer brand engagement: Exploring the loyalty nexus. *Journal of Marketing Management, 27*(7–8), 785–807.

Holmbeck, G. N. (1997). Toward terminological, conceptual, and statistical clarity in the study of mediators and moderators: Examples from the child-clinical and pediatric psychology literatures. *Journal of Consulting and Clinical Psychology, 65*(4), 599–610.

Hsieh, J., & Hsieh, Y. (2015). Dialogic co-creation and service innovation performance in high-tech companies. *Journal of Business Research, 68*(11), 2266–2271.

Jaakkola, E. (2014). The role of customer engagement behavior in value co-creation: A service system perspective. *Journal of Service Research, 17*(3), 247–261.

Jin, S.-A. A., & Phua, J. (2014). Following celebrities' tweets about brands: The impact of Twitter-based electronic word-of-mouth on consumers' source credibility perception, buying intention, and social identification with celebrities. *Journal of Advertising, 43*(2), 181–195.

Keller, K. (1993). Conceptualizing, measuring, and managing customer-based brand equity. *Journal of Marketing, 57*(1), 1–22.

Kline, R. B. (1998). *Principles and practice of structural equation modeling*. New York: Guilford Press.

Kozinets, R. V., de Valck, K., Wojnicki, A. C., & Wilner, S. J. S. (2010). Networked narratives: Understanding word-of-mouth marketing in online communities. *Journal of Marketing, 74*(2), 71–89.

Kunz, W., Schmitt, B., & Meyer, A. (2011). How does perceived firm innovativeness affect the consumer? *Journal of Business Research, 64*(8), 816–822.

Liljddal, K. (2016). The effects of advertising consumer co-created new products. *Journal of Advertising Research, 56*(1), 53–63.

Martin, W. C., & Lueg, J. E. (2013). Modeling word-of-mouth usage. *Journal of Business Research, 66*(7), 801–808.

Moreau, C. P., & Herd, K. B. (2010). To each his own? How comparisons with others influence consumers' evaluations of their self-designed products. *Journal of Consumer Research, 36*(5), 806–819.

Morgan-Thomas, A., & Veloutsou, C. (2013). Beyond technology acceptance: Brand relationships and online brand experience. *Journal of Business Research, 66*(1), 21–27.

Nambisan, S., & Baron, R. A. (2007). Interactions in vortual customer environments: Implications for product support and customer relationship management. *Journal of Interactive Marketing, 21*(2), 42–63.

Nunnally, J. C., & Bernstein, I. H. (1994). *Psychometric theory* (3rd ed.). New York: McGraw-Hill.

Nysveen, H., & Pedersen, P. E. (2014). Influences of co-creation on brand experience: The role of brand engagement. *International Journal of Market Research, 56*(6), 807–832.

Palmatier, R. W., Dant, R. P., Grewal, D., & Evans, K. R. (2006). Factors influencing the effectiveness of relationship marketing. *Journal of Marketing, 70*(4), 136–153.

Payne, A., & Frow, P. (2005). A strategic framework for customer relationship management. *Journal of Marketing, 69*(4), 167–176.

Podsakoff, P. M., & Organ, D. W. (1986). Self-reports in organizaitonal research: Problems and prospects. *Journal of Management, 12*(4), 531–544.

Podsakoff, P. M., MacKenzie, S. B., & Lee, J.-Y. (2003). Common method biases in behavioral research: A critical review of the literature and recommended remedies. *Journal of Applied Psychology, 88*(5), 879–903.

Prahalad, C. K., & Ramaswamy, V. (2000). Co-opting customer competence. *Harvard Business Review, 78*(1), 79–87.

Prahalad, C. K., & Ramaswamy, V. (2004). Co-creation experiences the next practice in value. *Journal of Interactive Marketing, 18*(3), 5–14.

Preacher, K. J., & Hayes, A. F. (2008). Asymptotic and resampling strategies for assessing and comparing indirect effects in multiple mediator models. *Behavior Research Methods, 40*(3), 879–891.

Putrevu, S., & Lord, K. R. (1994). Comparative and noncomparative advertising: Attitudinal effects under cognitive and affective involvement conditions. *Journal of Advertising, 23*(2), 77–91.

Rafiq, M., Fulford, H., & Lu, X. (2013). Building customer loyalty in online retailing: The role of relationship quality. *Journal of Marketing Management, 29*(3–4), 494–517.

Ramaswamy, V., & Ozcan, K. (2015). Brand value co-creation in a digitalized world: An integrative framework and research implications. *International Journal of Research in Marketing, 33*(1), 93–106. doi:10.1016/j.ijresmar.2015.07.001.

Reinartz, W., & Kumar, V. (2000). On the profitability of long-life customers in a no contractual setting: An empirical investigation and implications for marketing. *Journal of Marketing, 64*(4), 17–35.

Reynolds, F. D., & Darden, W. R. (1971). Mutually adaptive effects of interpersonal communication. *Journal of Marketing Research, 8*(4), 449–454.

Sashi, C. M. (2012). Customer engagement, buyer-seller relationships, and social media. *Management Decision, 50*(2), 253–272.

Sawhney, M., Verona, G., & Prandelli, E. (2005). Collaborating to create: The Internet as a platform for customer engagement in product innovation. *Journal of Interactive Marketing, 19*(4), 4–18.

Schreier, M., Oberhauser, S., & Prügl, R. (2007). Lead users and the adoption and diffusion of new products: Insights from two extreme sports communities. *Marketing Letters, 18*(1), 15–30.

Schreier, M., Fuchs, C., & Dahl, D. W. (2012). The innovation effect of user design: Exploring consumers' innovation perceptions of firms selling products designed by users. *Journal of Marketing, 76*(5), 18–32.

Shi, M., & Wojnicki, A. C. (2014). Money talks…to online opinion leaders: What motivates opinion leaders to make social-network referrals? *Journal of Advertising Research, 54*(1), 81–91.

Shrout, P. E., & Bolger, N. (2002). Mediation in experimental and nonexperimental studies: New procedures and recommendations. *Psychological Methods, 7*(4), 422–445.

Srinivasan, S. S., Anderson, R., & Ponnavolu, K. (2002). Customer loyalty in e-commerce: An exploration of its antecedents and consequences. *Journal of Retailing, 78*(1), 41–50.

Tripp, C., Jensen, T., & Carlson, L. (1997). The effects of multiple product endorsements by celebrities on consumers' attitudes and intentions. *Journal of Consumer Research, 20*(4), 535–547.

Urban, G. L., & von Hippel, E. (1988). Lead user analyses for the development of industrial products. *Management Science, 34*(5), 569–583.

van der Merwe, R., & van Heerden, G. (2009). Finding and utilizing opinion leaders: Social networks and the power of relationships. *South African Journal of Business Management, 40*(3), 65–77.

Vargo, S. L., & Lusch, R. F. (2004). Evolving to a new dominant logic. *Journal of Marketing, 68*(1), 1–17.

Vernette, E., & Hamdi-Kidar, L. (2013). Co-creation with consumers: Who has the competence and wants to cooperate? *International Journal of Market Research, 55*(4), 2–20.

von Hippel, E. (1986). Lead users: A source of novel product concepts. *Management Science, 32* (7), 791–805.
von Hippel, E. (2005). *Democratizing innovation*. Cambridge, MA: The MIT Press.
Wa, K., & Yiyan, S. (2010). Understanding consumer-to-consumer interactions in virtual communities: The salience of reciprocity. *Journal of Business Research, 63*(9–10), 1033–1040.
Wikström, S. (1996). The customer as co-producer. *European Journal of Marketing, 30*(4), 6–19.
Zeithaml, V., Berry, L., & Parasuraman, A. (1996). The behavioral consequences of service quality. *Journal of Management, 60*(2), 31–46.
Zhao, X., Lynch, J. G., & Chen, Q. (2010). Reconsidering Baron and Kenny: Myths and truths about mediation analysis. *Journal of Consumer Research, 37*(2), 197–206.

Knowledge and Innovation in Portuguese Enterprises

Vanessa Ratten, Carmem Leal, Marlene Loureiro, Rui Silva, and Alexandra Braga

Abstract This chapter discusses the role of knowledge and innovation in Portuguese enterprises. The role of family businesses in the Portuguese economy is stated, which highlights the link between knowledge creation and family entrepreneurship. The unique characteristics of the Portuguese economy are stated together with the reasons for the high level of family businesses. Suggestions for future research and practical implications are stated.

Keywords Family business • Innovation • Knowledge • Portugal • Small business

1 Introduction

Family businesses are considered as hybrid identity organisations as they combine the family with economic goals (Randerson, Bettinelli, Fayolle, & Anderson, 2015). The identity of family businesses is often captured in the founder who gave a sense of purpose to the emerging enterprise but also in the culture of the country in which the family business is located. Family businesses are a heterogeneous group of businesses due to differences in culture, industry, involvement, legal form and size (Kraus, Harms, & Fink, 2011). Family businesses are important parts of a countries identity as they involve social interactions that encourages a conducive environment for entrepreneurship. Jaskiewicz, Combs, and Rau (2014: 17) states "family firms are less entrepreneurial, on average, and those that are often become less so after one or two generations". Family businesses usually have a more flexible management structure. Family members play an important role in the

V. Ratten (✉)
La Trobe University, Melbourne, VIC, Australia
e-mail: v.ratten@latrobe.edu.au

C. Leal • M. Loureiro • R. Silva
University of Tras-os-Montes e Alto Douro, Vila Real, Portugal
e-mail: cleal@utad.pt; mloureiro@utad.pt; ruisilva@utad.pt

A. Braga
Polytechnic Institute of Porto, Porto, Portugal
e-mail: abraga@estgf.ipp.pt

V. Ratten et al. (eds.), *Knowledge, Learning and Innovation*, Contributions to Management Science, DOI 10.1007/978-3-319-59282-4_4

development of a family business depending on need and expertise. Family connections are important especially for internationalising family businesses who may require contacts in different countries.

The concept of family differs depending on the cultural, environmental and social context (Sharma, Melin, & Nordqvist, 2014). The cultural context of a country is dependent on family businesses to maintain social and economic connections (Martin-Reyna & Duran-Encalada, 2012). This has meant that family businesses are amongst the most common type of business and permeate society due to their linkages with the community. Family businesses tend to focus on their sense of identity for the long term viability of their brand and position in society (Patel & Chrisman, 2013). Most family businesses have a sense of uniqueness about them due to the inherent cultural considerations. Often family businesses will seek to maintain their goodwill in the community by foregoing short term gain for long term objectives. This has meant that family businesses are considered to be more loyal as they try to ensure their sense of trustworthiness (Miller, Le Breton-Miller, Lester, & Cannella, 2007). Miralees-Marcelo, Miralles-Quiros, and Lisboa (2014) in a study of Portuguese and Spanish family businesses found that the person who manages the firm influence risk exposure and financial performance because of the cultural considerations. The country context influences the performance of family businesses (Martin-Reyna & Duran-Encalada, 2012). This country context is an important way to understand how family businesses innovate, growth and internationalise.

Most existing research on family business has tended to use a generic definition of the family without taking into account cultural or social contexts (Randerson et al., 2015). This restricts a holistic understanding about family due to the issue of culture inherent in business. Families are products of the cultural setting and are conceptualised based on social factors. This has meant that there is a lack of consensus in the literature about how to define a family business. Some define a family business in terms of shareholdings. For example, Barantoni and Caprio (2006) define a family business as when the largest shareholder controls owns more than 10% of the ownership rights. Others define a family business in terms of family involved in management decision making. Miller et al. (2007) define them in this way by stating that family businesses occur when members of the same family comprise most of the management staff. More recently Miralees-Marcelo et al. (2014) stated that a family business is an organisation that is controlled and owned by a family. This definition is adopted in our chapter as it includes a wide and non-discriminatory definition of family.

Traditionally family businesses have been the main form of management in the global economy (Randerson et al., 2015). This is due to family businesses creating business revenue despite economic hardship. Due to the increase in the knowledge economy more people are becoming entrepreneurs and forming family businesses. This is due to self employment offering career prospects for people wanting to start new ventures. Steier (2009) suggests that most entrepreneurial behaviours start in a family context and are then influenced by the environment. Therefore, increasingly the family has been considered as important to understanding entrepreneurial activity (Randerson et al., 2015).

This chapter is structured as follows. The first section discussed family businesses with a focus on entrepreneurship. Next, the Portuguese shoe industry is discussed in terms of its composition of family owned and managed businesses. Lastly, the implications for practitioners including family business owners and future research suggestions are stated.

2 Family Business Theory

There are a number of main theories that are widely used to understand family business: agency, resource-based view, socioemotional wealth, stewardship and behavioural (Le Breton-Miller, Miller, & Bares, 2015). Agency theory is used to explain the work relationships between owners, employees and stakeholders of a business. Typically most agency theory has characterised one party doing the work and the other determining how the work is done. In family business, agency theory describes how the ownership and management are linked (Le Breton-Miller et al., 2015). This means that the monitoring of the work is low due to the personal and social relationships people have in family businesses. Fama and Jensen (1983) suggested that it is hard sometimes to separate the control and ownership of businesses due to personal relationships. This means that whilst agency costs might be low in family businesses there is a risk of resources being inadequately utilised. A reason for this might be due to family members exercising their control and power so that the agency relationship is unequal (Le Breton-Miller et al., 2015).

Agency theory incorporates positive, negative and neutral outcomes from family businesses (Randerson et al., 2015). The agency theory acknowledges that there are problems associated with family businesses such as balancing work and family life (Anderson & Reeb, 2003). Other issues that the agency theory seeks to understand are the nepotism and favouritism that is present in some family businesses (Lubatkin, Schulze, Ling, & Dino, 2005). An interesting study by Karra, Tracey, and Phillips (2006) discussed agency problems in the context of family businesses entering into international new ventures and suggested that family relationships can both help and hinder the internationalisation process. Randerson et al. (2015: 148) states that "no consensus exists as to whether entrepreneurial family firms have more agency constraints or agency advantages". Therefore, agency theory tends to focus on the presence of intra-family convergence and divergence depending on the stage of business development (Carney, 2005).

The resource based view is a popular theory both in family business but non-family business studies. The resource based view suggests that firm strategies are based on financial and non-financial considerations. This means that family firms manage their resources differently particularly their intangible resources such as brand image and reputation (Le Breton-Miller et al., 2015). Human resources are especially important for family businesses as people employed tend to stay longer because of social connections. This means that from a resource-based family businesses focus on long term objectives forsaking immediate gain for more strategic objectives (Habbershon, Williams, & MacMillan, 2003). The size of a family business affects its ability to access resources that might play a critical part in internationalization efforts.

Randerson et al. (2015: 149) defines socioemotional wealth as "affective endowments that family owners consciously or unconsciously establish with the firm". The socioemotional wealth theory of family business suggests that habitual entrepreneurship may emerge because of family dynamics (Gomez-Mejia, Hoskisson, Makri, Sirmon, & Campbell, 2011). Socioemotional wealth for family businesses means providing income and jobs to family members (Gomez-Meija et al., 2007). This can have positive affects as there is more long term orientation for family businesses but can influence the level of entrepreneurship. This means that to understand family business we need to focus on both the social aspects of a family but also on the emotional sides that are inherent in being part of a family.

Stewardship theory is another way to understand family business due to its emphasis on both individual and firm level behaviour (Randerson et al., 2015). The stewardship theory suggests that family owners act as stewards looking after value for all stakeholders (Miller, Le-Breton-Miller, & Scholnick, 2008). This means that family businesses seek to balance both internal and external stakeholder relationships.

Behavioral theory focuses more on the behavioural aspects inherent in family businesses. This can be an issue in terms of opportunity recognition and encouraging an entrepreneurial culture in a family business (Miller & Le Breton-Miller, 2005). There is some research that exists about behaviours in family businesses suggesting they are risk averse rather than innovative. Therefore, the behavioural agency theory has been helpful in explaining the changing societal context and attitudes towards family businesses. The behavioural agency theory is adopted in this chapter as it provides the best way to understand Portuguese family shoe businesses.

3 Family Business

There is an emphasis on communication in family businesses due to the need for consensus and greater understanding about potential economic effects (Le Breton-Miller et al., 2015). This means that in family businesses the decision making processes are usually more based on consultation that leads to a more holistic understanding about decisions (Miralees-Marcelo et al., 2014). The negative components of a family business refer to their focus on the business at the expense of other opportunities. This may mean that they can be too concentrated in a single asset and unwilling to divert assets into other projects (Gomez-Meija et al., 2007). The information contained in a family business is often difficult to obtain, which is a competitive strength but also a disadvantage in terms of takeovers or buyouts. The information tends to be less transparent as there is often no need to share it with outside parties.

Many businesses particularly small ones are founded with financial and human resources from family members (Chrisman, Chua, & Litz, 2003). Some family businesses are renewed by bringing in outside managers who have a new perspective. This helps to change the organisational culture in family businesses from being risk averse and conservative to entrepreneurial. The goals of family businesses may be different to non-family businesses due to the different conceptualisations of performance.

Family members usually share more information with each other leading to stronger network ties (Kraus et al., 2011). This means that there are different sources of family business capital including human capital, governance structures, and social capital (Sirmon & Hitt, 2003). These sources of capital impact the survivability of family businesses in terms of long term performance. Family businesses transfer capabilities across generations such as knowledge and core competences (Habbershon & Williams, 1999). Most family businesses take a long term orientation about their strategic direction (Le Breton-Miller & Miller, 2006). This can be a limitation as they focus on succession interests rather than business opportunities.

Familiness is a term used to describe the unique synergistic resources that are in families (Habbershon, Williams, & MacMillan, 2003). Familiness has been used to explain the way families are inseparable and interact with each other to create distinct capabilities (Kraus et al., 2011). Family businesses are a continuous development as they bridge culture with power in a business setting. This means that familiarity as a by-product of being in a family will help to increase trust in a business setting.

Wright, Chrisman, Chua, and Steier (2014) suggest there are different contexts that influence family business. The meso or organizational context focuses on the internal environment of a family business in terms of its policies and governance structures. The organizational context helps to understand the resources that a family business has and how they align with their goals and strategic direction. Some family businesses will have an organisational context more conducive to entrepreneurship depending on the attitudes of family members.

Most business ventures start with some kind of family backing in the form of financial and/or non-financial resources (Astrachan, 2003). Heck, Hoy, Poutziouris, and Steier (2008: 324) states that "family entrepreneurship involves the underpinnings and interactions of two systems, namely the family system and the business system". The word entrepreneuring family has been used to describe the innovativeness and risk taking of family businesses (Uhlaner, Kellermans, Eddleston, & Hoy, 2012). This word has been used due to families having a crucial role in influencing entrepreneurial behaviours of individuals (Bettinelli, Fayolle, & Randerson, 2014). This is due to some families viewing innovation as important and a way of life despite the failures they may occur.

The transmission of entrepreneurial values in a family is shared through communication about behaviour. Serial business families occur when an original family business is transformed into a new family business (Randerson et al., 2015). The process of entrepreneurship in a family business context involves exploiting opportunity internally using knowledge and expertise but also externally by forming partnerships (Randerson et al., 2015).

4 Portugal

Portugal has a leather manufacturing heritage similar to that of countries such as France and Italy but only recently has the industry gained international prominence (Mellery-Pratt, 2015). In Portugal, the historical regions of Guimaraes has grown in terms of the number of exports of leather shoes (Mellery-Pratt, 2015). The reason for this increase has been the greater attention placed on Portuguese shoes and the costs advantages compared to other European countries. Portugal has a similar cultural and social role of family enterprises, which is similar to Italy. There are many family owned shoe manufacturers that pride themselves on attention to detail and high quality products.

The family business sector has contributed significantly to the Portuguese economy (Howorth & Ali, 2001). Portugal has a large percentage of small family firms and many large firms are also family businesses. Casimiro and Chambel (2014) in a study about Portuguese family businesses found that cultural patterns and the founders academic level affects business performance. Many of the footwear family businesses took a traditional approach to new business opportunities but this has changed with newer generations entering the business.

Despite the cost advantages of shoes made in Portugal there has been an increase in high priced shoes. This became more known after Pippa Middleton, sister of the Duchess of Cambridge, wore Portuguese made shoes to the royal wedding. This has led to more global recognition of the 'Made in Portugal' label for shoes but it is still considered less known compared to the more famous Italian brands such as Tods. This has been an advantage as Portuguese shoe companies have increasingly focused on niche markets such as high fashion women's shoes or in the case of Wolf & Sons male contemporary shoes.

The Association of Portuguese manufacturers of Portuguese shoes has begun a marketing campaign aimed at focusing on the sexiness of Portuguese shoes (Eytan, 2015). This has produced some changing perceptions in consumer's eyes about the image of Portugal. Most of the shoes made in Portugal are exported as it is important to have a contemporary image associated with the country. The sexiness campaign for the 'Made in Portugal' brand has coincided with more interest in Portuguese fashion. Whilst leather shoes are the main fashion item associated with Portugal there has also been an increase in handbags and accessories. To further strengthen the 'Made in Portugal' brand there has been more focus on innovation in terms of colours and materials used (Eytan, 2015).

The launch of the 'Portuguese shoes: The sexiest industry in Europe' started after the global financial crisis, which affected the Portuguese economy. Most of the Portuguese shoe industry is concentrated in the north of the country. The shoe industry in Portugal has been amongst the most successful internationally orientated industry. As a country Portugal is seen as a neutral European country that does not have the large population of neighbouring countries such as Spain. There is also an emphasis in the Portuguese economy on sustainability and the environment, which has impacted the way shoes are produced. Recently Portugal was amongst the first countries in the world to run solely on renewable energy, which created global attention on the country as a leader in sustainability.

Portugal's entry into the European Union solidified its position as a manufacturer of cost efficient leather goods. The shoe industry in Portugal had to change its strategic direction after China became a global player and major manufacturer of shoes. Instead of competing on price Portuguese shoe companies focused on high-quality shoes. This enabled them to emphasise the heritage of many family owned shoe companies that are more interested in their reputation and brand image than price. This emphasis on quality also linked with the technological innovations and marketing capabilities of the Portuguese shoe businesses.

Alberto Sousa is a Portuguese shoe company located northeast of Porto that successfully changed its business strategy after losing business to China (Leiber, 2015). The company who is amongst the biggest shoe producer in Portugal employs 430 people and has an annual revenue of $28 million Euro (Leiber, 2015).

In Portugal, there are more than 1500 shoe factories mostly located in the North who export more than 1.8 billion euro of shoes every year (Leiber, 2015). The shoe industry is a significant component of the Portuguese economy as it employs more than 37,000 people (Leiber, 2015). The transformation of the Portuguese shoe industry from low cost to high cost is a successful economic story that can be applied to other industries. The rise in the exports of Portuguese shoes has been helped by the Portuguese Footwear Technology Centre, which helps shoemakers incorporate new innovations in their manufacturing processes. Portuguese shoe companies have continued to manufacture shoes instead of the increasing strategy favoured by Italian shoe companies of finishing shoes from imports (Leiber, 2015).

Howorth and Ali (2001: 232) states "Portugal has one of the highest rates of marriage and lowest divorce rates in Europe, indicating that traditional family stems may be more predominant". The focus on the family in Portugal may stem from the religious and societal environment that is part of the culture. This emphasis on traditional family values links to the large percentage of family businesses that are part of the Portuguese economy. In addition to the family owned Portuguese shoe businesses there are foreign owned shoe manufacturers in Portugal.

Shoemaking is amongst the oldest industries in Portugal that has played a central role in the economic performance of the country (Soares, 2013). In Guimaraes, which is the oldest city in Portugal the shoe industry has remained despite other industries leaving for emerging economies including China because of their lower labour rate (Soares, 2013). Some Portuguese shoe makers are innovating by adopting Anglo-Saxon names that are easier to remember for international customers (Soares, 2013). Examples of Portuguese shoe makers with Anglo-Saxon names include Camport, Fly London and Softwaves.

Portugal has a culture that exhibits strong family values that encourages the maintenance of family businesses. In the Portuguese shoe industry family members are tied to each other because of mutual economic interest. This facilitates cooperation and sharing amongst family members about the competitiveness of the shoe industry. Family relationships can ensure solidarity and reciprocity to ensure the ongoing future success of Portuguese shoes.

Portugal is in a convenient geographic location being close to the fashion and financial capitals of London and Paris. In the 1990s many textile producers moved to Asia due to cost advantages but many have returned to Portugal. This has been due to Portugal's locational advantages but also reputation of high quality and qualified textile manufacturers. Portugal has a textile industry heritage particularly in the shoe industry. Portuguese people are considered to be hardworking and trustworthy as business partners that have a strong focus on family business. In addition, due to Portugal being a member of the European Union there are lower customs and taxes compared to businesses from Asia and other geographic locations. The main shoe producers in Portugal are located in Felgueiras and Sao Joao de Madeira.

The shoe industry in Portugal helped the country overcome the austerity measures implemented after the global financial crisis. Helsar is a family shoe company located near Porto that became famous after Pippa Middleton commissioned shoes from them for the royal wedding. Manufacturing technology in Portugal has continually innovated enabling shoes to be made from cutting edge technology. The 'Made in Portugal' name has increased in prestige due to its association with high quality fashion conscious products. Globally, Portugal is amongst the top shoe manufacturers. Due to increased ease of doing business across borders in Europe, Portugal has become more concerned about their global competitiveness.

The Danish shoemaker Ecco has a Portuguese plant that is located in a geographic area known for shoe production. Paradigma is Portuguese family shoe business that is owned by second generation family members (www.paradigmafootwear.com). Paradigma has incorporated a family business ethos to produce shoes that have a distinct craftsmanship. The Portuguese shoe making business has been changed with the modernisation of factories and increase in creative ideas.

5 Future Research Suggestions

Further studies need to focus on the family dynamics of the Portuguese shoe industry to observe their innovative capacity. Future research on the 'Made in Portugal' role in invigorating family businesses might be useful. There are some interesting questions future research about Portuguese family business that should be explored including: How do family businesses in Portugal differ to other countries? Why have Portuguese family businesses been successful in the shoe industry? What is the role of Portuguese culture and society in influencing the success of family business?

6 Conclusion

This book chapter has discussed the role of entrepreneurship and innovation in the success of Portuguese shoe family businesses. The findings of this chapter can help to inform theories about how traditional textile industries can utilise family businesses in the global marketplace. The lack of research about Portuguese family business means that there is a need to study the processes that lead them to international success.

References

Anderson, R. C., & Reeb, D. M. (2003). Founding family ownership and firm performance: Evidence from the S&P 500. *Journal of Finance, 58*(3), 1301–1328.

Astrachan, J. H. (2003). The emergence of a field: Commentary on the special issue 'The evolving family/entrepreneurship relationship'. *Journal of Business Venturing, 18*(5), 567–572.

Barantoni, R., & Caprio, L. (2006). The effect of family control on firm value and performance: Evidence from continental Europe. *European Financial Management, 1*, 689–723.

Bettinelli, C., Fayolle, A., & Randerson, K. (2014). Family entrepreneurship: A developing field. *Foudnations and Trends in Entrepreneurship, 10*(3), 161–236.

Carney, M. (2005). Corporate governance and competitive advantage in family controlled firms. *Entrepreneurship Theory and Practice, 29*(3), 249–265.

Casimiro, M., & Chambel, M. J. (2014). Culture in small-sized Portuguese family businesses. *Management Research: The Journal of the Iberoamerican Academy of Management, 12*(1), 40–67.

Chrisman, J. J., Chua, J., & Litz, R. (2003). A unified perspective of family firm performance: An extension and integration. *Journal of Business Venturing, 18*(4), 467–472.

Eytan, D. (2015). *Portugal wants to be sexy, as it aims to rebrand 'Made in Portugal' image*. Last visited November 4, 2016, from www.forbes.com

Fama, E. F., & Jensen, M. C. (1983). Separation of ownership and control. *Journal of Law and Economics, 26*, 301–325.

Gomez-Meija, L. R., Haynes, K. T., Nunez-Nickel, M., Jacobson, K. J. L., & Moyano-Fuentes, J. (2007). Socioemotional wealth and business risks in family-controlled firms: Evidence from Spanish olive oil mills. *Administration Science, 52*, 106–137.

Gomez-Mejia, L. R., Hoskisson, R. E., Makri, M., Sirmon, D. G., & Campbell, J. T. (2011). *Innovation and the preservation of socioemotional wealth: The paradox of R&D investment in family-controlled high technology firms* (Working paper). College Station, TX: Mays Business School, Texas A&M University.

Habbershon, T. G., & Williams, M. L. (1999). A resource-based framework for assessing the strategic advantages of family firms. *Family Business Review, 12*, 1–25.

Habbershon, T. G., Williams, M., & MacMillan, J. C. (2003). A unified systems perspective of family firm performance. *Journal of Business Venturing, 18*(4), 451–465.

Heck, R. K. Z., Hoy, F., Poutziouris, P. Z., & Steier, L. P. (2008). Emerging paths of family entrepreneurship research. *Journal of Small Business Management, 46*(3), 317–330.

Howorth, C., & Ali, Z. A. (2001). Family business succession in Portugal: An examination of case studies in the furniture industry. *Family Business Review, XIV*(3), 231–244.

Jaskiewicz, P., Combs, J. G., & Rau, S. B. (2014). Entrepreneurial legacy: Towards a theory of how some family firms nurture transgenerational entrepreneurship. *Journal of Business Venturing, 30*(1), 29–49.

Karra, N., Tracey, P., & Phillips, N. (2006). Altruism and agency in the family firm: Exploring the role of family, kinship and ethnicity. *Entrepreneurship Theory and Practice, 30*(6), 861–877.

Kraus, S., Harms, R., & Fink, M. (2011). Family firm research: Sketching a research field. *International Journal of Entrepreneurship and Innovation Management, 13*(1), 32–47.

Le Breton-Miller, L., & Miller, I. (2006). Why do some family businesses out compete? Governance, long-term orientations and sustainable capability. *Entrepreneurship Theory and Practice, 30*(6), 731–746.

Le Breton-Miller, L., Miller, I., & Bares, F. (2015). Governance and entrepreneurship in family firms: Agency, behavioral agency and resource-based comparisons. *Journal of Family Business Strategy, 6*, 58–62.

Leiber, N. (2015). *Portuguese shoemakers get fancy*. Last visited November 4, 2016, from www.bloomberg.com

Lubatkin, M. H., Schulze, W. S., Ling, Y., & Dino, R. N. (2005). The effects of parental altruism on the governance of family-managed firms. *Journal of Organizational Behavior, 26*(3), 313–330.

Martin-Reyna, J., & Duran-Encalada, J. (2012). The relationship among family business, corporate governance and firm performance: Evidence from the Mexican stock exchange. *Journal of Family Business Strategy, 3*, 106–117.

Mellery-Pratt, R. (2015). *Made in Portugal' is on the rise*. Last visited November 4, 2016, from www.businessoffashion.com

Miller, D., & Le Breton-Miller, I. (2005). *Managing for the long run: Lessons in competitive advantage from great family businesses*. Boston: Harvard Business Press.

Miller, D., Le Breton-Miller, I., Lester, R. H., & Cannella, A. A. (2007). Are family firms really superior performers? *Journal of Corporate Finance, 13*, 829–858.

Miller, D., Le-Breton-Miller, I., & Scholnick, B. (2008). Stewardship vs stagnation: An empirical comparison of small family and non-family businesses. *Journal of Management Studies, 45*(1), 51–78.

Miralees-Marcelo, J. L., Miralles-Quiros, M., & Lisboa, I. (2014). The impact of family control on firm performance: Evidence from Portugal and Spain. *Journal of Family Business Strategy, 5*, 156–168.

Patel, R., & Chrisman, J. (2013). Risk abatement as a strategy for R&D investments in family firms. *Strategic Management Journal, 35*(4), 617–627.

Randerson, K., Bettinelli, C., Fayolle, A., & Anderson, A. (2015). Family entrepreneurship as a field of research: Exploring its contours and contents. *Journal of Family Business Strategy, 6*, 143–154.

Sharma, P., Melin, L., & Nordqvist, M. (2014). Scope, evolution and future of family business studies. In L. Melin, M. Nordqvist, & P. Sharma (Eds.), *Sage handbook of family business* (pp. 1–23). London: Sage.

Sirmon, D. G., & Hitt, M. A. (2003). Managing resources: Linking unique resources, management and wealth creation in family firms. *Entrepreneurship Theory and Practice, 27*, 339–358.

Soares, I. (2013). *How 'Made in Portugal' is expanding its footprint on global stage*. Last visited November 4, 2016, from www.edition.cnn.com

Steier, I. (2009). Where do new firms come from? Households, family capital, ethnicity and the welfare mix. *Family Business Review, 22*(3), 273–278.

Uhlaner, L. M., Kellermans, F. W., Eddleston, K. A., & Hoy, F. (2012). The entrepreneuring family: A new paradigm for family business research. *Small Business Economics, 38*(1), 1–11.

Wright, M., Chrisman, J. J., Chua, J. H., & Steier, L. P. (2014). Family enterprise and context. *Entrepreneurship Theory and Practice, 38*, 1247–1260.

Social Ties and Human Capital in Family SMEs' Internationalization

Masoud Karami, Cici Xiao He, and Shang Zhengang

Abstract While family business internationalization has been studied from different perspectives, we investigated the role of social ties, and human capital in internationalization of entrepreneurial family businesses. More importantly we have considered gender as an influential factor in applying human capital and social ties in internationalization efforts.

Keywords Social ties • Human capital • Internationalization • Family business

1 Introduction

Internationalization of family businesses is considered as an important topic in global economy (Ratten, Dana, & Ramadani, 2017). Entrepreneur's social ties play an important role in a family's SME internationalization. With the liability of limited resources, SMEs rely on entrepreneurs' social ties to explore international opportunities (Ellis, 2011; Schweizer, Vahlne, & Johanson, 2010). Considering the family ownership and involvement (Pukall & Calabrò, 2014), an entrepreneur's family relationships, especially the relationship between the first and second generation, is an important type of social ties that have an influence on the internationalization of firms (Lu, Au, Peng, & Xu, 2013; Saxena, 2013).

As extant literature shows, while female entrepreneurs are influenced by their skills, knowledge, and specifically the level of education (Carter, Brush, Greene, Gatewood, & Hart, 2003), they are generally excluded from social networks (Brush, 1990; Manolova, Carter, Manev, & Gyoshev, 2007; Woldie & Adersua, 2004), and therefore have some difficulties in leveraging networks to explore international opportunities. Indeed, developing social ties is more challenging for female than male entrepreneurs. Considering that men and women entrepreneurs' networking

M. Karami (✉) • C.X. He
University of Otago, Dunedin, New Zealand
e-mail: masoud.karami@postgrad.otago.ac.nz; cici.he@otago.ac.nz

S. Zhengang
Shanghai Jiaotong University Overseas Education Colleague, Shanghai, China
e-mail: szhengang@sjtu-oec.com

V. Ratten et al. (eds.), *Knowledge, Learning and Innovation*, Contributions to Management Science, DOI 10.1007/978-3-319-59282-4_5

behaviours are different (Hisrich & Fülöp, 1997; Manolova et al., 2007; Woldie & Adersua, 2004), investigating gender's effect on using social ties in the internationalization of family business remains under-researched. Based on this background, this research focuses on the following questions: How and why do two different genders of entrepreneurs use social ties in family SMEs' internationalization?

When combining gender and family entrepreneurship as the two perspectives in the study of SMEs' internationalization, entrepreneurs' human capital (Becker, 1993), that is, the level of education, business experience and business skills, is considered to be the concept that links these two perspectives. Human capital as representation of two critical, initial means of an entrepreneur, that is, "who I am and what I know" (Sarasvathy, 2001) influence the entrepreneur's networking behaviour. Considering that human capital is embodied in people (Becker, 1993), gender can play a critical role in a human being's self-recognition, and therefore in human capital. Given the importance of the entrepreneurs rather than the firm in developing international opportunity in SMEs (family businesses) (Ellis, 2011), the entrepreneur's networking behaviours play a critical role in these firms. In this vein and in response to a call for more research on the role of social ties in family SMEs' internationalization (Kontinen & Ojala, 2011; Mustafa & Chen, 2010), and the influence of human capital on women entrepreneurs' success (Davidsson & Honig, 2003), this study focuses on the role of human capital in the use of social ties by considering gender as the moderating factor in family SMEs' internationalization. By explaining this relationship, we contribute to the family business internationalization literature by highlighting the role of gender differences in terms of using human capital and networking behaviours when developing international opportunities.

Case studies are employed in this research to answer the "how and why" question (Eisenhardt & Graebner, 2007). We examine four internationalizing Chinese family SMEs including different genders of entrepreneurs. China is a suitable context for the aims of this research for two reasons. First, studying the internationalization of family businesses in dynamic environments with quick changes is considered as an important topic (Ratten et al., 2017). Second, the collectivist culture of China (Hofstede & Hofstede, 2005) provides a rich setting for studying firms' networking behaviours. As the literature shows, personal networks are often highlighted in the studies of Chinese entrepreneurs (e.g. Luo, 2007; Poutziouris & Chittenden, 1996; Shi & Dana, 2013). Third, although, the female-owned family SME is a relatively new phenomenon in China, there is a high growth of successful female-owned businesses in China (Kitching & Jackson, 2002).

We review the literature on networking, gender, and human capital in the internationalization of family business in the following part. Then, we describe the research method and summarise the four cases. After that, we will present the findings and discussion. Finally, the managerial applications will be provided.

2 Literature Review

2.1 *Networking and Internationalization*

A network perspective to internationalization has gained momentum after the revisited Uppsala model. According to this perspective, internationalization is not a matter of overcoming the liability of foreignness; rather it is the matter of networking and having the right position in related network(s). This implies that internationalization is a matter of overcoming the liability of outsidership (Johanson & Vahlne, 2009). Put simply, SMEs can enter foreign markets resting on contacts and network relationships and start their internationalization with scarce resources (Ruzzier, Antonci, Hisrich, & Konecnik, 2007). The revisited Uppsala model has been used to explain the internationalization of family businesses (e.g., Casillas, 2005; Graves & Thomas, 2008). There is a huge body of literature on the role of networks in the internationalization process of SMEs (e.g., Chetty & Agndal, 2008; Coviello & Munro, 1997). Empirical evidence shows that networks provide competitive advantage for internationalizing firms (Wright, Filatotchev, Hoskisson, & Peng, 2005). In these studies, networks provide the internationalization knowledge, opportunity, and experience (Kontinen & Ojala, 2010); help to avoid problems (Mainela & Puhakka, 2009); diminish the risks associated with crossing borders (Crick & Crick, 2016); facilitate growth in international markets (Gabrielsson & Gabrielsson, 2013), and accelerate entering into several markets in a relatively short time (Andersson, 2011). From an opportunity-based view, the core function of networking in the internationalization process is co-creation of an opportunity for internationalization through sharing available resources (Sarasvathy, Kumar, York, & Bhagavatula, 2014). However, there is not enough research on the process of the creation of networks (by family firms) in their internationalization process (Johanson & Vahlne, 2009).

2.2 *Family Business and Networking*

The importance of network analysis in family business has been emphasized in extant family business literature (Oswald, Muse, & Rutherford, 2009; Zamudio, Anokhin, & Kellermanns, 2014). Family kinship networks facilitate knowledge sharing and trust between family firms, and pool resources to pursue goals (Ratten, 2015). Shi and Dana (2013) observed that the entrepreneur's socialisation behaviors have an important influence on the firms operation. The network approach to SMEs' internationalization has been applied in the context of family SMEs (e.g., Kontinen & Ojala, 2010; Ratten et al., 2017). The basic idea is that the founder's personal networks and the family firm's business network facilitate its foreign market entry process (Manolova et al., 2010). In this perspective, social capital is considered as a resource for agents' actions (Coleman, 1988). The family's social network ties provide resources, and protect the family business from risks of being involved in external networks (Anderson, Jack, & Dodd, 2005). In family business, factors such as little international experience, resistance of managers towards internationalization, reluctance to make alliances with third parties, lack of technological and financial resources, and the reliance of family business on domestic market (Gallo & García Pont, 1996) prohibit internationalization. Thus, having access to related networks in foreign markets can play an important role in family businesses' internationalization by providing help to find new customers, suppliers, and employees, and for financing, business growth, introducing export opportunities, advertising, managing production operation, and legal issues (Anderson et al., 2005).

2.3 Human Capital and Internationalization

Human capital has been considered to be a critical resource for firms (Hitt, Biermant, Shimizu, & Kochhar, 2001), and it has long been argued to be an important factor in entrepreneurial firms' success (Unger, Rauch, Frese, & Rosenbusch, 2011). An SME's internationalization often relies on an entrepreneur as a key person (Ruzzier, Antoncic, & Konecnik, 2006). Therefore, the entrepreneur's personal factors are critical because they can influence a firm's performance. For instance, Hitt et al. (2001) observe that human capital can influence a professional service firm's performance and it can moderate the relationship between a firm's strategy and its performance. In a broad definition, human capital represents "an intangible resource (i.e., knowledge, education, skills and experience) that allows firms to add value to other tangible firm-specific resources in the pursuit of competitive advantage" (DeNoble, Ehrlich, & Singh, 2007). It is the result of experiential learning and formal and informal education such as particular training courses (Davidsson & Honig, 2003). Human capital leads to capabilities, skills and knowledge in people to help them to behave in new ways (Coleman, 1988), and to explore new opportunities and assemble resources to exploit them (Alvarez & Busenitz, 2001). That is, entrepreneurs with higher levels of human capital do better when exploring opportunities (Ruzzier et al., 2007). Greene and Brown (1997) observed that human capital along with social capital is critical for entrepreneurship in terms of entrepreneurs' capabilities and knowledge, as initial resources of business venturing. The entrepreneur's human capital is important because it shows the initial basis of the entrepreneur for gaining other sources in the process of venturing (Carter et al., 2003). Considering that human capital is embodied in people (Becker, 1993), and considering the importance of the individual in SMEs (family businesses) in developing international opportunities (Ellis, 2011), human capital plays a critical role in these firms.

A review of the extant literature on SME internationalization reveals that human capital plays an important role in SME internationalization (Manolova, Brush, Edelman, & Greene, 2002). Ruzzier et al. (2007) measured the impact of four dimensions of human capital: international orientation, environmental risk perception, international business skills and management know-how on SME internationalization (Ruzzier et al., 2007). Along this line, Javalgi and Todd (2011) observed that an entrepreneur's educational level and international experience as two dimensions of human capital affect the firm's degree of internationalization. The entrepreneur's experiential knowledge as an important part of her or his human capital plays an important role in successful internationalization (Johanson & Vahlne, 2009). Different scholars have talked about various types of experience in the international business context. Examples are international operations experience, and decision-specific experience (Padmanabhan & Cho, 1999). Other types of entrepreneur's knowledge, such as foreign market knowledge (Brennan & Garvey, 2009; Ruzzier et al., 2007) play important role in SMEs' internationalization. Internationalizing SMEs use these experiences to decrease the perceived uncertainty and develop internationalization opportunities (Johanson & Vahlne, 2006). Therefore, human capital plays an important role in internationalization of family businesses. However, the impact of human capital on firm's internationalization is under researched and needs to be more elaborated (Ruzzier et al., 2007).

2.4 Gender, Internationalization, and Networking Behaviours

Gender has always been considered as an important factor in international entrepreneurship studies. For instance, Manolova et al. (2007) observe that gender of entrepreneurs influences the relationship between entrepreneurs' human capital, networking behaviours and entrepreneurial growth expectancies. As mentioned in entrepreneurship literature, education as a critical part of human capital plays an important role for female entrepreneurs (Bates, 1990). An entrepreneur's gender can influence a firm's intention to internationalize such that female entrepreneurs may face some particular barriers in their internationalization decisions; these include cultural discrimination in foreign business relationships, getting legitimacy, securing financial resources, and accessing related networks (Alon, Yeheskel, Lerner, & Zhang, 2013).

While networks play a critical role in SME internationalization (Chetty & Agndal, 2008), extant literature shows that female entrepreneurs have difficulties in their networking efforts (Ramadani, Hisrich, & Gërguri-Rashiti, 2015; Woldie & Adersua, 2004), and while men entrepreneurs rely on advice from their network ties, women entrepreneurs have difficulties in accessing or creating high-quality business networks and getting business consultancies from network ties (Ramadani, Gerguri, Dana, & Tašaminova, 2013; Ramadani et al., 2015). Besides, when female entrepreneurs network, they interact more with female than with male entrepreneurs (Brush & Hisrich, 1991; Carter et al., 2003). Therefore, women entrepreneurs mainly rely on their own prior experience (Manolova et al., 2007), which is part of their human capital. However, reviewing the extant literature reveals that although gender is considered an important factor in entrepreneurship (McClelland, Swail, Bell, & Ibbotson, 2005), its influence on family SME internationalization in terms of founder's human capital and networking behaviours is not clear yet.

3 Research Method

This study conducted a series of case studies (Eisenhardt, 1989; Eisenhardt & Graebner, 2007) to answer the "how and why" question (Eisenhardt & Graebner, 2007). Case study is also used to explain relatively new phenomenon and facilitates proto-theoretic contributions that at least indicate directions or questions for subsequent theorizing (Woodside & Wilson, 2003). Studying international business combining gender and family entrepreneurship is relatively new to the entrepreneurship field. Thus, case study is appropriate in this research.

The authors chose four Chinese family SMEs following Eisenhardt's (1989) suggestion that choosing four to ten cases allows patterns to develop using replication logic. These SMEs should have more than 3 years of experience in international business and have entered more than two foreign markets. They are either manufacturers exporting products or trading companies in exporting or cooperation with foreign partners doing investment projects in China. The authors also follow the Chinese government's regulations, *Law of the People's Republic of China on Promotion of Small and Medium-sized Enterprises* (2003) and *Small and Medium-sized Enterprises Designated Standards* (2011) to define SMEs based on the number of employees and the category of firm. For manufacturers, the number of employees is under 1000 in China. For trading companies, the number of employees is under 300.

To achieve a thorough understanding of family business, the authors chose family business more broadly and inclusively as a firm that is controlled by the founders, or by the founders' families and heirs (Burkart, Panunzi, & Shleifer, 2003). Two of the SMEs were established by female entrepreneurs and the other two were founded by male entrepreneurs. These four founders are all considered to be the first generation in their families and their second generation are family members over 20 years old who have the potential of taking over the company.

The authors used their personal networks in China and 'snowballing' method to get access to the cases. Two of the authors are originally from China and now running an entrepreneur training programme in China. They have a strong relationship with the participants because of this programme. The reliability of the data also rested on the personal trust between these authors and participants. The main method to collect the data was semi-structured, face-to-face interview.

4 Data Analysis and Results

The author follows the data analysis step suggested in Eisenhardt (1989). The following part shows the case summaries of the four SMEs in this research. It provides basic information of the cases, their internationalization, and their family involvement.

Case A
It was established in 1994 by a male entrepreneur. The founder holds 90% of the company stock and his wife and son hold 10%. The main products are children's clothing and accessories. All the products are exported to Europe, mainly France. The companynow has about 400 employees and annual sales output value of RMB two billion yuan.

The company conducts only OEM products. The French client, the main client, takes 90% of the annual sales. This supplier-seller relationship has existed for more than 20 years. The entrepreneur visits France at least once a year and has developed a close relationship with this client, much like a family relationship.

The entrepreneur is around 60 years old and is the president of this company. His son is 20 years old and joined the company last year.

Case B
The company was established in 1992 by a male entrepreneur. The founder holds 90% of the stock, his wife holds 5%, and his son 5%. The value of company assets is 200 million RMB (31 million US). The main products are goose materials and goose bedding. The company now has around 80 people in the administration and 300 workers in the factory. Exports are directly to the US, Western European markets, Australia, New Zealand, Canada, and Japan.

The entrepreneur is about 50 years old. His son has studied and lived in New Zealand for more than 10 years. He is now involved in strategic decisions for this company and has explored the New Zealand market in recent years.

Case C
The female entrepreneur established a trading company in 1999. The main products are the equipment for real estate establishment. Since the company was established, it has mainly exported the products to the US market. Since the 2000s, the company has turned to cooperate with US companies to conduct some projects in China. The female entrepreneur owns 100% of this company.

The entrepreneur has lived in the US and China since 2000. Her son studied design in the US.

Case D
It is a company that provides overseas logistic services for multinational firms. This company was transferred from a state-owned company and is owned by a female entrepreneur. She now owns 100% of this company. The number of employees is up to 100. The clients are located in the US, Europe, and South East Asia.

The entrepreneur has a daughter who is 25 years old and is studying for an arts degree in the US.

The next step is to analyse the data based on the key concepts such as gender, human capital and social networks in firms' internationalization (see Table 1). The concept of human capital is coded in terms of internationalization knowledge, education background, overseas experience, and environmental perception. This code is adapted from the measurement of human capital in Ruzzier et al. (2007). Internationalization knowledge refers to the knowledge of foreign markets and the knowledge of conducting foreign operations (Johanson & Vahlne, 2006). The education background includes the education level of degree and level of language skills. Overseas experience is whether the entrepreneurs have lived overseas. The environment perception is coded to be whether the entrepreneur considers the risk of doing international business is high or low. The concept of social ties is coded to be the relationships for any internationalization efforts, for example, foreign market entry and conducting international effort, and the relationship with second generation. Then, the authors conducted within-case analysis and cross-case analysis to develop the patterns of explanation.

5 Findings and Discussion

This study finds that gender of entrepreneurs does matter in developing trust and using social ties in the context of family SMEs' internationalization. The role of gender in business is highlighted because it is related to associated personality and behavioural traits (Manolova et al., 2007), and the entrepreneurs as the founders and first generation play critical roles in family SME succession and internationalization (Ramadani, Bexheti, Rexhepi, Ratten, & Ibraimi, 2016; Ramadani & Hoy, 2015). The male and female entrepreneurs have different ways of developing trust in the relationships, negotiation in the business, and reducing the risk in the cooperation. Entrepreneurs of family SMEs do not have enough internationalization knowledge, language skills, and overseas experience; thus, they perceive conducting international business to be a high risk. However, female entrepreneurs are more likely to perceive the risk based on emotion, while male entrepreneurs are more likely to evaluate the risk based on the cost. The gender also matters in the succession of family SMEs. Although the first generations are likely to educate the second generation overseas, male entrepreneurs are more likely to let their second generation get involved in business than are female entrepreneurs.

Regarding the way of developing trust in the relationships, while female entrepreneurs are more likely to develop relationships based on emotions, the male entrepreneurs develop relationships with the people they think have same view of value. The entrepreneur of case A mentioned why he can keep a long-term relationship with his main client in the France,

> We share same view of value and world. When the client visited China 20 years ago, he faced several companies like my company at that time. He [the client] told me that he chose me because of my way of living, how I treated my employees, my habits and so on.

Table 1 Gender of entrepreneur, human capital, and social ties in case firms' internationalization

Case	Gender of entrepreneur	Developing social ties to enter foreign markets	Utilizing second generation in internationalization	Internationalization knowledge	Education background	Overseas experience	Environmental perception
A	Male	Developing trust based on same view of the value Developing long-term and strong relationship with one foreign client (the French client) to do exporting business	His son is working in the company The son is learning French to get more language skills	Limited international market knowledge due to exporting to only main client in France and only producing OEM products	College degree in law in 1985; master's degree in business 2016 No language skill	Never lived overseas	Perceives risk based on the cost Reduces the risk by following the basic rules and ethical norms
B	Male	Developing trust based on same view of the value Paying more attention to keeping the main client in the US	His son received a business degree in New Zealand He has explored new foreign markets and now working in this company	Limited internationalization knowledge due to only producing OEM products	No degree No language skills	Never lived overseas	Perceives risk based on the cost Reduces the risk by entering more foreign markets
C	Female	Developing close personal relationships before doing business Developing long-term and strong relationship with main partner in the US	Her son received degree majoring in design in the US Her son is not involved in her business	Limited international market knowledge due to only having business in the US	College degree in 2000 No language skills	Living overseas	Perceives risk based on the emotions Reduces the risk by showing feminine weakness
D	Female	Developing close personal relationships before doing business Paying more attention to keeping the main client in the US	Her daughter studying for a Master of Arts degree in the US Her daughter is not involved in her business	Limited internationalization knowledge due to providing logistic service	College degree No language skills	Never lived overseas	Perceives risk based on the emotions Developing relationships by showing feminine weakness

The entrepreneur of case B also highlighted the importance of sharing the same Chinese basic value, such as "*renqing*", as the condition for developing relationships. *Renqing* refers to the social resource that leverages the interpersonal favour exchange (Yang, 1994). In essence, reciprocity originates from *renqing* (Tsui & Farh, 1997). If a personal relationship partner gets into difficulties, the other partner should help him or her, and after the recipient has received the favour, he or she should return it when the opportunity arises (Lee & Dawes, 2005). In that case, if the partner does not obey the rules of reciprocity, the entrepreneurs in China would not believe that he or she has the same value system.

Compared to male entrepreneur, female entrepreneurs prefer to use emotions to develop trust. "*I like the person*" is more important than doing business. The entrepreneur of case C described her way of developing relationships in this term:

> I always begin with sharing some secrets with women. Once you both started to talk about family issues, you are indeed developing trust. For man, we start to become like brother and sister. Once we call each other brother or sister, everything is easy to negotiate.

In that case, developing an emotional link between partners is the way female entrepreneurs develop trust. The entrepreneur of Case D also highlights the importance of developing personal relationships in her business: "*For me, the priority is whether I like this person or not. If not, I will not think about doing business with him or her.*"

Female entrepreneurs have a priority of using social ties to develop opportunities more than do male entrepreneurs. In this study, when participants all have limited internationalization knowledge, low education background, and face a high risk environment, female entrepreneurs have the advantage of using cultural discrimination in foreign business relationships, getting legitimacy, and developing relationships. It is contradictory to the existing literature that female entrepreneurs have difficulties in accessing social networks (Alon et al., 2013; Ramadani et al., 2013). In this study, female entrepreneurs show weakness about increasing their bargaining power. As the entrepreneur of case C said,

> This is a society controlled by men. We need to accept that. Women are always weaker in the society [than men]. However, we can use this. No man will tease woman. They [men] will take care over of weakness. It is the human nature.

In her opinion, gender does help her to internationalize her business. She provided an example of the reason she won the first order from the US client was that she was the only woman among the competitors:

> We met in the trade exhibition. I had many competitors at that exhibition. We all came from China, so there was no big difference on price and quality. I think I got the order because I was the only woman at that time.

To reduce the perceived risk, male entrepreneurs prefer developing relationships based on the regulations and ethical norms, while female entrepreneurs pay more attention to developing personal relationships. The entrepreneur of case A said,

> The basic rules I follow in developing and using social relationships is whether the partners follow the rules and regulation. On one hand, the way of doing things should obey the

regulation. On the other hand, the people in the relationships should both have met the ethical norms.

Female entrepreneurs pay more attention to developing personal relationships, sharing secrets, family issues, and developing relationships between their families. They reduce risk by developing connections at a personal level. This finding explains the reason for the success of female entrepreneurs; this contrasts to the existing literature that finds that female entrepreneurs suffer from a lack of capability of getting consultancies and creating formal business relationships (Ramadani et al., 2013, 2015).

The matter of business succession is always the key issue for family SMEs. This study finds that female entrepreneurs, as the mothers, consider more than male entrepreneurs about the second generation's personal interests rather than business succession. The male entrepreneurs of Case A and B intentionally educated their sons to take over their business. The entrepreneur of case A is training his son by giving him a low position in the company. He planned to let his son work in different positions, from low to high management, to get experience and then take over the company. The entrepreneur of case B educated his son by having him earn a business degree and used the son's experience and networks overseas to explore new foreign markets. To the entrepreneur of case B, enhancing the capability and increasing the internationalization knowledge is more important than exploring new foreign markets.

However, the female entrepreneurs allow the next generation to do the job based on their interests. The entrepreneur of case C did not force her son to study for a business degree, but has allowed him to study design in the US. Also, she did not force her son to get involved in her business. The entrepreneur of case D also makes it clear that, *"As a mother, I always want my daughter to be happy. I don't want her to make money. She needs time to learn and finds her own interests of working and living."* This finding supports the understanding of female entrepreneurs that they have the responsibility for balancing work and family (Ramadani et al., 2013).

6 Managerial Implications

In explaining the role of human capital and social ties in internationalization of family businesses, findings of this study can be useful for both scholars and practitioners. From a practical perspective, entrepreneurs should consider the importance of gender in entrepreneurs' internationalization process. Developing relationship and trust with male and female entrepreneurs has different approaches. The female entrepreneur might use her own way to overcome the liability of outsidership (Johanson & Vahlne, 2009), for example, showing weakness and developing social relationships.

Considering the importance of human capital, family owners might take the benefits of the second generation's higher education and language skills. Adding the first generation's prior internationalization experience can be combined with the succession plans. The first generation may suffer from a lack of internationalization knowledge and language skills, but they have the experience. This experience can be combined with the language skills and capability of overcoming the cultural discrimination because of overseas living experience and high education background of the second generation.

For family SMEs, educating the second generation overseas is a useful way to gain the internationalization knowledge and explore new foreign markets. However, for a female entrepreneur, involving professional managers instead of family succession might be more important when the second generation has no interest on family business.

For scholars, studying human capital in more detail, for instance, by applying a psychological perspective, can provide a more fine-grained explanation of the role of different elements of human capital in a family business's networking and internationalization behaviours. In addition, considering the process of network formation by a family business in their internationalization efforts and how different genders enter and maintain themselves in related networks can be insightful.

This research focuses on the first generation of family SMEs in a transition economy. These entrepreneurs suffer from the lack of internationalization knowledge and high-level education. Their way of developing and using networks are influenced by the institutional transition. Future research can focus more on the institutional background and pay more attention to the family SMEs in a transitional economy.

7 Conclusion

The influence of human capital on networking behaviours of internationalizing family SMEs is alluring. The story becomes even more attractive when considering the entrepreneur's gender and difference between female and male entrepreneurs in their efforts for internationalization. This study considered the influence of gender in using human capital and social ties in internationalization of family forms. Our findings show that social networking plays a critical role in entering foreign markets for both women and men entrepreneurs. However, there are some interesting differences between female and male entrepreneurs in terms of their understanding of trust as a critical factor in networking efforts. Furthermore, different genders use different mechanisms to reduce their perceived uncertainty in the process of internationalization. Success female entrepreneurs have their advantage of developing and using relationships relying on the emotions, personal relationship development, and showing weakness. Finally, this research reveals the gender does matter in the succession planning of family SMEs. Maternity plays an important role here in that female entrepreneurs' succession motivation is weaker than male entrepreneurs'.

References

Alon, I., Yeheskel, O., Lerner, M., & Zhang, W. (2013). Internationalization of Chinese entrepreneurial firms. *Thunderbird International Business Review, 55*(5), 495–512.
Alvarez, S. A., & Busenitz, L. W. (2001). The entrepreneurship of resource-based theory. *Journal of Management, 27*(6), 755–775.
Anderson, A. R., Jack, S. L., & Dodd, S. D. (2005). The role of family members in entrepreneurial networks: Beyond the boundaries of the family firm. *Family Business Review, 18*(2), 135–154.
Andersson, S. (2011). International entrepreneurship, born globals and the theory of effectuation. *Journal of Small Business and Enterprise Development, 18*, 627–643.
Bates, T. (1990). Entrepreneur human capital inputs and small business longevity. *Review of Economics and Statistics, 72*, 551–559.
Becker, G. S. (1993). *Human capital: A theoretical and empirical analysis with specific reference to education.* Chicago: University of Chicago Press.
Brennan, L., & Garvey, D. (2009). The role of knowledge in internationalization. *Research in International Business and Finance, 23*(2), 120–133.
Brush, C. G. (1990). Women and enterprise creation. In *Enterprising women.* Paris: OECD.
Brush, C. G., & Hisrich, R. D. (1991). Antecedent influences on women-owned businesses. *Journal of Managerial Psychology, 6*(2), 9–16.
Burkart, M., Panunzi, F., & Shleifer, A. (2003). Family firms. *The Journal of Finance, 58*(5), 2167–2202.
Carter, N. M., Brush, C. G., Greene, P. G., Gatewood, E., & Hart, M. M. (2003). Women entrepreneurs who break through to equity financing: The influence of human, social and financial capital. *Venture Capital, 5*(1), 1–28.
Casillas, J. C. (2005). Internationalisation of Spanish family SMEs: An analysis of family involvement. *International Journal of Globalisation and Small Business, 1*(2).
Chetty, S., & Agndal, H. (2008). Role of inter-organizational networks and interpersonal networks in an industrial district. *Regional Studies, 42*(2), 175–187.
Coleman, J. S. (1988). Social capital in the creation of human capital. *American Journal of Sociology, 94*, S95–S120.
Coviello, N., & Munro, H. (1997). Network relationships and the internationalisation process of small software firms. *International Business Review, 6*, 361–386.
Crick, D., & Crick, J. (2016). The first export order: A marketing innovation revisited. *Journal of Strategic Marketing, 24*, 77–89.
Davidsson, P., & Honig, B. (2003). The role of human and social capital among nascent entrepreneurs. *Journal of Business Venturing, 18*(3), 301–331.
DeNoble, A., Ehrlich, S., & Singh, G. (2007). Toward the development of a family business self-efficacy scale: A resource-based perspective. *Family Business Review, 20*(2), 127–140.
Eisenhardt, K. M. (1989). Building theories from case study research. *Academy of Management Review, 14*(4), 532–550.
Eisenhardt, K. M., & Graebner, M. E. (2007). Theory building from cases: Opportunities and challenges. *Academy of Management Journal, 50*(1), 25–32.
Ellis, P. D. (2011). Social ties and international entrepreneurship: Opportunities and constraints affecting firm internationalization. *Journal of International Business Studies, 42*(1), 99–127.
Gabrielsson, P., & Gabrielsson, M. (2013). A dynamic model of growth phases and survival in international business-to-business new ventures: The moderating effect of decision-making logic. *Industrial Marketing Management, 42*, 1357–1373.
Gallo, M. A., & García Pont, C. (1996). Important factors in family business internationalization. *Family Business Review, 9*(1), 45–59.
Graves, C., & Thomas, J. (2008). Determinants of the internationalization pathways of family firms: An examination of family influence. *Family Business Review, 21*(2), 151–167.
Greene, P. G., & Brown, T. E. (1997). Resource needs and the dynamic capitalism typology. *Journal of Business Venturing, 12*(3), 161–173.

Hisrich, R. D., & Fülöp, G. (1997). Women entrepreneurs in family business: The Hungarian case. *Family Business Review, 10*(3), 281–302.

Hitt, M. A., Biermant, L., Shimizu, K., & Kochhar, R. (2001). Direct and moderating effects of human capital on strategy and performance in professional service firms: A resource-based perspective. *Academy of Management Journal, 44*(1), 13–28.

Hofstede, G., & Hofstede, G. J. (2005). *Cultures and organizations: Software of the mind*. London: McGraw-Hill.

Javalgi, R. R. G., & Todd, P. R. (2011). Entrepreneurial orientation, management commitment, and human capital: The internationalization of SMEs in India. *Journal of Business Research, 64*(9), 1004–1010.

Johanson, J., & Vahlne, J. E. (2006). Commitment and opportunity development in the internationalization process: A note on the Uppsala internationalization process model. *Management International Review, 46*(2), 165–178.

Johanson, J., & Vahlne, J. E. (2009). The Uppsala internationalization process model revisited: From liability of foreignness to liability of outsidership. *Journal of International Business Studies, 40*(9), 1–21.

Kitching, B. M., & Jackson, P. A. (2002). Female entrepreneurs in a transitional economy: Businesswomen in China. *The International Journal of Entrepreneurship and Innovation, 3* (2), 145–155.

Kontinen, T., & Ojala, A. (2010). The internationalization of family businesses: A review of extant research. *Journal of Family Business Strategy, 1*(2), 97–107.

Kontinen, T., & Ojala, A. (2011). Social capital in relation to the foreign market entry and post-entry operations of family SMEs. *Journal of International Entrepreneurship, 9*(2), 133–151.

Lee, D. Y., & Dawes, P. L. (2005). Guanxi, trust, and long-term orientation in Chinese business markets. *Journal of International Marketing, 13*(2), 28–56.

Lu, Y., Au, K., Peng, M. W., & Xu, E. (2013). Strategic management in private and family businesses. *Asia Pacific Journal of Management, 30*(3), 633–639.

Luo, Y. (2007). *Guanxi and business*. Singapore: World Scientific.

Mainela, T., & Puhakka, V. (2009). Organising new business in a turbulent context: Opportunity discovery and effectuation for IJV development in transition markets. *Journal of International Entrepreneurship, 7*(2), 111–134.

Manolova, T. S., Brush, C. G., Edelman, L. F., & Greene, P. G. (2002). Internationalization of small firms personal factors revisited. *International Small Business Journal, 20*(1), 9–31.

Manolova, T. S., Carter, N. M., Manev, I. M., & Gyoshev, B. S. (2007). The differential effect of men and women entrepreneurs' human capital and networking on growth expectancies in Bulgaria. *Entrepreneurship Theory and Practice, 31*(3), 407–426.

Manolova, T. S., Manev, I. M., & Gyoshev, B. S. (2010). In good company: The role of personal and inter-firm networks for new-venture internationalization in a transition economy. *Journal of World Business, 45*(3), 257–265.

McClelland, E., Swail, J., Bell, J., & Ibbotson, P. (2005). Following the pathway of female entrepreneurs: A six-country investigation. *International Journal of Entrepreneurial Behavior and Research, 11*(2), 84–107.

Mustafa, M., & Chen, S. (2010). The strength of family networks in transnational immigrant entrepreneurship. *Thunderbird International Business Review, 52*(52), 97–106.

Oswald, S. L., Muse, L. A., & Rutherford, M. W. (2009). The influence of large stake family control on performance: Is it agency or entrenchment? *Journal of Small Business Management, 47*, 116–135.

Padmanabhan, P., & Cho, K. R. (1999). Decision specific experience in foreign ownership and establishment strategies: Evidence from Japanese firms. *Journal of International Business Studies, 30*(1), 25–41.

Poutziouris, P., & Chittenden, F. (1996). *Family business or business families*. Leeds: Institution for Small Business Affairs.

Pukall, T. J., & Calabrò, A. (2014). The internationalization of family firms: A critical review and integrative model. *Family Business Review, 27*(2), 103–125.

Ramadani, V., & Hoy, F. (2015). *Context and uniqueness of family businesses. Family businesses in transition economies*. Cham: Springer International Publishing.

Ramadani, V., Gerguri, S., Dana, L. P., & Tasaminova, T. (2013). Woman entrepreneurs in the Republic of Macedonia: Waiting for directions. *International Journal Entrepreneurship and Small Business, 19*(1), 95–121.

Ramadani, V., Hisrich, R. D., & Gërguri-Rashiti, S. (2015). Female entrepreneurs in transition economies: Insights from Albania, Macedonia and Kosovo. *World Review of Entrepreneurship, Management and Sustainable Development, 11*(4), 391–413.

Ramadani, V., Bexheti, A., Rexhepi, G., Ratten, V., & Ibraimi, S. (2016). Succession issues in Albanian family businesses: An exploratory research. *Journal of Balkan and Near Eastern Studies, 19*(3).

Ratten, V. (2015). Family business in sport organizations: Western experiences as lessons for transitional economies. In *Family businesses in transition economies* (pp. 305–317). Cham: Springer International Publishing.

Ratten, V., Dana, L. P., & Ramadani, V. (2017). Internationalisation of family business groups in transition economies. *International Journal of Entrepreneurship and Small Business, 30*(4), 509–525.

Ruzzier, M., Antončič, B., & Konečnik, M. (2006). The resource-based approach to the internationalisation of SMEs: Differences in resource bundles between internationalised and non-internationalised companies. *Zagreb International Review of Economics and Business, 9* (2), 95–116.

Ruzzier, M., Antonci, C. B., Hisrich, R. D., & Konecnik, M. (2007). Human capital and SME internationalization: A structural equation modeling study. *Canadian Journal of Administrative Sciences/Revue Canadienne des Sciences de l'Administration, 24*(1), 15–29.

Sarasvathy, S. D. (2001). Causation and effectuation: toward a theoretical shift from economic inevitability to entrepreneurial contingency. *Academy of Management Review, 26*, 242–263.

Sarasvathy, S., Kumar, K., York, J. G., & Bhagavatula, S. (2014). An effectual approach to international entrepreneurship: Overlaps, challenges, and provocative possibilities. *Entrepreneurship Theory and Practice, 38*, 71–93.

Saxena, A. (2013). Transgenerational succession in business groups in India. *Asia Pacific Journal of Management, 30*(3), 769–789.

Schweizer, R., Vahlne, J. E., & Johanson, J. (2010). Internationalization as an entrepreneurial process. *Journal of International Entrepreneurship, 8*, 343–370.

Shi, H. X., & Dana, L. P. (2013). Market orientation and entrepreneurship in Chinese family business: A socialisation view. *International Journal of Entrepreneurship and Small Business, 20*(1), 1–16.

Tsui, A. S., & Farh, J. L. L. (1997). Where guanxi matters. *Work and Occupations, 24*(1), 56–79.

Unger, J. M., Rauch, A., Frese, M., & Rosenbusch, N. (2011). Human capital and entrepreneurial success: A meta-analytical review. *Journal of Business Venturing, 26*(3), 341–358.

Woldie, A., & Adersua, A. (2004). Female entrepreneurs in a transitional economy: Businesswomen in Nigeria. *International Journal of Social Economics, 31*(1/2), 78–93.

Woodside, A. G., & Wilson, E. J. (2003). Case study research methods for theory building. *Journal of Business and Industrial Marketing, 18*(6/7), 493–508.

Wright, M., Filatotchev, I., Hoskisson, R. E., & Peng, M. W. (2005). Strategy research in emerging economies: Challenging the conventional wisdom. *Journal of Management Studies, 42*(1), 1–33.

Yang, M. M. H. (1994). *Gifts, favors, and banquets: The art of social relationships in China*. Ithaca, NY: Cornell University Press.

Zamudio, C., Anokhin, S., & Kellermanns, F. W. (2014). Network analysis: A concise review and suggestions for family business research. *Journal of Family Business Strategy, 5*(1), 63–71.

Perceived Social Support and Social Entrepreneurship: Gender Perspective from Turkey

Ayşe Gökçen Kapusuz, Mustafa Fedai Çavuş, and Nazmiye Ülkü Pekkan

Abstract Entrepreneurship can be defined as a process of creating value by searching and creating some opportunities. Entrepreneurial organizations are known as the firms which do not abstain from taking risks while trying to create something new from different opportunities on the basis of organization, product, foundation, service, and process. Environment and society are the main factors for the entrepreneurs who should perfectly analyze the society for being beneficial to others. Gender is becoming popular as a new entrepreneurial field for creating an original idea. Today's business world needs the coordination between personal issues and social issues while acting entrepreneurial. In this point, women become popular and play vital roles to be able to create different beneficial and entrepreneurial acts as a part of the society and global business environment. Besides men, the number of women entrepreneurs increase seriously day by day. The main purpose of this chapter is to find out and emphasize the importance of social entrepreneurship in business and social environment based on the perceived social support and its dimensions. Besides, traditional and social entrepreneurship, the status of male and female entrepreneurs, the features of entrepreneurs, and the relationship between perceived social support and social entrepreneurship with the participation of 302 undergraduate students from Mersin Toros University/Turkey will be emphasized and some suggestions will be noted to encourage people to become successful in the society and to develop upcoming future studies.

Keywords Entrepreneurship • Social entrepreneurship • Perceived social support

---

A.G. Kapusuz
Selcuk University, Konya, Turkey
e-mail: aysegokcen07@hotmail.com

M.F. Çavuş (✉) • N.Ü. Pekkan
Osmaniye Korkut Ata University, Osmaniye, Turkey
e-mail: mfcavus@osmaniye.edu.tr; nazmiyeulku.pekkan@gmail.com

V. Ratten et al. (eds.), *Knowledge, Learning and Innovation*, Contributions to Management Science, DOI 10.1007/978-3-319-59282-4_6

1 Introduction

Economic development of countries depend on different sides and perspectives. Entrepreneurs have an important place and are the large part of economies. Both male and female entrepreneurs in a society perform beneficial and necessary tasks to be able to fill a gap in social needs. Women entrepreneurs besides men started to play a significant role to be able to be located in production for finding a solution to the social problems and needs.

At the present time, the interest of entrepreneurial issues is gradually increase among people besides researchers. Bringing social and personal benefits into the forefront is a main factor for entrepreneurship and individual tendency of entrepreneurship consists of creating new idea for innovation and social benefits (Ratten, 2012). In today's world, gender became an important point to be able to emphasize the meaning and significance of entrepreneurship. Women entrepreneurs play some different and important roles as a part of today's globalized business world to develop social and economic progress.

The term 'social entrepreneur' is used to define people who realize an aim to get a social profit and benefit instead of financial profit and this term came into use by researchers with the phenomenon of social entrepreneurship (Shaw & Carter, 2007). These people who are called "socially entrepreneurial", focus and create the innovative attempts and new social regulations to be able to find some solutions on the social problems and needs (Alvord, Brown, & Letts, 2004).

Entrepreneurship is called as a process of creating different value by searching some opportunities and aims to gather all sources to be able to provide different and new benefits from these opportunities. As Reyhanoğlu and Akın (2012) emphasized that entrepreneurship is a key and main concept; social and commercial entrepreneurship are the sub-concepts which are defined as the types of this main concept. This value creation process (Ratten, 2011) aims to provide some solutions to the necessary conditions (Mair & Marti, 2006) and some specific needs and requirements.

In this study, entrepreneurship and entrepreneurs besides social entrepreneurship which is important for social change and social development for the society and countries, the features of both traditional and social entrepreneurs, gender perspectives and differences of perceived social support and social entrepreneurship, and examples from Turkey will be emphasized and suggestions will be noted for the future news.

2 Personality Traits of Entrepreneurs

Entrepreneurs are generally valued as a person who are not afraid of taking some different risks while making their own dreams come true. These people are also creative and powerful besides their good communication technics in different areas and topics (Smith, 1999). They motivate themselves with these positive personality traits and features and their believes. These proactive people who have innovative capabilities (Ratten, 2012) also are skillful always open to new experiences in life and to create new and original ideas. Providing the continuity of creative and new products depends on these motivational features, dreams, traits and ideas (Ford & Gioia, 1995).

On the other hand, some difficulties are also situated for entrepreneurial steps and entrepreneurs as well. Being resistant for difficulties and obstacles is necessary and important feature for these innovative people (Barendsen & Gardner, 2004). Roberts and Woods (2005) noted and emphasized that social entrepreneurs act similar and almost same with commercial and traditional entrepreneurs but they pay more attention to the social issues without aiming to get some economic profit. As Ratten (2012) noted that individuals with entrepreneurial features are generally associated with being supportive and adoptive of new ideas, social values, and innovations. They have both creative and practical skills to make actual their dreams and ideas to be able to satisfy the social needs and requirements (Thompson, Alvy, & Lees, 2000).

Most-known personality traits of entrepreneurs can be aligned as follows (Dees, 1998; Kılıç Kırılmaz, 2014; Kümbül Güler, 2011; Mort, Weerawardena, & Carnegie, 2003):

- These creative people work on the new mission to improve value for the society.
- Entrepreneurial people are good at seeing new opportunities.
- They are open to learning something new.
- They do always seek new opportunities and focus on serving.
- Their behaviors are in accord and balanced for their goals, ideas, and acts.
- Entrepreneurial people act to help others in a society.
- They are good risk-takers to create new and innovation.
- These innovative and proactive people easily realize social problems and needs.
- Entrepreneurial people draw more attention to the social needs than personal needs.
- These mission-oriented people establish the economic, social, environmental organizations by adopting novelty.
- They do not like being limiting with the current sources. They always seek the new ones to be able to reach current markets in the society.
- Social and traditional entrepreneurs also support productive and beneficial production of goods and services.

3 Overview of the Traditional and Social Entrepreneurship Under the Gender Perspective

It should be known that all solutions about social problems and needs are coming from focusing on determining and understanding both personal and social needs for social development and improvement (Koçak & Kavi, 2014).

Entrepreneurship can be seen as an interdisciplinary approach contains economics, psychology, sociology, management, environment, business, technology, and so on (Mitchell et al., 2002). Either traditional or social, entrepreneurship is generally used to define new desiring and building process such as product, business, opportunity, service... etc. In social literature, these processes are called as "social entrepreneurship" which aims to design and create social benefits for the society and social needs. According to Bygrave and Hofer (1992), entrepreneurship is used to understand today's needs by redefining a dynamic, integrative, and unique process which also involves the yesterdays. As mentioned before, people who socially contribute to others' life by creating different value to be able to improve social and economic life without profit making purpose are generally called as a "social entrepreneur".

Individuals' entrepreneurial behaviours are affected by different internal and external environmental factors, such as organizational and social culture, other people, needs and problems, gender perspectives, social support, organizational climate, job satisfaction, organizational, personal and social justice, personal experiences... etc. (Basım, Meydan, & Şeşen, 2009).

Men are always thought as an outside person and they work to earn a living for the family. In today's World, people either man or woman can easily be a part of countries' economic situations. Besides men, women are also thought as a mom in general but as Anis and Hašan (2013) emphasized that women also have a significant place in a society and they perform two kinds of jobs both at home and outside. They can do whatever men do as well. Poor educational and practical knowledge and experiences can be an obstacle for developing women entrepreneurs of a society but it can easily be a surmountable issue if they want to.

Gender discrimination was really clear and distinct before but societies and of course individuals and their perspectives were gradually changed and in today's life women have a voice as much as men. It is known that women and women entrepreneurs, who are willing to overcome different and difficult roles, gradually increase in the economies of countries. Today, it was recognized that women entrepreneurs as much as men, play an important role and are an important source of economic and social growth of countries. Gender-based barriers and obstacles are always seen in communities while starting new businesses.

As Lock and Smith (2015) noted in their research paper that the role of women is much more comprehensive than being a mother, child bearer, food provider or housewife/housekeeper even though it is traditionally known and accepted as that. It has started to shift for last years from these counted roles towards business women, entrepreneurs, job creators, designers, decorators... etc. through governmental supports, perceived social supports, gender-focused developments. By the way Humbert, Drew, and Kelan (2009) also emphasized that the roles and importance of women were not taken into consideration till 1970s; but in recent years this importance and positive effects of women entrepreneurship has been realized and understood with the increase of the number of women entrepreneurs (Weiler & Bernasek, 2001).

Entrepreneurial organizations and individuals do not abstain from taking risks to create something new, seek different and new opportunities for being the first of evaluating environmental advantages and opportunities (Lumpkin & Dess, 2001). These actions and aims help both organizations and individuals to create entrepreneurial culture, make new moves, and take risks (Knight, 1997).

Studies and researches have shown and emphasized the positive impacts of entrepreneurship and specifically female entrepreneurship on economic and social development of different countries. People and governments gradually realize the importance and positive effects of women entrepreneurs who have double role at work and home (Brush, Carter, Gatewood, Greene, & Hart, 2006) as a business woman and a mother in the society besides males.

Social entrepreneurship is first used and mentioned in a book was written by H. Bowen in 1953 (Koçak & Kavi, 2014). Since 1953, different and various explanations and definitions by different authors and researchers in different fields of social literature have been made. On the other hand, it cannot be said that social entrepreneurship context has been really understood in different fields and by different researchers because of the various and different perspectives (Mulyaningsih & Ramadani, 2016).

As Ersen, Kaya, and Meydanoğlu (2010) emphasized two dimensions of social entrepreneurship called as being 'social' and 'entrepreneurial'. By the way, Kılıç Kırılmaz (2014) also noted that social entrepreneurship is shaped by the combination of 'socialness' and 'entrepreneurship'. All these mentioned terms are supposed or determined as the dimensions of social entrepreneurship and are also discussed and emphasized by different researchers (Aslan, Araza, & Bulut, 2012).

On the other hand, people who socially act in a society generally offer some suggestions through their devotion towards the social needs and aims. These socially entrepreneurial people are often identified as follower or chaser to find some opportunistic values and resources to be able to transform to benefit of society. Social entrepreneurship and social entrepreneurs are differentiated by their vision, practices, ability to generate social value and social network, ability to transformational change in a society, and limited resources by various researchers from past to today (Thompson, 2002).

It can easily be seen in many studies and researches that entrepreneurs either men or women are always faced with some difficulties and different problems/barriers/obstacles while trying to balance their personal and work life. From this point of view, women face much more difficulties than men in balancing their family life and business life (Moore & Buttner, 1997). As Pines, Lerner, and Schwartz (2010: 192) noted that "from the perspective of diversity, equality and inclusion, entrepreneurship can be viewed as a means of inclusion for women and other marginalized groups in countries, ..." and entrepreneurial issues are generally mentioned with masculine characteristics. Women who do not care about masculinity and masculine characteristics in business life or can exhibit masculine traits and features are generally inclined to entrepreneurial aims and purposes (Gupta, Turban, Wasti, & Sikdar, 2009).

Murphy and Coombes (2009) defined social entrepreneurship as a process of creating new value with some special aims. From this point of view, innovative, practical, beneficial, and sustainable attitudes can be defined as social entrepreneurship which aims to be an answer for social needs and problems.

In today's increasingly globalized business world, innovative and creative people based on perceived social support play a vital role upon the social effects of new ideas and behaviors for improvement and development of the societies. On the other hand, Hibbert, Hogg, and Quinn (2002) noted and emphasized non-profit entrepreneurial behaviors which contain social benefits and change to be able to find some results for the social needs.

Entrepreneurial people are defined as a leader of social activities by Barendsen and Gardner (2004), and they also described these people as socially sensitive and believer. Social entrepreneurs display non-profit activities while traditional or commercial entrepreneurs are profit-oriented people. Reaching and gaining profit is the main goal of commercial entrepreneurship; but social entrepreneurship aims to be socially beneficial for the people and society by creating social value (Austin, Stevenson, & Wei-Skillern, 2006). Profit is not a mission for social entrepreneurship, it can merely be a motivational factor for social aims.

As mentioned earlier, social entrepreneurs improve their vision and mission for creating social change and improving the social and personal life quality (Elkington & Hartigan, 2008). In contrast to the commercial entrepreneurship, social entrepreneurship and social entrepreneurs are mainly focused on the social value and basic human needs to be able to improve perceived social supports. Frequently noted personality characteristics and traits of entrepreneurs will be emphasized on the following pages and parts of this chapter.

There are five mostly used and cited dimensions of social entrepreneurship, such as "social vision, sustainability, social networking, innovativeness, and financial returns" (Malecki & Demaray, 2002).

From this point of view, first dimension named as *social vision* can be briefly described as "the sense of destiny" and also sense of requirement to be able to see the social opportunities, provide social change, and supply personal needs (Barendsen & Gardner, 2004). *Sustainability* refers the long-term survival of humans beings and other organisms in an environment or in a community (Machan, 1999). *Social networks* are the other dimension of social entrepreneurship. As a social being, people have to communicate others to reach social well-being and to benefit from others' knowledge. At this juncture, social networks refer the sharing of different knowledge and perspectives to be able to improve relations. As Chen and Wang (2008) emphasized that sharing information will help to find innovative solutions to different social needs and problems in a community and society. Building support for socially entrepreneurial mission and vision is important and possible by communicating others and relying on personal contacts and experiences. Reputation and recognition come from social networks and play a significant role and hold a mediatory position between social entrepreneurship and social networks (Shane & Cable, 2002). The fourth dimension of social entrepreneurship is *innovation* which refers to the way to create something new and valuable. As Hart and Christensen (1992) noted that social entrepreneurs generally apply to innovative and technological processes for creating a social values and making strategic decisions about the social needs. *Financial returns* are the last dimension of social entrepreneurship. Social entrepreneurship is non-profit organizations as mentioned before but shareholders can possibly get some financial return but this is not a main point of being a social entrepreneur. As Gunn, Durkin, Singh, and Brown (2008) emphasized that social entrepreneurship may be distinguished from traditional or commercial entrepreneurship by emphasizing social value and social returns instead of financial returns.

3.1 Perceived Social Support

Individuals, as a social being, need support in every step of life. Besides adults, this becomes more of an issue for the youth to be able to begin to work and gain a place in society and social life. Polatçı (2015) emphasized that perceived social support has an important effect in both personal and business life.

It is possible to see the several definitions about social and perceived social support in different literature and researches. The most common and accepted definition created by Cobb in 1976 and defined as personal beliefs in respect of being loved, valued, and being considered important. This definition is originated with three components or dimensions such as feeling loved, feeling valued, and belonging to a social network (Malecki & Demaray, 2002).

Network is commonly used as a dimension of social support by different researchers. As mentioned before, networks are the bridge/connector between individual and social life.

Eker, Arkar, and Yaldız (2001) characterised social support as a coping guide or source based on personal feelings. According to other definition, social support can be defined as an opportunity to be able to get some advices, suggestions and help (Morgeson & Humphrey, 2006). Besides all these, social support can be defined as an interpersonal correlation system (Toepfer, 2010). Based on Truxillo, Cadiz, Rineer, Zaniboni, and Fraccaroli (2012)'s definition, social support is a guiding light for people to be able to get out of hole.

It is possible to say that perceived social support is effective to satisfy the social needs which are the third step of Maslow's Theory of Hierarchy of Needs. From this point of view, perceived social support has a vital role to be able to get used to a new situation and environment and gain self-confidence (Polatçı, 2015). Based on different researches and literature reviews of Malecki & Demaray (2002), it is noted that social support and perceived social support levels have significant effects to decrease some adjustment problems in a society.

Social support is a complicated and multidimensional concept (Duru, 2007) which is important for personal life adjustments (Gurung, Sarason, & Sarason, 1997) and adding value. The lack of social support is a risk factor for individuals' physical and emotional problems (Çavuş, 2009).

Perceived Social Support Consists of Three Components Family, friends, and special persons/partners (Çeçen, 2008). It is a fact accepted by everybody that family is the most important source of social support for the person as a social being (Işık, 2013). It is obvious enough that people who provide social support to others also need support for themselves as much as others who receive social support (Eker et al., 2001).

4 Methodology

The lack of the similar researchers analyzed the relationship between social entrepreneurship and perceived social support is the main feature to show the originality and uniqueness of this research. From this viewpoint, the fundamental contribution of this study will be the examination of the relationship between social entrepreneurship and perceived social support under the gender perspective.

4.1 Instruments: Participants and Procedures

The relationship between social entrepreneurship and perceived social support under the gender perspective has been examined in this study and multidimensional scale of perceived social support (MSPSS) and scale of social entrepreneurship translated into Turkish have been used to be able to conduct a survey. Based on the conceptual literature reviews, strong and significant relationship is awaited from the survey results gathered from 302 undergraduate students in Mersin/Turkey.

Besides demographic factors and questions, the multidimensional scale of perceived social support (MSPSS) generated by Zimet and co-workers in 1990 and translated into Turkish by Eker and Arkar (1995) contains 12 items in total, 4 items for each dimension and 3 dimensions/components (family, friends, and special persons) and the scale of social entrepreneurship generated by Koe Hwee Nga and Shamuganathan (2010) contains 33 items and 5 dimensions (social vision, sustainability, social networks, innovativeness, and financial returns) but first four dimensions except financial returns (it was improper for the participations) have been used (27 items and 4 dimensions) and attached to the survey in this research with Likert-type scale from 1 to 5, indicating responses of "strongly disagree (1)" to "strongly agree (5)". Structured 350 questionnaire forms have been distributed to the students and 302 of them returned (86%) to contribute to the analyses process and all returned forms have been added to the analyses structure.

4.2 Data Analyses and Results

First of all, demographic factors of students have been classified and following findings obtained. The demographic background of 302 participations of questionnaire ranged from 18 to 24 years old but the majority are located between 20 and 22 years old. It is categorized by a proportion of females 62.3% and males 37.7%. The proportion of single students are 94%; so the majority of participants ($n \approx 284$) were single.

Then, correlation analysis has been done to be able to see the relationship between each dimensions of perceived social support and social entrepreneurship's dimensions. Afterwards, regression analysis has been used to test the effects of perceived social support's dimensions upon the dimensions of social entrepreneurship.

Based on the results of factor analysis about the social entrepreneurship, predicted and predetermined factor structure has been obtained with 4 dimensions (one was exempted from the original version) of social entrepreneurship and explained 54.2% of total variance. Three dimensions of multidimensional scale of perceived social support explained 66.2% of total variance as well. Results of factor analyses can be seen on the Tables 1 and 2 below:

Cronbach alpha coefficient is used to evaluate the reliability of variables and dimensions. Reliabilities for two main variables and each basic components of them have been tested. Based on that, results present that used scales considerably are reliable (0.815 and 0.910) as can be seen on the Table 3 below:

For the purpose of analyzing the relationship between perceived social support and attitudes of social entrepreneurship of students', correlation analysis has been used and the result of pearson correlation of this research as can be seen below showed that perceived social support of students' is positively related to the social entrepreneurship ($r = 0.362$; $p < 0.01$).

Highest-level positive relationship ($r = 0.398$ at the $p < 0.01$ level) is found between social support from a special person and social entrepreneurship and that indicates a linear increase in social support coming from a special person with increasing values of social entrepreneurial attitudes. Familial social support ($r = 0.351$) and right after supports from the friends ($r = 0.205$) are following that result with the same high-level correlations at the $p < 0.01$ level.

Medium-level positive relationship between social vision and special person support ($r = 0.340$; $p < 0.01$) can easily be seen on the correlation table as well. On the other hand, low-level positive relationship has been found between social vision and supports from family ($r = 0.278$) and friends ($r = 0.189$).

In general, positive and significant relationships among variables have been found but there is a positive, weak-level and insignificant relationship between social networks and second component of perceived social support named as friends as well ($r = 0.097$; insignificant) (Table 4).

To be able to understand which one of the independent variables are much more effective and related to the dependent variable, regression analysis has been used in

Table 1 Factor analysis results of social entrepreneurship

Items	Factor 1 Social vision	Factor 2 Innovativeness	Factor 3 Sustainability	Factor 4 Social networks
SS1	0.512			
SS4	0.589			
SS8	0.558			
SS10	0.524			
SS20	0.568			
SS21	0.589			
SS26	0.657			
SS27	0.701			
SS2		0.541		
SS3		0.675		
SS5		0.447		
SS6		0.533		
SS12		0.711		
SS14		0.478		
SS17		0.480		
SS25		0.662		
SS7			0.381	
SS9			0.538	
SS11			0.529	
SS13			0.517	
SS23			0.614	
SS24			0.638	
SS15				0.475
SS16				0.604
SS18				0.609
SS19				0.377
SS22				0.633

Extraction method: Principal component analysis rotation method: Varimax with Kaiser normalization

this research. Mathematical relationships and the forms of these relationships between social entrepreneurship and perceived social support and their components have been tested by regression analysis and results can be seen as follows (Table 5):

5 Conclusion and Discussion

The chapter draws conclusion and discussion about entrepreneurship and gender-based perceptions and perspectives that is supported for economic growth. This research has already mentioned some of the personal traits and characteristics of entrepreneurship and entrepreneurs. As emphasized before, entrepreneurship is

Table 2 Factor analysis results of multidimensional scale of perceived social support

Items	Factor 1 Family	Factor 2 Friends	Factor 3 Special persons
SS3	0.736		
SS4	0.873		
SS8	0.772		
SS11	0.883		
SS6		0.857	
SS7		0.720	
SS9		0.771	
SS12		0.836	
SS1			0.890
SS2			0.853
SS5			0.756
SS10			0.797

Extraction method: principal component analysis rotation method: Varimax with Kaiser normalization

Table 3 Results of reliability analysis

	Cronbach's Alpha	N of items
Perceived social support	**0.815**	**12**
*Family	0.771	4
*Friends	0.766	4
*Special persons	0.715	4
Social entrepreneurship	**0.910**	**27**
*Social vision	0.829	8
*Sustainability	0.819	6
*Innovativeness	0.824	8
*Social networks	0.909	5

dealed and discussed with its different forms and types in the literature of social sciences.

Participants of this research have been choosed from the university students who are really young and they are out of the starting gate for business life. It is thought that personal behaviours, attitudes, emotions, and ideas of youth are shamed by not only psychological factors, but also economic and social factors of the current situations and environment. Social support has an important place for people especially for youth while participating in different social tasks to create social value and raising environmental awareness.

Baughn, Chua, and Neupert (2006) noted that entrepreneurs are generally associated with males who are risk takers, aggressive, creator, innovator... etc. But in today's globalized World, there is a great awareness of women entrepreneurship and their impact on economic and social life besides men. Thus, entrepreneurship may be characterised as finding and creating new focuses for the main and essential needs of human beings. Traditional and also social entrepreneurs no matter what its

Table 4 Means, standard deviations, and Pearson correlations among variables

	1	2	3	4	5	6	7	8	9
1. Family	1								
2. Friends	000	1							
3. Special persons	000	000	1						
4. Social vision	0.278**	0.189**	0.340**	1					
5. Sustainability	0.379**	0.234**	0.397**	0.763**	1				
6. Innovativeness	0.297**	0.199**	0.376**	0.785**	0.761**	1			
7. Social networks	0.285**	0.097	0.281**	0.559**	0.620**	0.589**	1		
8. Perceived social support	0.796**	0.864**	0.854**	0.308**	0.385**	0.332**	0.244**	1	
9. Social entrepreneurship	0.351**	0.205**	0.398**	0.900**	0.891**	0.906**	0.788**	0.362**	1
Mean	4.17	4.12	4.04	3.61	3.83	3.62	4.01	4.11	3.74
Standard deviation	0.98	1.42	1	0.67	0.68	0.65	0.94	0.95	0.52

**Correlation is significant at the 0.01 level (2-tailed)

Table 5 The result of regression analysis

Dependent variables	Independent variables	β	p	R^2
Social vision	Family	0.07	0.099	
	Friends	−0.01	0.602	
	Special persons	**0.19**	**0.000**	0.124
Innovativeness	Family	0.07	0.103	
	Friends	−0.02	0.432	
	Special persons	**0.22**	**0.000**	0.150
Sustainability	Family	**0.15**	**0.001**	
	Friends	−0.01	0.592	
	Special persons	**0.18**	**0.000**	0.187
Social networks	Family	**0.19**	**0.004**	
	Friends	−0.09	0.045	
	Special persons	**0.22**	0.002	0.111
Social entrepreneurship	Family	**0.11**	**0.008**	
	Friends	−0.03	0.258	0.180
	Special persons	**0.20**	**0.000**	

Among the components of perceived social support as independent variables, social entrepreneurship as a dependent variable is optimally explained by the support from special person (β = 0.19; 0.22; 0.18; 0.22; overall 0.20)

gender is, are easily see and utilize the opportunities, find and focus on the solution for the needs and problems. As Ratten (2011) emphasized that the development of social entrepreneurship and entrepreneurs is significant to be able to share social ideas, values, and innovations for proactively being social entrepreneurs. But the main different point between social and traditional entrepreneurs is that traditional entrepreneurs generally aim to get an economic profit and create an economic value; conversely social entrepreneurs target to focus on social needs and creating social value. As Kotetska and Berezyak (2014) noted that social entrepreneurship is a field of application which is innovative, solution-oriented, open to change and development.

It is the fact that social developments and changes are mostly coming from the social entrepreneurs. Social entrepreneurs differentiate from traditional or commercial entrepreneurs with their social aims to create social value by pursuing social effect instead of economic profit (Kılıç Kırılmaz, 2014). Social entrepreneurship is generally associated with innovation, social value, sustainability, social responsibility, and so on by aiming social benefits and social changes for the society and social development (Kılıç Kırılmaz, 2014; Marshall, 2011).

Individual behaviors are shamed not only personal psychological world but also social environment surrounding people as mentioned before. Personal and mental factors and elements are in a relationship and an interaction with environmental factors (Çavuş, 2009; Keskin & Orgun, 2006). It is possible to say that people achieve success in a supportive environment. When the means about all dimensions of perceived social support and social entrepreneurship are considerated, the highest mean score comes from the family support in this study. This result provide support to the previous similar studies as well. Based on the social entrepreneurship behaviours and attitudes, the mean value of females (3.764) is different from males (3.706). According to this survey results, all dimensions of the perceived social support of participant students (family, friends, and special persons) are positively related to all dimensions of social entrepreneurial attitudes.

This study/research has showed that women display successful operations and effects as an entrepreneur in business life and they also compete against other women and men. Our study also aimed to extinguish gender biases about entrepreneurship. It should not be forgotten that different results can be found in different sectors and industries with broader participant groups.

References

Alvord, S. H., Brown, L. D., & Letts, C. W. (2004). Social entrepreneurship and societal transformation. *The Journal of Applied Behavioral Science, 40*(3), 260–282.

Anis, Z., & Hasan, M. (2013). Woman entrepreneurs of small and medium enterprises in Rajshahi area: Opportunities and challenges. *Intermational Journal of Scientific and Research Publications, 3*(8), 1–13.

Aslan, G., Araza, A., & Bulut, Ç. (2012). Sosyal Girişimciliğin Kavramsal Çerçevesi. *Girişimcilik ve Kalkınma Dergisi, 7*(2), 69–88.

Austin, J., Stevenson, H., & Wei-Skillern, J. (2006). Social and commercial entrepreneurship: Same, different, or both? *Entrepreneurship Theory and Practice, 30*(1), 1–22.

Barendsen, L., & Gardner, H. (2004). Is the social entrepreneur a new type of leader? *Leader to Leader, 34*, 43–50.

Basım, H. N., Meydan, C. H., & Şeşen, H. (2009). Bireyin Örgütsel Adalet Algısının İç Girişimcilik Davranışı İle İlişkisi: Kamuda bir araştırma. *İktisat İşletme ve Finans, 24*(274), 79–99.

Baughn, C., Chua, B. L., & Neupert, K. (2006). The normative context for women's participation in entrepreneurship: A multicountry study. *Entrereneurship Theory and Practice, 30*(5), 687–708.

Brush, C. G., Carter, N. M., Gatewood, E. J., Greene, P. G., & Hart, M. M. (2006). *Growth oriented women entrepreneurs and their businesses: A global research perspective*. Cheltenham: Edward Elgar.

Bygrave, W. D., & Hofer, C. W. (1992). Researching entrepreneurship. *Entrepreneurship Theory and Practice, 16*, 91–100.

Chen, M., & Wang, M. (2008). Social networks and a new venture's innovative capability: The role of trust within entrepreneurial teams. *R&D Management, 38*(3), 253–263.

Çavuş, M. F. (2009). Gençlerde Algılanan Sosyal Desteğin Özyeterlilik İnancına Etkileri. *Çağ Üniversitesi Sosyal Bilimler Dergisi, 6*(2), 1–11.

Çeçen, A. R. (2008). Öğrencilerin Cinsiyetlerine ve Anababa Tutum Algılarına Göre Yalnızlık ve Sosyal Destek Düzeylerinin İncelenmesi. *Türk Eğitim Bilimleri Dergisi, 6*(3), 415–431.

Dees, J. G. (1998). *The meaning of social entrepreneurship* (Draft report for the Kauffman Center for Entrepreneurial Leadership, pp. 1–5). Stanford University.

Duru, E. (2007). Re-examination of the psychometric characteristics of the multidimensional scale of perceived social support among Turkish University students. *Social Behavior and Personality, 35*(4), 443–452.

Eker, D., & Arkar, H. (1995). Çok Boyutlu Algılanan Sosyal Destek Ölçeğinin Faktör Yapısı, Geçerlik ve Güvenirliği. *Türk Psikoloji Dergisi, 34*, 45–55.

Eker, D., Arkar, H., & Yaldız, H. (2001). Çok Boyutlu Algılanan Sosyal Destek Ölçeği'nin Gözden Geçirilmiş Formunun Faktör Yapısı, Geçerlik ve Güvenirliği. *Türk Psikiyatri Dergisi, 12*(1), 17–25.

Elkington, J., & Hartigan, P. (2008). *The power of unreasonable people*. Boston: Harvard Business Press.

Ersen, T. B., Kaya, D., & Meydanoğlu, Z. (2010). *Sosyal Girişimler ve Türkiye (İhtiyaç Analiz Raporu)*. İstanbul: TÜSEV Yayınları.

Ford, M. C., & Gioia, D. A. (1995). *Creative action in organizations: Ivory tower visions, real world voices*. London: Sage Publications.

Gunn, R., Durkin, C., Singh, G., & Brown, J. (2008). Social entrepreneurship in the social policy curriculum. *Social Enterprise Journal, 4*(1), 74–80.

Gupta, V. K., Turban, D., Wasti, S. A., & Sikdar, A. (2009). The role of gender stereotypes in perceptions of entrepreneurs and intentions to become an entrepreneur. *Entrepreneurship Theory and Practice, 33*(2), 397–417.

Gurung, R. A., Sarason, B. R., & Sarason, I. G. (1997). Personal characteristics, relationship quality, and social support perceptions and behavior in young adult romantic relationships. *Personal Relationships, 4*, 319–339.

Hart, S. L., & Christensen, C. M. (1992). The great leap: Driving innovation from the base of the pyramid. *MIT Sloan Management Review, 44*(1), 51–56.

Hibbert, S. A., Hogg, G., & Quinn, T. (2002). Consumer response to social entrepreneurship: The case of the big issue in Scotland. *International Journal of Nonprofit and Voluntary Sector Marketing, 7*(3), 288–301.

Humbert, A. L., Drew, E., & Kelan, E. (2009). Gender identity and ICT entrepreneurship in an Irish context. In A. M. Pines & M. F. Ozbilgin (Eds.), *Handbook of research on high-technology entrepreneurs*. Cheltenham: Edward Elgar.

Işık, E. (2013). Mesleki Sonuç Beklentisinin Yordayıcıları Olarak Algılanan Sosyal Destek ve Denetim Odağı. *Kuram ve Uygulamada Eğitim Bilimleri Dergisi, 13*(3), 1419–1430.

Keskin, G. Ü., & Orgun, F. (2006). Öğrencilerin Öz Etkililik-Yeterlilik Düzeyleri ile Başa Çıkma Stratejilerinin İncelenmesi. *Anatolian Journal of Psychiatry, 7*, 92–99.

Kılıç Kırılmaz, S. (2014). Sosyal Girişimcilik Boyutlarına Kuramsal Bir Bakış. Ekonomive Yönetim Araştırmaları Dergisi, 3(2), 55–74.

Knight, G. (1997). Cross-cultural reliability and validity of a scale to measure firm entrepreneurial orientation. *Journal of Business Venturing, 12*, 213–225.

Koçak, O., Kavi, E. (2014). Sosyal Politika Aktörü Olarak Sosyal Girişimci Belediyecilik. *HAK-İş Uluslararası Emek ve Toplum Dergisi*, 3(3). ISSN:2147-3668.

Koe Hwee Nga, J., & Shamuganathan, G. (2010). The influence of personality traits and demographic factors on social entrepreneurship start up intentions. *Journal of Business Ethics, 95*, 259–282.

Kotetska, I., & Berezyak, I. (2014). Social entrepreneurship as an innovative solution mechanism of social problems of society. *Management Theory and Studies for Rural Business and Infrastructure Development, 36*(3), 569–577.

Kümbül Güler, B. (2011). Yoksullukla Mücadelede Sosyal Girişimcilik: ASHOKA üyelerinden sosyal yenilikçi örnek uygulamalar. *Dokuz Eylül Üniversitesi Sosyal Bilimler Enstitüsü Dergisi, 13*(3), 79–111. ISSN:1302-3284, E-ISSN:1308-0911.

Lock, R., & Smith, H. L. (2015). *The impact of female entrepreneurship on economic growth in Kenya* (CIMR research working series, Working Paper No:26). ISSN 2052-062X.

Lumpkin, G. T., & Dess, G. G. (2001). Linking two dimensions of entrepreneurial orientation to firm performance: The moderating role of environment and industry life cycle. *Journal of Business Venturing, 16*, 429–451.

Machan, T. R. (1999). Entrepreneurship and ethics. *International Journal of Social Economics, 26*(5), 596–608.

Mair, J., & Marti, I. (2006). Social entrepreneurship research: A source of explanation, prediction and delight. *Journal of World Business, 41*, 36–44.

Malecki, C. K., & Demaray, M. K. (2002). Measuring perceived social support: Development of the child and adolescent social support scale (CASSS). *Psychology in the Schools, 39*(1), 1–18.

Marshall, R. S. (2011). Conceptualizing the international for-profit social entrepreneur. *Journal of Business Ethics, 98*, 183–198.

Mitchell, R. K., Busenitz, L., Lant, T., McDougall, P. P., Morse, E. A., & Smith, B. (2002). Toward a theory of entrepreneurial cognition: Rethinking the people side of entrepreneurial research. *Entrepreneurship Theory and Practice, 27*(2), 93–104.

Moore, D. P., & Buttner, E. H. (1997). *Woman entrepreneurs – Moving beyond the glass ceiling*. Thousand Oaks, CA: Sage Publications.

Morgeson, F. P., & Humphrey, S. E. (2006). The work design questionnaire (WDQ): Developing and validating a comprehensive measure for assessing job design and the nature of work. *Journal of Applied Psychology, 91*(6), 1321–1339.

Mort, G. S., Weerawardena, J., & Carnegie, K. (2003). Social entrepreneurship: Towards conceptualisation. *International Journal of Nonprofit and Voluntary Sector Marketing, 8*(1), 76–88.

Mulyaningsih, H. D., & Ramadani, V. (2016). *Social entrepreneurship in an Islamic context. Entrepreneurship and management in an Islamic context* (pp. 143–158). Heidelberg: Springer.

Murphy, P. J., & Coombes, S. M. (2009). A model of social entrepreneurial discovery. *Journal of Business Ethics, 95*, 259–282.

Pines, A. M., Lerner, M., Schwartz, D. (2010). Gender differences in entrepreneurship: Equality, diversity and inclusion of global crisis. *Equality, Diversity and Inclusion: An International Journal, 29*(2), 186–198. Emerald Group Publishing Limited 2040–7149.

Polatçı, S. (2015). Örgütsel ve Sosyal Destek Algılarının Yaşam Tatmini Üzerindeki Etkisi: İş ve evlilik tatmininin aracılık rolü. *Ekonomik ve Sosyal Araştırmalar Dergisi, 11*(2), 25–44.

Ratten, V. (2011). Social entrepreneurship and innovation in sports. *International Journal of Electronic Finance, 1*(1), 42–54.

Ratten, V. (2012). Entrepreneurship, E-finance and mobile banking. *International Journal of Electronic Finance, 6*(1), 1–12.

Reyhanoğlu, M., & Akın, Ö. (2012). Ticari Girişimciler Ne Kadar Sosyal Girişimcidir? *YÖNETİM: İstanbul Üniversitesi İşletme İktisadı Enstitüsü Dergisi, 23*(71), 8–23.

Roberts, D., & Woods, C. (2005). Changing the world on a shoestring: The concept of social entrepreneurship. *University of Auckland Business Review, 7*(1), 45–51.

Shane, S., & Cable, D. (2002). Network ties, reputation and financing of new ventures. *Management Science, 48*(3), 364–381.

Shaw, E., & Carter, S. (2007). Social entrepreneurship: Theoretical antecedents and empirical analysis of entrepreneurial processes and outcomes. *Journal of Small Business and Enterprise Development, 14*(3), 418–434.

Smith, S. S. (1999, January). Rebirth of a salesman, losing your edge? *Entrepreneur Magazine*.

Thompson, J., Alvy, G., & Lees, A. (2000). Social entrepreneurship a new look at the people and the potential. *Management Decision, 38*(5), 328–338.

Thompson, J. L. (2002). The world of the social entrepreneur. *The International Journal of Public Sector Management, 15*(5), 412–431.

Toepfer, S. M. (2010). Family social support and family intrusiveness in young adult women. *Family Science Review, 15*(2), 57–65.

Truxillo, D., Cadiz, D. M., Rineer, J. R., Zaniboni, S., & Fraccaroli, F. (2012). A lifespan perspective on job design: Fitting the job and the worker to promote job satisfaction, engagement, and performance. *Organizational Psychology Review, 2*(4), 340–360.

Weiler, A. S., & Bernasek, A. (2001). Dodging the glass ceiling? Networks and the new wave of women entrepreneurs. *Social Science Journal, 38*, 85–103.

Entrepreneurship Challenges and Gender Issues in the African Informal Rural Economy

Paul Igwe, Robert Newbery, and Afam Icha-Ituma

Abstract In Africa the majority of businesses operate as informal sector in the rural economy. With relevant current debates encompassing informality and the family firm and employing data from a national survey that captures over 18 million entrepreneurs and business owners, this chapter examines the social, economic, environmental, cultural and wider barriers to female entrepreneurship in rural Nigeria. This chapter describes how lack of capital, low levels of literacy and education, inadequate transport facilities and poor access roads are the most important barriers that face female entrepreneurship in rural African communities. These are magnified by traditions and cultural barriers that favour men over women in many African countries, including Nigeria.

Keywords Knowledge • Entrepreneurship • Informal rural economy

1 Introduction

Gender issues in business have gained increasing attention over recent years in terms of theory, practice and policy. Female-owned enterprises make up an important segment of sub-Saharan Africa's micro and small business sector (USAID, 2010). In Africa, majority of family business activities takes place in the form of informal business activities in the farm and non-farm sector. The literature highlights the importance of female entrepreneurs to the economy in terms of their contributions to employment creation, poverty/inequality reduction, and sustainable development. USAID (2010) revealed that micro-enterprises with less than ten employees constituted over 99% of

P. Igwe (✉)
Faculty of Business and Society, University of South Wales, Treforest Campus, Wales, UK
e-mail: paul.igwe@southwales.ac.uk

R. Newbery
Newcastle Business School, Newcastle University, Newcastle upon Tyne, UK
e-mail: newbery@ncl.ac.uk

A. Icha-Ituma
Federal University Ndufu-Alike, Ndufu-Alike, Ikwo, Ebonyi State, UK
e-mail: afamituma@yahoo.com

V. Ratten et al. (eds.), *Knowledge, Learning and Innovation*, Contributions to Management Science, DOI 10.1007/978-3-319-59282-4_7

the countries' micro-, small and medium-sized enterprises in Ethiopia, Kenya and Tanzania. Of that, the report showed that the share of women business owners was about 65% in Ethiopia, 45% in Kenya and 43% in Tanzania, 73% in Lesotho, 84% in Swaziland, 62% in South Africa, and 67% in Zimbabwe (USAID, 2010). Despite the large share of female business owners in most Africa countries, women in Africa face challenges that arise from traditions and customs which combine with unfavourable cultural, economic, legal, political, technological and regulatory environments that result in unequal access to opportunities.

This chapter explored the issues, challenges, barriers and gender issues in the context of the contemporary rural informal African economy and will address a bias in the entrepreneurship literature towards the developed world (Naudé, 2013; Newbery, Siwale, & Henley, 2017). It brings together three areas of literature that have been hitherto disconnected, namely research on family businesses, informality and research on female entrepreneurship. According to African Development Bank (2013), the fact that the informal sector has for a long time been neglected by policy-makers has not helped in generating knowledge on this sector. The concepts, issues and challenges articulated in this book chapter are intended to support those involved in Small-Medium Enterprises (SMEs) and female entrepreneurship promotion: policymakers who want to create the right conditions; non-governmental organisations who fund and support start-ups; academics and researchers exploring and applying the theories and paradigms that underpin SMEs and informality.

There are many reasons for the broad support given to SMEs and entrepreneurship promotion in Africa, but two are most often cited. First, the high rate of population growth requires investment to increase economic activities to address the problem of the high rate of unemployment in Africa. Second, increasing economic activities through promoting entrepreneurship will increase income earning opportunities that offer the long-term path to poverty reduction. In this regard, female entrepreneurship has been attracting special interest, not only because women stand to benefit from the benefits of entrepreneurship, being the poorer and more discriminated against gender, but also because they are seen as a critical driver of entrepreneurship in light of their unique role in the household (Minniti & Naudé, 2010). It has been proven by much research that entrepreneurship is a key driver of economic development and growth (e.g. Bandiera et al., 2013). As the economy of developing countries grows, SMEs receive increased attention at both local and national levels. However, while high on most government priorities, little is known about female entrepreneurs in terms of traits, motivations, behaviour, experiences, cultural issues and the business environment.

In this chapter, we approach entrepreneurship from an economics and social view by adopting a behavioural and occupational view. This approach leads us to three perspectives. First, we adopt a view that entrepreneurship is either what an entrepreneur does, such as starting or managing a business, or a person's occupational choice to be self-employed (as defined by Naudé, Amorós, & Cristi, 2013). Second, given the dynamics of underdevelopment and poverty in African rural communities, we adopt another view of entrepreneurship that includes the informal micro and small business activities. These informal activities are mostly ignored, rarely supported and sometimes discouraged by policy makers and governments (Becker, 2004). Above all, their role in economic development remains controversial, despite being a means of livelihood for billions of people (La Porta & Shleifer, 2014). The African Development Bank (ADB, 2013) noted that little attention has been paid to the role of the informal sector in fostering growth and creating jobs in Africa. Third, we adopt a social entrepreneurship view (as defined by Arribas, Hernández, Urbano, & Vila, 2012) by referring to innovative, social value-creating activities that occur across social enterprises, private sector and community groups in the society.

In the last few years, a large number of studies have focused on family firms and SMEs. Within these areas, the issues, concepts and barriers are well known. These concepts have been explored in depth by studies such as Global Entrepreneurship Monitor (GEM), World Bank—Doing Business, etc. Despite a growing literature on the field of entrepreneurship, we still need more research on female entrepreneurship—particularly in the African context where we are seeing a growing number of initiatives aimed at promoting entrepreneurship and empowering women (Minniti & Naudé, 2010). The majority of female enterprises in developing countries take in the form of informal businesses. There is little comparable knowledge on African informal sector despite its contribution to economic development in the African region. One key reason for the lack of information is the difficulty in collecting data on informal business activities in African rural communities. This chapter attempts to fill these gaps.

This chapter progresses as follows: in Sect. 2, the definitions of the terms informality, family business and female businesses, particularly in relation to entrepreneurship are reviewed, and multidimensional understanding of the concepts articulated. Here we focus on the nature and composition of the important agricultural sector that is vital to rural Nigeria. In this regard, rural informal activities are important sources of local economic growth. This leads to Sect. 3, which examines the social, economic, cultural and wider barriers to female entrepreneurship in the African rural society. In this context, this chapter explores the impact on women and families where opportunities to engage in economic activities are hindered or removed through unfavourable economic, social, political and environmental conditions. It examines how access to opportunities or resources can be constrained by poverty, culture and many other institutional and environmental factors. These institutional factors include the regulatory framework; market conditions; banking and finance system; access to education; and lack of roads, transportation and electricity. We link these conditions to the concepts of rural livelihood strategies, fragility, resilience and sustainability. Finally, some avenues for future research are outlined.

2 Definitions and Characteristics of Informal Activities and Female Entrepreneurship

There is a growing interest in the informal sector, family firms and female entrepreneurship in developing countries, mainly due to the high rate of poverty and unemployment. These are the dominant forms of business ventures in developing regions and they play a significant role in the social and economic development of many African nations. These are important since existing business knowledge, structures and policies have failed to address critical issues such as unemployment, climate change, inequality and a high rate of poverty. Entrepreneurship is a multifaceted phenomenon that manifests itself throughout the economy in different forms and with different outcomes, such as the creation of wealth; increasing employment; and tackling of inequalities and environmental issues (OECD, 2016).

2.1 *Definition of the Informal Sector*

The majority of entrepreneurs in Nigeria (like in many African countries) operate in the form of micro/small enterprises in the informal sector. According to the World Bank (2012), there are a number of possible definitions of informality, and various authors have adopted different approaches. The 'informal economy' refers to "all economic activities by workers and economic units that are—in law or in practice—not covered or insufficiently covered by formal arrangements (ILO, 2014). In this context, we associate the informal sector with all legal and illegal business activities that are unregistered with government and are untaxed. Oviedo (2009) maintains that informality takes many forms, from the unregistered small firm, to the street vendor, to the large, registered-formal firm that employs a share of its workers without offering them written contracts with access to benefits and unemployment protection.

2.2 *The Current Debate on the Importance of the Informal Economy*

The literature highlights the importance of the informal sector to the economies of many developing countries. Many studies highlight these roles in the form of the economic role that the informal sector performs in stimulating the growth of the market economy, promoting a flexible labour market and absorbing retrenched labour from the formal sector (Onwe, 2013).The importance of the informal sector in most African economies stems from the opportunities it offers to the most vulnerable populations such as the poorest households, women and youths (ADB, 2013). In Kenya, the National Bureau of Statistics estimate that, as of 2014, the informal sector represents 82.7% of employment (World Bank, 2016). According to ADB (2013), the informal sector contributes about 55% of Sub-Saharan Africa's GDP and 80% of the labour force. It has been found that nine in ten rural and urban workers have informal jobs in Africa and most employees are women and youth (ADB, 2013).

Despite its importance being acknowledged by many researchers and studies, the views on the nature and characteristics of the informal sector have been changing with recent developments (Onwe, 2013). As illustrated in Table 1, the informal

Table 1 Views on informal sector

The traditional view	The current view
The informal sector is the traditional economy that will wither away and die with modern, industrial growth	The informal economy is increasing with modern, industrial growth—accounting for more than half of the new jobs in Latin America and 80% of new jobs in Africa. In India, more than 90% of the labour force is in it. It is a feature of economic transition as well as capitalist industrialisation
It is only marginally productive	Virtually everywhere the informal economy is efficient and resilient, creating jobs. It is a major provider of employment, goods and services for lower-income groups. It contributes significantly to GDP
It exists separately from the formal economy	It is linked to the formal economy—it produces for, trades with, distributes for, and provides services to the formal economy
It represents a reserve pool of surplus labour	Much of the recent rise in informality reflects the decline in formal employment associated with structural adjustment and global competition. It reflects not only the incapacity of formal firms to absorb labour, but also their unwillingness to do so
Most of those in the sector are entrepreneurs of illegal and unregistered enterprises seeking to avoid regulation and taxation	It should not be equated with the criminal or illegal economy. It is made up of non-standard wageworkers as well as entrepreneurs and self-employed persons producing legal goods and services, albeit through irregular or unregulated means. Most entrepreneurs and the self-employed are amenable to, and would welcome, efforts to reduce barriers to registration and related transaction costs and to increase benefits from regulation
Work in the informal economy is comprised mostly of survival activities and thus is not a subject for economic policy	Informal enterprises include not only survival activities but also stable enterprises and dynamic growing businesses. All informal enterprises are affected by economic policies
It comprises mainly of unregistered business	It comprises not only of informal enterprises but also of informal jobs, including employees of informal firms, casual day labourers, and domestic workers as well as industrial outworkers and other non-standard workers in both informal and formal firms
It comprises mostly of street traders and very small-scale producers	It is made up of a wide range of informal arrangements- both "resilient old forms" and "emerging new ones" (temporary and part-time jobs plus home-based work for high tech industries). Its two basic segments are informal enterprises and informal jobs
It is unregulated	Some informal enterprises-such as street vendors-are highly regulated, so much so that

(continued)

Table 1 (continued)

The traditional view	The current view
	regulations are impossible to enforce or comply with and are often not clear either to local authorities or to vendors. Regulations become a tool of harassment and control, not a way to encourage economic contributions of street vendors. On the other hand, the employers of most informal workers often seek to avoid complying with labour legislation
Because it is unregulated and untaxed, many working in the informal sector are wealthy	Average incomes are lower in the informal economy than in the formal economy. A higher percentage of people working in the informal economy are micro entrepreneurs who hire others. The poorest are, typically, informal wageworkers, especially industrial outworkers
To regulate the informal economy is unnecessary interference with its workings	In today's globalised economy, the active role of government is needed in the regulation of economic activities, including the informal economy. Clear rules and appropriate legislation are needed to regulate the relationship between governments, foreign investors, local enterprises, and the workforce
Street traders are to blame for crime in the inner sites	Criminals are a threat to business interests of both formal and informal enterprises
It does not contribute to economic growth	It contributes substantially to the economy and needs to be encouraged and facilitated

Source: Onwe (2013, p. 64)

sector is interpreted in different situations with different causes, posing different problems that require different solutions. As such ILO described the informal sector as activities that are unrecognised, unrecorded, unprotected or unregulated by public authorities, and was not confined to marginal activities but also included profitable enterprises (Becker, 2004). The World Bank (2016) stresses that the informal sector across Africa is ubiquitous, with a significant number of people engaged in small household enterprises outside formal wage employment. Some authors have described informal activities as parasites competing unfairly with law-abiding formal firms (La Porta & Shleifer, 2014).

Many associate the informal sector with illegal and unregistered enterprises seeking to avoid regulation and taxation. Although this definition could apply to informal activities in developed countries, this is untrue for developing countries. As Oviedo (2009) put it, in developed economies, informality tends to involve tax evasion and undeclared labour rather than a significant share of unregistered businesses. In developing countries, tax and regulation avoidance are not the main reasons as to why most of the economic activities remain informal. As Oviedo (2009) stressed, an important component of informality relates to the rational choices of firms and workers to remain informal based on the relative costs and benefits of being in each sector.

2.3 The Transition from an Informal to a Formal Economy

It has been shown that as countries develop, informality becomes less important. Important as the informal sector is in low-income countries, it becomes much less significant in high-income ones (La Porta & Shleifer, 2014). The authors maintain that there is a strong negative correlation between per capita income and the share of economic activity that is informal as measured by the share of self-employment in total employment. The informal economy operates in a complex environment of linkages between the formal and informal economies, with workers and producers in the informal economy being linked to the global economy in various ways (global production networks, migration, global economic cycles and variations in global commodity and food prices) (ILO, 2014). Formalization, or bringing the informal firms within the fold of the formal sector, is suggested as a possible solution to low-income levels, according to the World Bank (2016). However, the move to the formal sector has been notoriously difficult to achieve and slow in most countries. Hence, an important question here is how and when do informal activities transform to the formal sector, and what kinds of informal sector are more likely to do so. The transition from informal to formal activities will differ in different sectors and in different economies. However, it has been suggested that informal firms almost never become formal. As La Porta and Shleifer (2014) put it, an average surveyed informal firm has been in business for nearly a decade without attempting to become formal. Understanding informality is important since majority of female entrepreneurs in Nigeria and African rural communities undertake their activities in the informal sector.

In explaining, the nature and the roots of informal economic activity across countries, Oviedo (2009) distinguished between informality as the result of "exclusion" and "exit" as follows: Informality as a result of 'exclusion' is due to (i) stringent and costly regulations, and (ii) lack of opportunities, especially for certain demographic groups in the formal sector. Also, Oviedo (2009) state that informality as a result of 'exit' is due to (i) mediocre benefits of being formally employed (or formally registered), (ii) individual preference for self-employment, and (iii) lack of trust in public institutions. In developing and developed countries, informality describes two contrasting forms as presented in Table 2.

Table 2 The Informal sector from developed and developing countries' point of view

Developing countries	Developed countries
Informal businesses are mostly very small (with five or fewer employees, often operating from the household); Some with little or no intention of, or potential for growth, while others facing serious barriers to expansion due to excessive regulation and lack of access to resources such as capital	Informality mostly involves formal firms and workers who underreport their income to the tax authorities, or the use of undeclared labour, often undocumented foreigners, especially in certain activities (construction, home repair, etc.)

Source: Adapted from Oviedo (2009, pp. 10–11)

Some authors suggest that informal firms inhabit an economic space of their own, disconnected from the formal space (for example, La Porta & Shleifer, 2014). Others associate formal and informal sectors as complementary, rather than segmented sectors and that although individuals' motivations to become informal may differ, the common denominator in the informal sector is low scale and low productivity (Oviedo, 2009). The overwhelming evidence supports the second notion that formal and informal sectors complement each other especially in the low and medium income countries. There are degrees of informality and formality in the developing economies and this changes as an economy grows. As Onwe (2013), noted, the term informal economy also emphasises the existence of a continuum from the informal to the formal ends of a given economy and thus, the interdependence between informal and formal economic activities.

2.4 *The Size, Characteristics and Roles of the Informal Sector in Developing Countries*

The informal economy in many African countries is big business. The World Bank and other studies estimate that between 80 and 90% of total employment is informal (World Bank, 2012). It suggests that official statistics from West African countries indicate that up to 60% of the GDP of these countries is produced from informal activities. Using the World Bank benchmarking for measuring the size of the informal economy, ILO (2006) estimates that its average size as a percentage of gross domestic product in sub-Saharan Africa ranges from under 30% in South Africa to 60% in Nigeria, Tanzania and Zimbabwe. The literature provides strong evidences that supports the economic role that informal business activities play in stimulating the growth of the market economy, promoting a flexible labour market, stimulating productive activities, and absorbing unskilled labour from urban and rural sectors. Across the globe, informal business activities provide the livelihood for billions of people (La Porta & Shleifer, 2014). In low and middle-income countries, informal firms make up the majority of all enterprises (World Bank, 2016). In all developing regions, self-employment constitutes a greater share of informal employment (non-agriculture) than wage employment (ILO, 2014). In Kenya, the total number of persons enrolled in both the formal and informal sectors increased from 13.5 million in 2013 to 14.3 million in 2014, and of the 799,700 new jobs, 700,000 were created by the informal sector (World Bank, 2016). In Nigeria, the informal sector has been noted as accounting for about 38% of the gross domestic product (GDP), as well as accounting for 21% of total employment in Sub-Saharan African countries (Onwe, 2013). Informal employment represents nearly one-third of total non-agricultural employment worldwide, and accounts for as much as 53% of non-agricultural employment in sub-Saharan Africa, 44% in Latin America, 32% in Asia and 31% in North Africa (ILO, 2014).

The World Bank Enterprise Surveys collects business data in both formal and informal firms on their sales and inputs, employee and manager education, as well as a variety of assessments of the institutional environment. This data provides considerable evidence on the determinants of productivity and characteristics of firms in developing countries. La Porta and Shleifer (2014, p. 113) provides a summary of characteristics that distinguish informal and formal businesses based on the World Bank surveys as follows:

- Informal businesses are much smaller than formal firms.
- On average formal firms employs 126 people, informal firms employ only four.
- Informal firms are much less productive, with productivity calculated as value added (sales net of expenditures on raw materials and energy) per employee.
- Informal firms add only 15% of the value per employee of formal firms, whereas, the ratio of value added by informal firms to that by formal firms ranges from 1% in Congo to 70% in Cape Verde.
- There is a sharp productivity difference between informal firms and formal firms of the same size, whereas productivity increases with size within the formal sector.
- Wages in informal firms are roughly one-half of those in small formal firms and less than one-third of those in large formal firms, another indication of low productivity.

3 Family Firm and Female Entrepreneurship

In the rural African economy, family firms develop through the form of diversification driven either by pull or push factors. In this context, two forms of diversification—opportunity-driven and survival-driven diversification. The first describes people who diversify to accumulate wealth and the second refers to individuals who diversify in order to survive. Accumulation of wealth becomes the motive for diversification once survival has been overcome, according to Mishra (2002). According to Fabusoro, Omotayo, Apantaku, and Okuneye (2010), diversification is a household survival strategy for risk reduction, overcoming income instability caused by seasonality and improving food security. Three factors of rural livelihood circumstances are mentioned as determining the nature and extent of diversification—seasonality, risk and vulnerability (Mishra, 2002). The author suggests that the rural economy in which farming is wholly dependent on climatic conditions suffers from all three factors. To plan against these factors, households becomes less dependent on agriculture. Such a strategy according to Mishra (2002) involves diversification, to reduce the risk of income failure as well as intra year and inter year income variability by diversifying economic activities.

Several authors suggest that given the importance of farming as the major source of livelihood for both the landless and small farmers, the non-farm sector offers capacity for diversification (IFAD, 2009; Reardon, Haggblade, & Hazell, 2002).

Rural households may engage in the non-farm sector as employers, self-employed entrepreneurs or as employees (IFAD, 2009). According to Mishra (2002) such diversification by rural households is less of a planned strategy and more of a coping behaviour. Several authors maintain that the end result of this coping behaviour is one of managing complex portfolios of not only capital but also time (Mishra, 2002). Entrepreneurial opportunities are thought to develop when aforementioned environmental factors support and not hinder any group of people from fulfilling or participating in the economic activities. In many developing countries women are the most vulnerable group that tend to be affected by these entrepreneurship environmental constraints. A few of women that break the barriers to start and operate a business do so often in the form of informal activity.

4 Nigerian Rural/Peasant Economic Activities

Subsistence farming is the dominant economic activity that is captured in the National Bureau of Statistics surveys in Nigeria. In this section, we analyse the composition of farming activity based on the National Agricultural Sample Survey (NASS). This survey by three Nigerian government agencies—National Bureau of Statistics (NBS), Federal Ministry of Agriculture and Rural Development (FMA&RD) is conducted every 10 years as recommended by Food and Agriculture Organization (FAO) across 36 states of Nigeria and Federal Capital Territory.

4.1 Characteristics and Composition of Rural Economic Activities

Four main activities captured in the NASS survey include—crops, livestock, poultry and fishery. The data shows distribution of the activities by holders, state, gender, age group, size of land, tenure type, sources of fund, level of education, etc. The results of the NASS reveals male dominance of agricultural activity at peasant level in Nigeria. The data captured 36,573,214 farming enterprise which when disaggregated by gender showed that enterprises operated by male were 31,090,789 and female 5,482,425 (Fig. 1). Several studies have shown that Nigeria has one of the lowest women entrepreneur rates in sub-Saharan Africa and women entrepreneurs in Nigeria face discriminatory sociocultural values and traditions that are embedded in the policy and legal environment and in institutional support mechanisms that pose as barriers to female entrepreneurship (British Council, 2012; Nnamdi, 2009).

The results grouped according to crop farmer population showed male domination with about 15,629,709 (85.99%), while females were 2,546,371 (14.01%) as shown in Table 3. In terms of the age group's distribution of crop farmers, the age

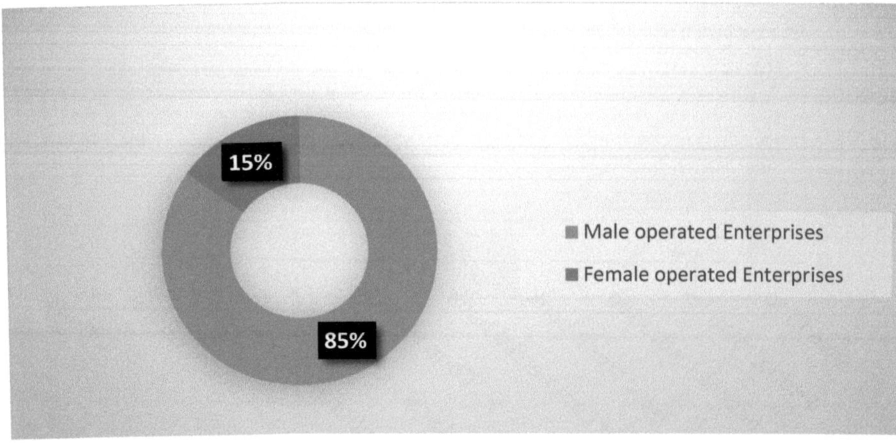

Fig. 1 Enterprise activities by gender. Source: Adapted from NBS (2012)

Table 3 Nigerian National distribution of activities by gender

	Male	Female	Total
Crops	15,629,709	2,546,373	18,176,082
Livestock	10,367,831	1,941,801	12,309,631
Poultry	4,196,945	866,126	6,393,094
Fishery	896,304	128,125	1,024,428
Total	31,090,789	5,482,425	36,573,214

Source: Adapted from NBS (2012)

group (30–49 years) had the highest number of 9,873,229 (54.32%), followed by age group (50–64 years) which was 5,376,031 (29.58%), whereas age group (65 years and above) was 1,892,314 (10.41%), and age group (15–29 years) accounted for 1,034,510 (5.69%).

The NASS survey also revealed information related to source of capital/funds for crop production activities. The total amount committed to crop farming was 570,063 million naira and the national average amount was thirty-one thousand, three hundred and sixty-three naira (N31, 363). Of the total amount, the biggest share of 513,577 million naira (90.09%) came from their own funds, followed by sources from friends/relatives 27,475 million naira (4.82%), traditional contribution 15,861 million naira (2.78%), local money lenders 5291 million naira (0.93%) and cooperative societies 3694 million naira (0.65%) (Fig. 2).

In terms of distribution of farmers by livestock, livestock farming followed a similar pattern to that of crops. An estimated 12,309,631 peasant livestock holders were captured in the survey during 2010/2011. Of this figure, males were 10,367,831 (84.2%) while females were 1,941,801 (15.8%) as shown in Table 3. In terms of distribution of livestock holders by age, the survey revealed that the

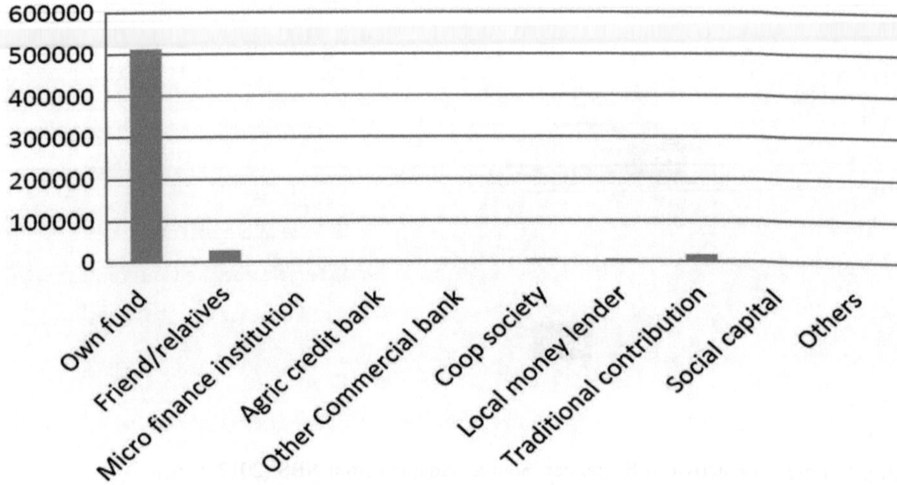

Fig. 2 Funds committed by source (national). Source: Adapted from NBS (2012, p. 21)

average age of holders was 49 years. Of the total population, age group 45–54 years accounted for the highest number of 3,783,578 (30.7%), this was closely followed by age groups 35–44 years with 3,483,090 (28.3%). A total of 6,393,094 holders were poultry farmers of which male were 4,196,945 (82.9%) while female holders were 866,126 (17.1%) (See Table 3). A total of 1,024,428 were fish farmers, of which 896,304 (87.49%) were male and 128,125 (12.51%) female in 2010/2011.

One of these discriminatory factors that limit women from taking part in economic activity is literacy and education attainment. As noted by the CIA (2013), about 61.3% of the population over the age of 15 years can read and write, although male/female split show that about 72.1% of men able to write, but only 50.4% of women. The result of NASS farm survey related to the distribution of fish farmers by level of education is shown in Fig. 3 and Livestock farmers by gender and education level is shown in Fig. 4. One of the main features of informal economic activities in many rural African communities is that operations are typically on a small scale with only a few workers and skills required for the business activities are usually gained outside formal education (ILO, 2006).

Out of the total 12,309,508 livestock holders, those with primary education constituted the highest number with 3,686,865 (29.95%) followed by those who had pre-school education with 2,947,317 (23.94%) whereas those with non-formal education were 2,943,656 (23.91%). Those with secondary education were2,195,035 (17.83%) while those with tertiary education made up only 536,758 (4.36%) of the entire livestock farmers, as shown in Fig. 4.

Similarly, in a survey of aquaculture operators in Ogun and Lagos State of Western Nigeria, the results showed that aquaculture operators in both states are

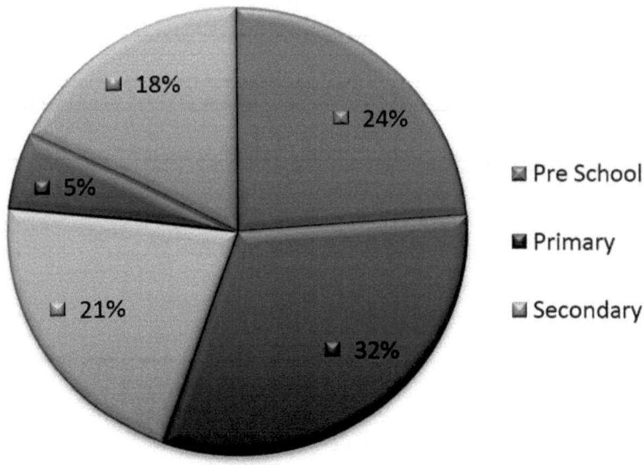

Fig. 3 Distribution of farmers by Level of Education. Source: Adapted from NBS (2012, p. 35)

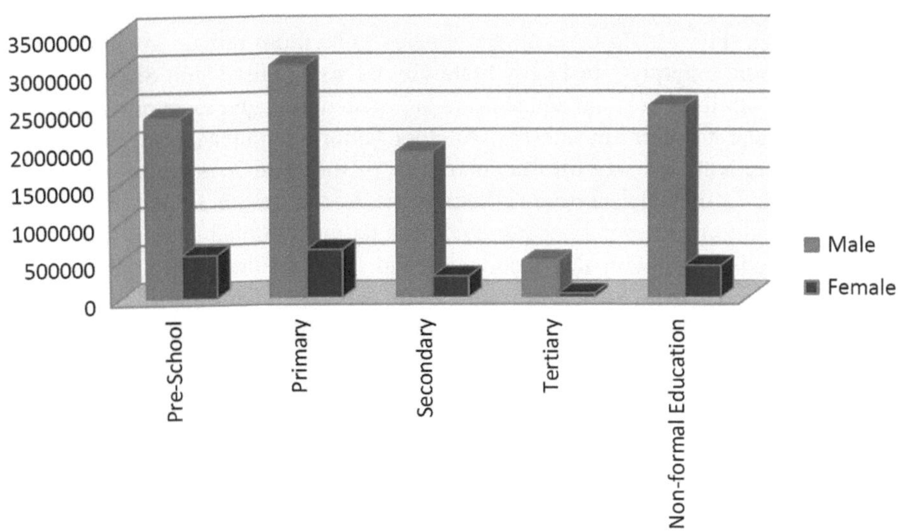

Fig. 4 Distribution of Livestock Farmers by Educational Level & Gender. Source: Adapted from NBS (2012, p. 31)

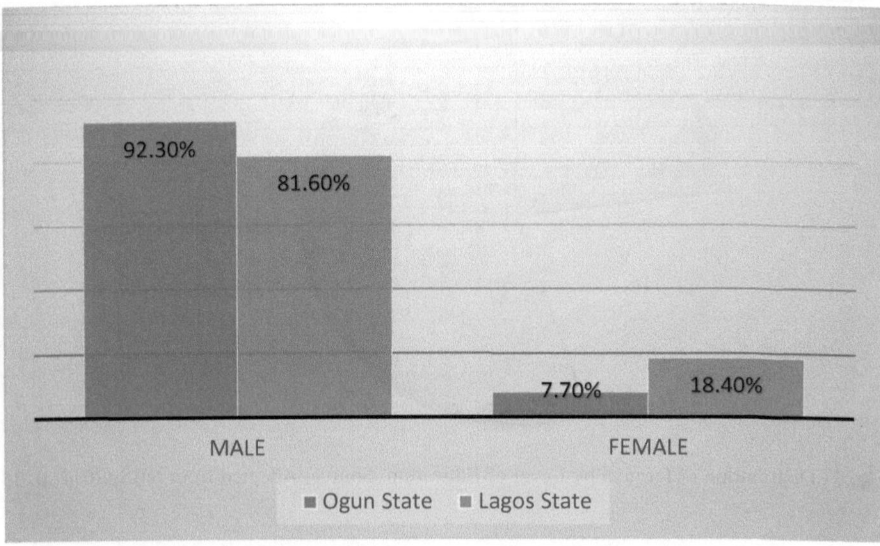

Fig. 5 Gender of aquaculture operators. Source: Adeoye (2016)

mainly males (Fig. 5). However, there appears to be more female involvement in the aquaculture enterprise in Lagos State (18.4% as against Ogun State (7.70%). Therefore, both livestock and aquaculture are male dominated as in other forms of agriculture and non-farm businesses. Another features of aquaculture business as with other agricultural activities is small size of the farms. As suggested by the World Bank (2012), the reasoning behind the size criterion is that small-scale activities tend to be informal because they lack the institutional and organizational capacity needed to obtain the accounting and financial documents required by government authorities. Most proponents of this approach consider informal activities to be survival strategies, providing income to poor households with little marketable skills (World Bank, 2012).

4.2 *Distribution of Rural Activities in Nigeria*

The national distribution of livestock holders by form of ownership showed that of the 12,309,631 that owned livestock, individual ownership was 11,760,063 (representing almost 96% of the population); jointly with another member of the household 529,662; jointly with members of other households were 19,906. The distribution of holdings by land size (hectare) of tenure type were as follows: Owner-like possession (26,877,847 ha, representing about 84% of total holding); family land (3,393,597 ha); rented/royalty (1,326,713 ha); squatter (322,283 ha) and others (111,380 ha). The number of working proprietors were dominated by

Table 4 Distribution of number of persons engaged in activities and by gender

Number of working proprietors ('000)		Number of unpaid family members ('000)		Number of paid employees ('000)	
Male	Female	Male	Female	Male	Female
8239	2421	9347	6047	1442	160

Source: Adapted from NBS (2012, p. 60)

men with 77% of the total population and women with 23% (as shown in Table 4). The number of unpaid family members were: males (about 61%) and females (about 39%), while the number of male paid employees were about 90%, with females 10% of the total number of employees (as shown in Table 4). This results shows that a higher proportion of the female population in Nigeria was engaged in unpaid family activities, whereas only small proportion of females was engaged in paid employment activities. This is one of the gender issues that has been highlighted in the literature regarding the bias in employment in developing countries.

The various marketing channels for peasant farmers to sell their products were: in the farm (4,207,603), in the open market (13,897,197), co-operative society (147,454), direct to the industry (15,516) and others (131,692). This result shows that the open market and in the farm are the two main options for peasant farmers to sell their produce. The market channels offer little opportunity for the farmers in term of achieving better prices, as they have to sell at farm gate prices or risk losing their produce to spoilage due to lack of storage facilities.

5 Socio-economic and Cultural Barriers to Female Entrepreneurship

In the Nigerian rural economy (as in the majority of other African rural communities), men dominate ownership of assets, the position of head of households and participation in paid employment. Low representation of women as heads of households could be related to strong cultural and traditional values within the rural communities, which tend to exclude women from major responsibilities such as ownership of land and businesses and being head of a household (Igwe, 2013). According to Woldie and Adersua (2004, pp. 80–81) "gender divide exists in Nigeria, hence aspiring Nigerian women entrepreneurs feel obstructed by the gender divide". USAID (2010) stated that gendered division of labour in the household, low value attached to women's work, together with simultaneous clustering of women in low-paid jobs, contribute to female poverty. In many rural communities of Nigeria, some culture and tradition only permit male households from inheriting family wealth and asset when the head of household is dead. Likewise, some culture tends to favour male households in terms of access to education than females.

Some culture in Nigeria permits early marriages for young girls as early as 14–16 years (e.g. in the Northern Nigeria), thereby preventing young girls from schooling and engaging in employment or business activities. Also, some traditions state what women can do and cannot in terms of their roles, jobs, employment, status, association and rights. In extreme cases, some culture tends to exclude or prevent women from travelling on the same public taxi or buses with men or travelling at night times in public transport and operating businesses at nights. These and many other cultural barriers discriminate against women in Nigeria. Lack of mobility, as a result of women's domestic responsibilities and other restrictions prevent women from running a business out of the home, thereby limiting direct interaction with customers. The results from the Nigerian National Agricultural Sample Survey (2010/2011) as shown in Sect. 2 and in Tables 3 and 4 revealed a wide gender disparity and bias against females in ownership and employment in all economic activities (such as crops production, land, livestock, poultry and fishery). It has been reported that this exclusion affects all categories of women; married, divorced or widowed, which translates to little or no access to assets of production and decision-making (Stephen & Lenihan, 2010).

"Women entrepreneurs in Nigeria are often prevented from running competitive businesses by their relatively low education and skill levels, which generally limit their access to the various support services" (Woldie & Adersua, 2004, pp. 80–81). Stephen and Lenihan (2010) observed that culturally defined gender-based divisions of labour do prescribe certain high-return activities for men and low-return occupations for women, thereby creating gender-based inequalities in livelihood opportunities and constraints. In Nigeria, wider gender disparity is caused by a range of issues that include—financial barriers; poor quality of roads; lack of availability of public transport services; limited capacity (for people and goods) on transport services; services not going to required destinations; services at inconvenient times; expensive services; and safety issues. This problem is recognised nationally, as many rural roads are in poor condition, and are often unpaved. This creates particular problems in the wet season when heavy rain can render them impassable (Igwe, 2013). Another prohibitive factor in the overall success of rural businesses operated by women is the high cost of public transport which led to increase the final cost of their products for the end user—impacting upon their overall competitiveness (Mijinyawa & Adetunji, 2005).

Economic pressures result from poorly developed rural policies, which lead to a harsh business environment and lack of economic security. As a result, the economic activities that take place in the rural sector and in which women participate take the form of peasant farming and small/micro scale non-farm activities. For example, farming is practiced by the majority of the households on a small scale (less than 2.0 ha) and there are only a few commercial farms in the study area (Igwe, 2013). This average is even lower when measured by ownership by women. The NASS survey showed several factors that constitute major obstacles and barriers to operating and managing businesses and farming in the rural villages, as shown in Table 5. The distribution of holdings by problems encountered when purchasing farm input showed that lack of funds and high cost of input as the most reported problems (see Table 5).

Table 5 Nigerian National distribution by problems encountered

A. National distribution of holding by problems encounter when purchasing farm input								
Too costly/ high cost	Lack of funds/ money	Don't know where to obtain	Not available/scarce	Too far to obtain	Lack of transport	Bad roads	Adulteration of inputs	Others
11,530,801	14,355,081	2,043,651	2,924,647	5,306,546	8,105,623	9,780,316	5,598,875	604,353
B. National distribution of holdings by problems encounter during production process								
Lack of personnel	Lack of fund	Far distance	Lack of infrastructure/frequent outage of electricity	Ineffective/inadequate extension service	Lack of encouragement from government		Others	
7,823,238	3,568,878	6,672,059	9,071,929	8,768,997	11,485,419		720,276	
C. National distribution of holding by problems encountered during storage								
Theft	Pests		Lack of modern storage facilities		Inadequate market		Others	
4,809,061	8,311,646		9,597,540		7,064,611		786,696	
D. Distribution of holdings by problems encountered during marketing								
Poor prices	Poor access roads		High cost of transport		Far distance to market		Others	
11,244,283	10,495,195		10,680,774		8,166,264		910,892	
E. Distribution of ways that government can assist farmers								
Credit	Land development		Improved input supplies/subsidies		Provision of infrastructure		Others	
14,307,033	10,223,017		12,050,370		11,799,751		1,469,430	
F. Distribution of access to information and communication (ICT)								
Radio	Television	Telephone (fixed)		Telephone (mobile)	Personal computer (PC)	Internet		Website
Access	Access	Ownership	Access	Access	Access	Ownership	Access	Access
14,276,702	6,239,630	422,915	893,180	10,114,474	638,954	228,189	405,771	215,998

Source: Adapted from NBS/NASS (2012)

Poor prices, high cost of transportation and poor access roads were the three most cited problems encountered during marketing (see Table 5). When these factors are further analysed based on gender, women, being the more vulnerable group, are more affected than men in terms of access to capital/credit, access to transport, market and storage facilities. These barriers and challenges that exclude women from participating in economic activities have a pronounced effect on household income leading to wider inequality and poverty in rural areas. According to USAID (2010), restrictive regulatory and legal environments (such as labour laws) that relegate women and other vulnerable groups to the informal sector; high taxes; unequal property rights; and male-biased and non-transparent procurement procedures. Past public legislation in Nigeria, focused on agricultural development as a means of achieving growth, and rural development policies have not achieved the desired result due to poor polices and implementation (Gaurba, 2006). As a result, the rural sector lacks access to good roads, electricity, market, credit and education, all of which affect productivity and well-being.

The literature shows that another major barrier to family firms and female entrepreneurship in rural areas of Nigeria is source financial capital. For example, Fabusoro et al. (2010) state that one of the principal problems of rural households and individuals wishing to start a business, whether in the farm or non-farm sector, is access to financial capital. They conclude that, without start-up funds, or with little cash available for investment, households are limited to a smaller number of activities that typically yield poorer returns. The problem of lack of capital is even worse for female entrepreneurs since women are less likely to obtain loan or credit than men from the informal lending organisations that operate in the rural areas. The NASS survey (2010/2011) revealed that the main source of financial capital is mainly own capital in the forms of cash savings, storage of farm produce, livestock, and land sales (see Fig. 2). The provision of financial services has been a long-standing challenge in developing countries, a fact reflected in the general lower penetration of financial services into rural areas (World Bank, 2010). As a result of lack of sources of formal capital, the informal financial sector, comprising money lenders and thrift associations, receives wide patronage because of the accessibility and flexibility of services, but the loans are usually short term, since the scale of operation of the average individual lender is small (Attah, 2008). According to the World Bank (2008), financial constraints are more pervasive in agriculture and related activities than in many other sectors, reflecting both the nature of the agricultural sector and the average size of firms.

Female entrepreneurship and family firms also face other challenges associated with levels of poverty, environmental degradation, conflict, wars and fragility in many African countries. Conflict, poverty and inequality in Nigeria have strong geographical concentrations, resulting in significant levels of regional disparity between the six regions of Nigeria. The characteristics of poverty provided by the World Bank (2003) include lack of control over resources, lack of education and skills, poor health, malnutrition, lack of shelter, poor access to water and sanitation, vulnerability to shocks, violence and crime, and the lack of political freedom and voice. There have been several studies on the link between poverty and conflict in the last three decades (Cramer, 2001; Draman, 2003; Justino, 2002). Beyond poverty and social issues, the prevalence of informal activities is closely associated to an environment characterized by weaknesses in three institutional areas, namely taxation, regulation and private property rights (ADB, 2013). Environmental conditions are the other important factors determining entrepreneurial capabilities in rural areas, since farming still depends on rain fed agriculture. Natural disasters (incidents of flood, fire, death and illness) are not rampant but there are no insurance provisions to cover such incidents if they do occur.

6 Conclusion

The informal sector matters because of its sheer size in African rural economy. For example, about half of national output, more than 80% of total employment and 90% of new jobs in African low income countries comes from informal sector (Mbaye, 2014). As USAID (2010, p. 1) put it: "gender, informal work, and poverty often co-exist, and the informal economy remains an important source of employment and income for women throughout the developing world". It is clear from the literature that the rural development policies in Nigeria and most of African countries has not been effective in terms of supporting women entrepreneurs. For many women, access to education, capital and rural transport are the many innumerable barriers that face women in trying to become entrepreneurs and generate income. For many women who aspire to become entrepreneurs or want to start their own business, access to capital is a major problem in the rural areas in developing countries such as Nigeria. According to Mishra, Igwe, Johnathan, and Megicks (2015) rural credit markets are characterized by high rates of interest, small volumes of credit availability and the problem of asymmetric information.

In many African rural economies, female entrepreneurship takes in the form of activities in the informal sector comprising mainly of subsistence farming and micro/small business activities. In contextualizing informality, this chapter focused on exploring the contrasting views as to the roles of informal economy in different regions. There are some suggestions that informal firms inhabit an economic space of their own and are disconnected from the formal sector (e.g. La Porta & Shleifer, 2014). However, the overwhelming evidence support the notion that informal and formal sectors are linked. However, the degree of informality and formality will differ from one region to another depending on many factors. These factors are poverty level, cultural issues, regulatory framework, market conditions, and access to finance, access to education, lack of roads, transportation and electricity. From this perspective, we recommend that policies should focus on reducing the barriers that limit or prevent women from participating fully in economic activities such as culture, access to finance and transport issues. Finally, policies designed to support only large scale agriculture and promote formality should be introduced with caution as many rural populations depend on small scale farming and micro non-farm enterprise activities for their livelihood. Future research should explore Africa informal sector in the West, East, South and North Africa to determine the differences and similarities. This will provide a more in-depth knowledge of the African entrepreneurs and the informal sector from non-western views.

References

Adeoye, D. (2016). *Survey of Hatchery farms in Western States of Nigeria*. University of Agriculture Abeokuta, unpublished.

African Development Bank (ADB). (2013). *Recognizing Africa's informal sector*, March 27, 2013. https://www.afdb.org/en/blogs/afdb-championing-inclusive-growth-across-africa/post/recognizing-africas-informal-sector-11645/

Arribas, I., Hernández, P., Urbano, A., & Vila, J. E. (2012). Are social and entrepreneurial attitudes compatible? A behavioral and self-perceptional analysis. *Management Decision, 50*(10), 1739–1757.

Attah, J. A. (2008, January–June 7). Micro-finance Banking needs for proper orientation. *The Nigerian Micro-finance Newsletter*.

Bandiera, O., Burgess, R., Das, N., Gulesci, S., Rasul, I., & Sulaiman, M. (2013). *Can basic entrepreneurship transform the economic lives of the poor?* (IZA Discussion Papers IZA DP 7386). Bonn.

Becker, K. F. (2004). *The informal economy: A fact finding study*. Stockholm: Swedish International Development Cooperation Agency (Sida).

British Council. (2012). *Gender in Nigeria report 2012: Improving the lives of girls and women in Nigeria*. Available from https://www.gov.uk/government/uploads/system/uploads/attachment_data/file/67333/Gender-Nigeria2012.pdf

Central Intelligence Agency. (2013). *Nigeria*. Available from https://www.cia.gov/library/publications/the-world-factbook/geos/ni.html

Cramer, C. (2001). *Economic inequalities and civil conflict* (CDPR Discussion Paper 1501). School of Oriental and African Studies.

Draman, R. (2003, May 19–23). *Poverty and conflict in Africa: Explaining a complex relationship*. Prepared for: Experts Group Meeting on Africa-Canada Parliamentary Strengthening Program, Addis Ababa.

Fabusoro, E., Omotayo, A. M., Apantaku, S. O., & Okuneye, P. A. (2010). Forms and determinants of rural livelihoods diversification in Ogun State, Nigeria. *Journal of Sustainable Agriculture, 34*(4), 417–438.

Gaurba, D. (2006). Survival at the margins: Economic crisis and coping mechanisms in Rural Nigeria. *Local Environment, 11*(1), 17–36.

IFAD. (2009). *Rural enterprise and poverty reduction*. Asia and the Pacific Division, International Fund for Agricultural Development.

Igwe, P. A. (2013). *Rural non-farm livelihood diversification and poverty reduction in Nigeria*. Ph. D. research, University of Plymouth, Rural Micro and Small Enterprises.

ILO. (2006). *The impact of globalization on the informal sector in Africa*. International Labour Organization, Report VI, ILO, Geneva.

ILO. (2014). *Transitioning from the informal to the formal economy*. International Labour Conference 103rd Session 2014, Report V (1). Geneva: International Labour Office.

Justino, P. (2002, February). Poverty, inequality and conflict. *Poverty Research Unit at Sussex (PRUS) notes, 6*.

La Porta, R., & Shleifer, A. (2014, Summer). Informality and development. *Journal of Economic Perspectives, 28*(3), 109–126.

Mbaye, A. A. (2014). *The informal sector, employment, and structural transformation some operational recommendations for a productive policy*. Prepared for the International Organization of La Francophonie. http://www.francophonie.org/IMG/pdf/secteur_informel_emplois_et_transformation_structurelle_english_.pdf

Mijinyawa, Y., & Adetunji, J. A. (2005). Evaluation of farm transportation system in Osun and Oyo States of Nigeria. International Commission of Agricultural Engineering (CIGR, Commission Internationale du Genie Rural). *E-Journal, 7*.

Minniti, M., & Naudé, W. (2010). Female entrepreneurship across countries and in development. *The European Journal of Development Research, 22*(003), 172.

Mishra, A. (2002). *Start-up and survival of rural non-farm activities*. Ph.D. Thesis, Department of Economics, University of Reading.

Mishra, A., Igwe, P. A., Johnathan, L., & Megicks, P. (2015). Microfinance – Supporting micro and small enterprises, Chapter 28. In T. Harrison & H. Estelami (Eds.), *The Routledge companion to financial service marketing*. London: Taylor & Francis.

National Bureau of Statistics (NBS). (2012). Report based on surveys in Nigeria by National Bureau of Statistics (NBS). Federal Ministry of Agriculture and Rural Development (FMA&RD).

Naudé, W. (2013). *Entrepreneurship and economic development: Theory, evidence and policy*. IZA DP No. 7507. Institute for the Study of Labour.

Naudé, W. A., Amorós, E., & Cristi, O. (2013). Surfeiting the appetite may sicken: Entrepreneurship and the happiness of nations. *Small Business Economics*, early online.

Newbery, R., Siwale, J., & Henley, A. (2017). Editorial: Special issue on rural entrepreneurship theory in the developed and developing context. *International Journal of Entrepreneurship and Innovation, 18*(1), 14–24.

Nnamdi, O. M. (2009). Breaking the glass ceiling in Nigeria: A review of women's entrepreneurship. *Journal of African Business, 10*(1), 51–66. doi:10.1080/15228910802701361.

OECD. (2016). *Entrepreneurship at a glance, organization for economic co-operation and development*. Paris: OECD. doi:10.1787/entrepreneur_aag-2016-en.

Onwe, O. J. (2013). Role of the informal sector in development of the Nigerian economy: Output and employment approach. *Journal of Economics and Development Studies, 1*(1), 60–74.

Oviedo, A. M. (2009, June). *Economic informality: Causes, costs, and policies: A literature survey of international experience*. Background Paper prepared for Country Economic Memorandum (CEM) – Informality: Causes, Consequences, Policies.

Reardon, T., Haggblade, S., & Hazell, P. (2002). *Strategies for stimulating poverty-alleviating growth in the rural non-farm economy in developing countries*. Washington, DC: International Food Policy Research Institute/Rural Development Department, The World Bank.

Stephen, O., & Lenihan, E. (2010). Rural livelihood insecurity in Eksako East of Edo State, Nigeria. *Journal of Sustainable Development, 5*(1/2), 1–11.

USAID. (2010, June 17). *Constraints to female entrepreneurship in sub-Saharan Africa*. USAID Knowledge Services Center, U.S. Agency for International Development.

Woldie, A., & Adersua, A. (2004). Female entrepreneurs in a transitional economy: Businesswomen in Nigeria. *International Journal of Social Economics, 31*(1/2), 78–93.

World Bank. (2003). *Sustainable development in a dynamic world – Transforming institutions, growth, and quality of life (world development report)*. Washington, DC: World Bank/Oxford University Press.

World Bank. (2010). *World development report: Development and climate change*. Washington, DC: The World Bank.

World Bank. (2012). *The informal sector in francophone Africa, firm size, productivity, and institutions*. Washington, DC: International Bank for Reconstruction and Development/The World Bank.

World Bank. (2016). *Informal enterprises in Kenya*. Washington, DC: World Bank Group Trade and Competitiveness.

World Development Report. (2008). *Agriculture for development*. Washington, DC: The World Bank.

The Construction of a Professional Identity of a Female Entrepreneur

Qiuhong Boers and Börje Boers

Abstract The construction of professional identity of an entrepreneur involves many factors. In this chapter, the case study of a Chinese female immigrant entrepreneur in Sweden illustrates the complexity of professional identity which intertwines with the gender identity and the cultural identity in all levels from personal, professional and socio-cultural. The methods of participant observation and discourse analysis are used. The results reflect the impacts of gender and culture factors in the construction and communication of professional identity, which can contribute to the integration process of Chinese immigrants in Sweden.

Keywords Professional identity • Gender identity • Cultural identity • Chinese entrepreneur • Female entrepreneur • Sweden • Integration

1 Introduction

Female entrepreneurs are common across the globe and also gains more and more resonance in the entrepreneurship literature (Jennings & Brush, 2013; Minniti & Naudé, 2010; Poggesi, Mari, & De Vita, 2016). However, scholars also maintain that the subject as such is still understudied and requires further attention (Ramadani, Fayolle, & Gërguri-Rashiti, 2015). Entrepreneurship is socially embedded (Davidsson, 2003; Steyaert & Katz, 2004) as well as it is embedded in different contexts (Welter, 2011) where gender is a particular context (Welter, Brush, & De Bruin, 2014). Already Shane (1993) found that national cultural patterns influence entrepreneurs and entrepreneurial behavior. This becomes in particular relevant, when an entrepreneur is working cross-culturally, e.g. as immigrant entrepreneur (Cooke, Zhang, & Wang, 2013; Halkias, Thurman, Caracatsanis, & Harkiolakis, 2016). In this chapter we argue that this becomes especially interesting with regard to what Gesteland (2012) framed as two iron rules, i.e. first, the seller has to adapt to the buyer and second, the visitor has to observe local customs.

Q. Boers • B. Boers (✉)
School of Business, University of Skövde, Skövde, Sweden
e-mail: qiuhongboers@gmail.com; borje.boers@his.se

V. Ratten et al. (eds.), *Knowledge, Learning and Innovation*, Contributions to Management Science, DOI 10.1007/978-3-319-59282-4_8

We argue that these rules could be considered as an obstacle for conducting business particularly for immigrant entrepreneurs. However, entrepreneurs seize opportunities and try to exploit these. The success in regards of these conventions is not at least dependent on the entrepreneurs' ability to handle these, which in turn can be shaped by their identity. However, integration and success as entrepreneur do not go hand in hand and challenges are unavoidable (Hjerm, 2004; Kloosterman & Rath, 2001; Preston & Man, 1999). Foss introduced the concept of entrepreneurial identity (Foss, 2004). Foss argues that such an identity relates to the self of the individual entrepreneur (Mead, 1934). Other research argues that entrepreneurship itself is gendered towards masculinity (Bruni, Gherardi, & Poggio, 2004) and that the stereotypical entrepreneur is male (Ahl, 2002, 2006; Ahl, Berglund, Pettersson, & Tillmar, 2016). More recent research underlines the importance of identity and its construction for entrepreneurs which can be considered even more relevant for female entrepreneurs (Essers & Benschop, 2007).

As cultural factors play important roles on the communication patterns of an entrepreneur with immigrant background (Cooke et al., 2013; Halkias et al., 2016), this report presents findings on cultural influences on the communicative activities in relation to the construction of professional identity in the business context. Based on the observation and documentation of the professional practices, and the reflection on the communicative activities in this organization, communication patterns, professional identity are discussed and analyzed in relation to communication theories, cultural theories and identity theories.

Extensive researches on professional identity have been focus on the language in use and social interactions (Benwell & Stokoe, 2012). Allwood's (1995, 2000) also characterizes commutative activity as cultural and social institutional acts. The cultural influences on the communication activities under the intercultural business context are therefore crucial in the construction of professional identities, especially for a female immigrant entrepreneur. How do the cultural factors influence the communication patterns in relation to the construction of professional identity?

This chapter contributes to the discourse on entrepreneurial identity with a special consideration of female entrepreneurs. It does so by drawing on communication theory (Allwood, 2000) and discourse analysis (Fairclough, 1992). The main theme in this chapter focuses on intercultural communication between a Chinese female entrepreneur and her customers in their business activities. The methods of content analysis, discourse analysis and narrative analysis are applied on the empirical data to illustrate the influences of cultural factors in relation to the construction of professional identity.

2 Theoretical Background

There is a limited understanding of specific processes of identity construction in and around organizations and the topic of identity can be addressed on multiple levels, such as organizational, professional, social and individual (Sveningsson & Alvesson, 2003).

A professional identity is embedded in a personal identity, which Gecas and Burke (1995, p. 42) define as 'the various meanings attached to oneself by self and others'. Thus, an identity becomes important in fixing an individual's place in society in relation to others and the meanings individuals adopt for themselves.

Slay and Smith suggest by reviewing the literature that a professional identity is shaped in three ways, namely socialization, adaptation during phases of career transition and thirdly, through life and work experiences (Slay & Smith, 2011). Slay and Smith also note the "...absence is the voice of minority professionals who often face stigma and discrimination as they enter career fields." (Slay & Smith, 2011, p. 87). This has also been argued for in the recent literature on entrepreneurial identity (Foss, 2004; Henry, Foss, & Ahl, 2016).

The discursive approach on professional identity is to 'examine people's own understandings of identity and how the notion of inner/outer selves is used rhetorically to accomplish social action' with the focus on spoken and written talk and text, images and interaction (Benwell & Stokoe, 2012, p. 5).

3 Methods

The study follows a narrative case study approach, which has been called for as suitable approach for studying female entrepreneurship (Henry et al., 2016). The qualitative data analyses are used in this paper. The material recorded in this diary is treated as a source of information which reflects some aspects of social reality (Treadwell, 2014). The content analysis of this diary is employed to examine the texts and identify relevant characteristics.

According to Fairhurst (2007), discourse analyses focus on the details of language in use and interaction. As Foucault (1980) suggests that power and knowledge are intertwined; the social reality can be represented through the language and practices in the study of Discourse, which focuses on the cultural and historical forces. The discourse analysis method is therefore interplay between discourse and Discourse (Fairhurst, 2007).

As identity can be constructed through the analysis of narrative stories, in which people recall, recount and reflect on their lives, Benwell and Stokoe (2012) recommends analysing narrative stories from the personal, interpersonal and social level which offers a framework for understanding the narrations in this field study (Benwell & Stokoe, 2012) which has also been called for in the entrepreneurship literature (Ahl, 2006; Henry et al., 2016).

To sum up, the content analysis of the diary with the focuses on discourse analysis and narrative analysis are the major methods employed in this chapter.

4 Data Collection

The study involves both historical narration on the past events and ethnographic observation on the current activities. Diary with reflective notes is therefore the 'natural' way to record detailed information and 'minimized recall and memory errors' (Alaszewski, 2006) in order to provide important insights into understanding of the theme. This field study is conducted from 28th September to 26th November 2015 with a total period of 80 h. The field notes include narration, interviews and e-conversation recording.

Besides the authenticity as a responsibility of the researcher, the confidentiality is very important especially involving business activities (Treadwell, 2014). Therefore the participants including the entrepreneur, the suppliers and the customers appeared in the observation data are anonymous; and the description of the major products is rather general as well.

5 Context

The intercultural context in which this study is located is of great relevance for the theme of intercultural communication, it is therefore necessary to describe the background information of the entrepreneur and the company. The entrepreneur in focus is a middle-aged female Chinese who came to Sweden in 2005. She established her company in 2007 and has been doing importing engineering equipment from China and whole-selling those products in Sweden. In 2009, she became a Swedish citizen. The company started as a self-employed small-sized company and is currently composed of two employees besides the employer, which include one accountant and one administrator who are paid by working hours. The company had a turnover of around five millions in the year of 2014.

To investigate the cultural factors on the communication activities in intercultural business setting, it must be aware of the cultural differences between Chinese and Swedish communication patterns in relation to business behaviours.

In this study, the cultural differences first of all involve multiple languages which include Chinese, Swedish and English, which constitute different semantic meanings and power through communication (Dirven & Verspoor, 2004). Besides the language as surface culture (Van Vianen, De Pater, Kristof-Brown, & Johonson, 2004), Gesteland (2012) classifies the cross-cultural business behaviour, in which Chinese and Swedish business people are contrasted by the different focus on relationship or deal but found the commonality of reserved communication style.

The gender issue is also classified by Hofstede's (2001) cultural taxonomies, which rank high femininity in Sweden and high masculinity in China. However gender may become a barrier in doing business in hierarchical cultures like in China; being 'a foreigner may lower that barrier significantly (Gesteland, 2012, p. 17)' for a Chinese female in Sweden.

Other cultural differences include dissimilarities in basic values between home and host cultures are more difficult to adjust (Van Vianen et al., 2004); and various cultural elements may mix together, which adds the complex during the contact of Swedish and Chinese culture.

6 Results

As the communication activities between the entrepreneur and her customers can be viewed as a process of demonstrating her leadership, the professional identity is therefore can be examined through the leadership discourse.

1. Linguistic strategies to gain power in the leadership discourse

The following data is the recording of the communication between the entrepreneur and one of her customers during a delivery activity on 9th of October, 2015.

> I got access to one of their delivery activity today. The entrepreneur would deliver generators and LED lamps to the customer company warehouse. After we parked the car at the company parking lot, we entered the company office from the other side. The boss of the customer company greeted her with smile and warm touch on the back. She responded to him also with a warm touch on the shoulder. Then she introduced me as her friend and we exchanged hand-shake and names with each other. After a brief talk, they went through the office to the warehouse. They started to unload the trailer while chatting and making jokes. Everyone on the site helps. It took only ten minutes that unload almost all the goods. Then one employee with the entire working outfit came out. The entrepreneur made a joke with him "When the real boss comes, only one box for you to carry". So everyone there burst into laugh. The atmosphere was really relaxing. After the trailer was emptied, she went to the car to take the delivery note. Then she suddenly noticed that there were some boxes packed in the trunk of the car. She then said: "Sorry, I forgot here still some of your stuff" with a big laugh. The boss seemed not surprised and together with his employee unloaded the rest of the goods. After all the goods were moved to the customer's warehouse, she asked about one order of headphones she made from the customer's company. He checked with the office stuff and answered it was not in stock yet. Then she wished him a nice weekend and we drove off.

There are two linguistic strategies that can be identified from the communication between the entrepreneur and the customer during this communication activity.

The first linguistic strategy is the language she used throughout the communication is English. During the communication, it is not possible for the entrepreneur to speak her mother tongue Chinese. Although she has acquired sufficient knowledge in Swedish after 10 years living experience in Sweden, she decides on speaking English instead of Swedish as the communication language, which enables her sense of power as neither of them speaks their native language. This communication phenomenon is afterwards, by her explanation, that the best way to avoid misunderstanding and to build self-confidence. She even takes English as a language advantage as she mentioned in a later interview that *sometimes she pretends that she doesn't understand the conversation in Swedish between her customers since most of her customers are used to that she speaks English, but she does capture important information, especially when they are not equipped with caution.* According to the entrepreneur, "*You don't have to adjust to the local language in every situation and it works efficiently for me for almost eight years*", she maintains her own way of communication in her business as an immigrant in Sweden.

The second linguistic strategy is the use of humour in her business. The joke in this scene to call the employee "real boss" downplays the power of the Swedish boss and creates a relaxing atmosphere, which is also considered as an appropriate humour in Swedish culture rather than in Chinese culture.

2. The manipulation of gender to gain power in the leadership discourse
Consider the above scene of the delivery activity in 9th of October, 2015. The body contact during the greeting between the entrepreneur and the boss in the above delivery scene involves the concept of gender related to power. The warm touch between the entrepreneur and the boss put the two parties in an equal and friendly position with the ignorance of gender issue. First of all, as both Chinese and Swedish cultures are considered low-contact culture, people normally do not approach each other so closely. The body contact shows a long-term friendly relationship established between them. Secondly, even in a close relationship in China, women are expected to show permission or initiative in bodily communication during business. The entrepreneur performs "brotherhood" with a male to maintain power in a way against traditional Chinese gender concept in business.

However, she would resort to the femininity when necessary in business. As recorded in 12th of October, the entrepreneur mentioned that she often gets the payment done earlier than agreed as Swedish business men often show their soft side to women especially when "*you have tears in your eyes*" in spite of their feminist culture. The entrepreneur as a woman sees the gender factor offers her both advantages and disadvantages in her business. The advantage of being a female in this industry is also described in her trip to an industry exhibition to Stockholm:

> The moment I jumped on the bus, all the people clapped their hands. Then I noticed that I was the only female among the Swedish businessmen. They really admired me and showed their respect to me. As a result, I often won the bud on the contract easier than other owners. That is the reason that after 8 years, I still keep great passion for all those welding, generators and wind wheels. It is a job against traditional women's image, at least in China; however, it is a prominent business for me. I love my job as I claimed quite often.

At this moment, she feels prestigious as a female and proud of her gender identity. She is able to "manipulate" the identity of gender to either perform weakness or become strong based on the judgement of cultural values and business occasions in the intercultural context.

3. The combination of cultural elements in the leadership discourse
Consider the following scene of selling porcelain to Chinese customers in Sweden in 3rd of November.

As the entrepreneur has a Chinese background, the business and customers involve Chinese products and Chinese customers. Besides the engineering equipment such as generators, she also has a collection of Chinese fine porcelain. By this way, she also supplies Chinese customers in Sweden. The entrepreneur prepared quite some in stock and sells them as a side business when there are interests and demands for them. And often those customers are from the Chinese community in Sweden.

> After several previous exchange of information, the entrepreneur took out the porcelain samples in the morning and displayed them in the office early before the sale. The business started with warm greeting by hugging each other and a long Chinese lunch. They talked about many things including news and cooking techniques, followed by Swedish coffee and Chinese "bullar" and then a round trip around the house and the office, even the warehouse. Eventually they got to the main tasks today which I even thought was forgotten by them. They checked carefully about every sample and gave praises to everything here. When it came to the price, although the previous information was given to each other, the entrepreneur mentioned again that she offered a good deal by reduced 20% just because they got along well with each other today. The atmosphere was quite warm and friendly. The customers showed their appreciation, and they never discuss price on the spot. Eventually, the customers took more than they planned and the business ended with a positive impression. At the departing time, the entrepreneur invited the customers for a ballet show performed by her daughter in the next two weeks. Later on that evening, they exchanged thanks through telephones and the customers showed their satisfaction, and the entrepreneur showed her warm welcome again to her more collections.

Although the entrepreneur has been living in Sweden for more than 10 years and the business setting is in Sweden, the way of doing business still follows Chinese tradition, but with a trace of Swedish culture. The lunch together before business is a very important occasion for establishing relationships and creating a friendly atmosphere. The indirect way of doing business, which makes the meeting almost like a friend gathering is also crucial in long term relationship. Compared with doing business with Swedish customers, it takes longer time and seems more complicated. However, the results are often more than expected. This long term relationship will often spread within the Chinese community and establish wider network. The avoidance to negotiate face to face is a typical way to maintain harmony. However, Swedish culture also has an influence on this occasion. The warm greeting is obviously westernized. They greet each other with a warm hug instead of Chinese hand shake. The Swedish "tack" everywhere seems become a habit of Chinese immigrants as well. Even Swedish coffee would be accompanied with Chinese "bullar". Some elements of Chinese culture and Swedish culture are "melted" together and serve for the concern for both task and relationships.

7 Discussion

The construction of professional identity as an entrepreneur can find some commonalities across cultures, however, it involves more aspects in an intercultural setting (Essers & Benschop, 2007; Slay & Smith, 2011). In this study for instance, the language issue, the relationship issue and cultural issue become complicated as suggested by Gesteland (2012) through the comparison of different business behaviours across cultures. Special attention should be paid to power in the leadership process for an entrepreneur as Fairclough (1992) states that 'power is axiomatic of leadership.' Foucault (1980) also suggests that power and leadership can be understood from the critical discourse perspective. In this study, the construction of professional identity is not simply achieved by learning to speak Swedish in the Swedish society as suggested that local language is 'legitimized "in the process of social integration (Hinnenkamp, 2005, p. 65); an avoidance of Swedish, instead to use English is an effective strategy in some occasion for an immigrant entrepreneur to gain power in the contact with the local competitor.

Besides the language, the use of humour in this study, according to Rickards (2008), first functions to 'ease internal differences (p. 94)' as the entrepreneur and the customers have different cultural background; this joke also reflects 'the relationship between relevant setting and professional engagement (p. 95)' as she makes a distinction on different roles; this joke further establishes the affiliation within this business group (p. 110), as it is considered as an appropriate humour in Swedish culture rather than in Chinese culture. Even if this humour is not shared by everyone in the scene, it still facilitates a 'mild amusing (p. 110)' atmosphere. The cultural background of the immigrant has a great influence on her identity as many home cultural elements are taken for granted. The Chinese way of doing business may be viewed as self-evident and rational (Fairhurst, 2007) for Chinese. However, the Swedish cultural elements are also adopted and integrated well.

8 Conclusions and Recommendations

The analysis is based on the cultural differences between Chinese and Swedish culture and in relation to the construction of professional identity of the Chinese female entrepreneur.

The results indicate that first of all, the linguistic strategies including the use of English and humour and the manipulation of gender concept to gain power are used appropriately in the construction of professional identity. The useful combination of different cultural elements is also visible in the construction of leadership discourse, which respects the convention while uses the new cultural resources constructively.

The discussion based on the results shows that cultural factors play a significant role in the construction of professional identity in the intercultural business setting. The implication for organizational communication is to take cultural factors in consideration and to develop intercultural communication competence.

This study suggests the value of using narrative in understanding the process of professional identity construction. Further studies should continue on this avenue (Henry et al., 2016). In addition, the use of intercultural communication and discourse analysis appear suitable for studying questions of identity construction in entrepreneurial and other contexts.

References

Ahl, H. (2002). *The making of the female entrepreneur: A discoursive analysis of research texts on women's entrepreneurship*. Jönköping: JIBS.

Ahl, H. (2006). Why research on women entrepreneurs needs new directions. *Entrepreneurship Theory and Practice, 30*(5), 595–621.

Ahl, H., Berglund, K., Pettersson, K., & Tillmar, M. (2016). From feminism to FemInc.ism: On the uneasy relationship between feminism, entrepreneurship and the Nordic welfare state. *International Entrepreneurship and Management Journal, 12*(2), 369–392.

Alaszewski, A. (2006). *Using diaries for social research*. London: Sage Publications.

Allwood, J. (1995). Language communication and social activity. In K. Junefelt (Ed.), Special session on activity theory. *Proceedings of the XIVth Scandinavian Conference of Language and the VIIIth Conference on General Linguistics, in Gothenburg; Papers of Theoretical Linguistics, 73*, Department of Linguistics, Göteborgs University.

Allwood, J. (2000). An activity based approach to pragmatics. In H. Bunt & W. Black (Eds.), *Abduction, belief and context in dialogue: Studies in computational pragmatics* (pp. 47–80). Amsterdam: Benjamins.

Benwell, B., & Stokoe, E. (2012). *Discourse and identity*. Edinburgh: Edinburgh University Press.

Bruni, A., Gherardi, S., & Poggio, B. (2004). Doing gender, doing entrepreneurship: An ethnographic account of intertwined practices. *Gender, Work and Organization, 11*(4), 406–429.

Cooke, F. L., Zhang, J., & Wang, J. (2013). Chinese professional immigrants in Australia: A gendered pattern in (re) building their careers. *The International Journal of Human Resource Management, 24*(13), 2628–2645.

Davidsson, P. (2003). The domain of entrepreneurship research. In J. Katz & D. Shephard (Eds.), *Cognitive approaches to entrepreneurship research* (pp. 315–372). Howard House: Emerald Group Publishing Limited.

Dirven, R., & Verspoor, M. (2004). Language, culture and meaning: Cross-cultural semantics. In R. Dirven & M. Versppor (Eds.), *A cognitive exploration of language and linguistics*. Amesterdam: Benjamins.

Essers, C., & Benschop, Y. (2007). Enterprising identities: Female entrepreneurs of Moroccan or Turkish Origin in the Netherlands. *Organization Studies, 28*(1), 49–69.

Fairclough, N. (1992). *Discourse and social change*. Cambridge, UK: Polity Press.

Fairhurst, G. T. (2007). *Discursive leadership: In conversation with leadership psychology*. Thousand Oaks, CA: Sage Publications.

Foss, L. (2004). *'Going against the grain...' construction of entrepreneurial identity through narratives*. University of Illinois at Urbana-Champaign's Academy for Entrepreneurial Leadership Historical Research Reference in Entrepreneurship. Available at SSRN: https://ssrn.com/abstract=1497284

Foucault, M. (1980). *Power/knowledge: selected interviews and other writings 1972–1977*. Brighton: Harvester Books.

Gecas, V., & Burke, P. J. (1995). Self and identity. In K. Cook, G. A. Fine, & J. S. House (Eds.), *Sociological perspectives on social psychology* (pp. 41–67). Boston: Allyn and Bacon.

Gesteland, R. R. (2012). *Cross-cultural business behavior – A guide for global management* (5th ed.). Copenhagen: Copenhagen Business School Press.

Halkias, D., Thurman, P., Caracatsanis, S., & Harkiolakis, N. (2016). *Female immigrant entrepreneurs: The economic and social impact of a global phenomenon*. Boca Raton: CRC Press.

Henry, C., Foss, L., & Ahl, H. (2016). Gender and entrepreneurship research: A review of methodological approaches. *International Small Business Journal, 34*(3), 217–241.

Hinnenkamp, V. (2005). *Semilingualism, double monolingualism and blurred genres-on (not) speaking a legitimate language*. Hebbani & Frey, Sharone 2013, Burton.

Hjerm, M. (2004). Immigrant entrepreneurship in the Swedish Welfare State. *Sociology, 38*(4), 739–756.

Hofstede, G. (2001). *Culture's consequences: Comparing values, behaviours, institutions and organizations across nations*. Thousand Oaks, CA: Sage Publications.

Jennings, J. E., & Brush, C. G. (2013). Research on women entrepreneurs: Challenges to (and from) the broader entrepreneurship literature? *Academy of Management Annals, 7*(1), 663–715.

Kloosterman, R., & Rath, J. (2001). Immigrant entrepreneurs in advanced economies: Mixed embeddedness further explored. *Journal of Ethnic and Migration Studies, 27*(2), 189–201.

Mead, G. H. (1934). *Mind, self and society* (Vol. 111). Chicago: University of Chicago Press.

Minniti, M., & Naudé, W. (2010). What do we know about the patterns and determinants of female entrepreneurship across countries? *The European Journal of Development Research, 22*(3), 277–293.

Poggesi, S., Mari, M., & De Vita, L. (2016). What's new in female entrepreneurship research? Answers from the literature. *International Entrepreneurship and Management Journal, 12*(3), 735–764.

Preston, V., & Man, G. (1999). Employment experiences of Chinese immigrant women: An exploration of diversity. *Canadian Woman Studies, 19*(3), 115.

Ramadani, V., Fayolle, A., & Gërguri-Rashiti, S. (2015). Introduction: Female entrepreneurship in transition economies as a significant but understudied field. In V. Ramadani, S. Gërguri-Rashiti, & A. Fayolle (Eds.), *Female entrepreneurship in transition economies: Trends and challenges* (pp. 1–8). London: Palgrave Macmillan.

Rickards, K. (2008). *Language and professional identity. Aspects of collaborative interaction*. Basingstoke: Palgrave MacMillan.

Shane, S. (1993). Cultural influences on national rates of innovation. *Journal of Business Venturing, 8*(1), 59–73.

Slay, H. S., & Smith, D. A. (2011). Professional identity construction: Using narrative to understand the negotiation of professional and stigmatized cultural identities. *Human Relations, 64*(1), 85–107.

Steyaert, C., & Katz, J. (2004). Reclaiming the space of entrepreneurship in society: geographical, discursive and social dimensions. *Entrepreneurship and Regional Development, 16*(3), 179–196.

Sveningsson, S., & Alvesson, M. (2003). Managing managerial identities: Organizational fragmentation, discourse and identity struggle. *Human Relations, 56*(10), 1163–1193.

Treadwell, D. (2014). *Introducing communication research: Paths to inquiry* (2nd ed.). London: Sage Publications.

Van Vianen, A. E., De Pater, I. E., Kristof-Brown, A. L., & Johonson, E. C. (2004). Fitting in: Surface-and deep-level cultural differences and expatriates' adjustment. *The Academy of Management Journal, 47*(5), 697–709.

Welter, F. (2011). Contextualizing entrepreneurship—Conceptual challenges and ways forward. *Entrepreneurship Theory and Practice, 35*(1), 165–184.

Welter, F., Brush, C., & De Bruin, A. (2014). *The gendering of entrepreneurship context* (Working Paper 01/14). Bonn: Institut für Mittelstandsforschung Bonn (Hrsg.). Available at SSRN: https://ssrn.com/abstract=2557272

Knowledge Creation and Relationship Marketing in Family Businesses: A Case-Study Approach

Veland Ramadani, Lutfije Ademi, Vanessa Ratten, Ramo Palalić, and Norris Krueger

Abstract In Bosnia and Herzegovina, family businesses operate successfully as the backbone of the countries' economies. We also know that even successful firms differ widely in use of best management practice. Smaller, newer firms in less developed countries should benefit from exposure to best practice. To this end we offer provide and present the advantages of using one of the newest and most successful approaches in marketing, that of relationship marketing. This chapter presents the theoretical aspects of relationship marketing, the advantages of using it and its specifics. Furthermore, in this chapter we discuss how relationship marketing affects the business development on two family businesses from two disparate industries in Bosnia and Herzegovina. AS Group is a group, including food, trade and textile, whereas Pharmamed Ltd. operates in the pharmaceutical industry. Relationship marketing concepts and specifics explained in this chapter will not help only the owners of family businesses, but also, the non-family businesses,

V. Ramadani (✉)
Faculty of Business and Economics, South East European University, Tetovo, Macedonia
e-mail: v.ramadani@seeu.edu.mk

L. Ademi
International Trade Support Service, Tetovo, Macedonia
e-mail: itss.export@gmail.com

V. Ratten
La Trobe Business School, La Trobe University, Melbourne, VIC, Australia
e-mail: v.ratten@latrobe.edu.au

R. Palalić
International University of Sarajevo, Sarajevo, Bosnia and Herzegovina

Dhofar University, Salalah, Sultanate of Oman
e-mail: ramopal@gmail.com

N. Krueger
Center for Management and Entrepreneurship, School of Advanced Studies, University of Phoenix, Phoenix, AZ, USA

Entrepreneurship Northwest, Boise, ID, USA
e-mail: norris.krueger@mail.phoenix.edu

V. Ratten et al. (eds.), *Knowledge, Learning and Innovation*, Contributions to Management Science, DOI 10.1007/978-3-319-59282-4_9

policy-makers and researchers who want to know more about advancing use of proven managerial practices in a transition economy.

Keywords Relationship marketing • Family business • Transition countries • Bosnia and Herzegovina

1 Introduction

Today, when the competition is a very fierce and when globalization touches every corner in the world, production may seem the easiest activity, whereas selling the hardest one, especially, if we consider the changing ways of selling (see Bloom, Eifert, Mahajan, McKenzie, & Roberts, 2011; Bloom & Van Reenen, 2010 about management best practices). It is much easier to gain a new costumer than to maintain the old one. The processes of buying and selling have changed a lot, making the purchase process more complicated. Our decision to buy something comes from a lot of factors and why we buy is not only because we need a specific product or service, or even want it. Rather, the issue of being related in any way to the product or brand can stimulate buying (Veseli, Ramadani, & Rexhepi, 2010).

Models of consumer behavior in the process of buying have shown that before the consumers buy a particular product, they need to have a positive attitude towards that brand and/or organization (Pope & Voges, 2000). Somehow, this means that purchasing is the last part of the buying process, stimulated by a lot of factors, separated from the actual sales process.

The traditional transactional marketing is becoming a past, and what today presents value for companies, is maintaining the old customers, developing loyalty and commitment. Essentially, this is the relationship marketing (RM). The concept of managing relations in marketing is deepening and it seems that it is at the top of marketing nowadays. It is not a new phenomenon, but it has started to be a part of the marketing theory very late, even though it is not limited to the theory. It is impossible to imagine any business activity in business-to-business (B2B) or business-to-customer (B2C) relations that does not use any element of the relationship marketing, both in consumer goods and services. But, how these approaches work in family-owned businesses (FOB), which are more unique? Some studies have shown that approaches used in FOB's can be converted into an unbelievable competitive advantage (Cooper, Upton, & Seaman, 2005; Miller, Le Breton-Miller, & Scholnick, 2008; Ward, 1997). Based on this, Carrigan and Buckley (2008) call it "familiness". Marketing departments in FOB, as in other firms try to create, communicate, and deliver value to their own customers (Dashew, 1996). In return, they expect sincerely responses from their customers, which will be translated into: sales, purchase, and patronage (Srinivasan & Hanssens, 2009). The "familiness" is more expressed in those societies where different cultural habits are much more present, such as Bosnia and Herzegovina (BiH), where people are much linked to their cultural habits, the way they live, the way they eat, wear or spend the time.

Those characteristics make them very familiar with some products or services, especially with their well known "Bosnian coffee" or the traditional ways of cooking. For instance, there are a lot of companies in BiH that pay a lot of attention to the cultivation of traditional items, products and services.

The relationship marketing in family businesses is the main topic in this chapter. We based our research on two BiH's family businesses, respectively in AS Group from Tesanj, and Pharmamed Ltd from Travnik. We raised the following research questions in this chapter:

1. Which are the ways that family businesses use to maintain and develop loyalty, trust and commitment, both in B2B and B2C relations?
2. Which are the ways that family businesses use to maintain and develop customer satisfaction approaches with special emphasis on motivational and cooperation elements, both in B2B and B2C relations?
3. In which way, do family businesses cooperate with their competition, and which are the benefits they see from these relations?
4. Which are the economic benefits derived from using the relationship marketing approaches in the industry where they belong instead of traditional marketing ones, both in B2B and B2C relations?
5. Do and how the relationship marketing approaches of family businesses change with regards to the cultural differences, both in B2B and B2C relations?

The purpose of this chapter is to highlight a correlation among the relationship marketing and companies' development, based on data evidence from concrete family businesses. The study will describe in details the most important elements of the relationship marketing which influence the development of the family businesses, both for B2B and B2C relations.

In BiH, as well as in the region, this concept is not very well studied. Thus, this research will provide information about the relationship marketing benefits and aim to influence family companies to implement relationship marketing activities. Moreover, this aim is becoming stronger if we consider the structure of our businesses, mostly of which are the family businesses. Even that like a practice, the relationship marketing is used here; this research aims to awake people and their family businesses about its importance, and to influence the use of high quality in every aspect of the firm's activity.

There are only a few issues in marketing that have drawn as much attention in the last few years, like the relationship marketing has. It is considered by economists and marketers as one of the top topics, if not the first one, that should be seriously studied and implemented in the future.

Because of the globalization, all the consumers in the most places of the world are exposed to every company and organization of the world at the same time. In most cases, to customers are offered the lowest prices. Thus, to be loyal and trusted consumers to companies, in the long-term, is the hardest thing. So, the study considers that to gain the knowledge, and to see practices how to maintain loyal consumers and associates, is a really valued advantage that all our companies need. This chapter will provide the essential rules of the relationship marketing and benefits of being a part of this kind of strategies and plans. The relationship marketing policies are based on the pure relationship rules and benefits, no matter what is your field of working or studying.

2 Literature Review

2.1 *The BiH Context*

Bosnia and Herzegovina (BiH) is an independent state in the Balkans Peninsula, bordering Serbia and Montenegro in the east, Croatia in the north, west and the south. It has a coastline of about 20 km on the Adriatic Sea. Bosnia's capital city is Sarajevo. BiH's population is about 3,802,000 people (UN Data, 2016). As most of the states in the Balkans, BiH is recovering from a 3-year war which accompanied the break-up of Yugoslavia in the early 1990s and which resulted with devastating effects. The conflict of 1992–1995 had to choose on whether BiH will stay in the Yugoslav Federation, or whether it should become an independent state. It is now an independent state, under the international administration. There are three main ethnic groups, Bosnian Muslims—50.11%, Croats—15.43% and Serbs—30.78% (Zavod za statistiku Bosne i Herzegovine, 2016). Around two million people or about half the population—were displaced during the war, mostly of them abroad. The consequences are still evident.

The Dayton accord set up two different and separated entities, Bosnian-Croat Federation of Bosnia and Hercegovina and Bosnian Serb Republic (RepublikaSrpska). Both have their own president, government, parliament, police and other bodies and institutions. In addition, there is the district of Brčko, a self-governing administrative unit created as a neutral area, which is placed under joint Serb, Croat and Bosnians authorities (BBC, 2016) (Fig. 1).

As is stated in the Worlds Bank Overview of Bosnia and Herzegovina, the political system in BiH is complex. In July 2015, the Council of Ministers of BiH, Government of Republika Srpska, and Government of the Federation of BiH established a joint program of reforms—known as the Reform Agenda. This Reform Agenda presents a big window of opportunity for structural reforms in BiH. The most important economic challenge for BiH is the imbalance of the country's economic model: public policies are oriented towards the public sector more than the private sector; consumption much more than investment; and imports further more than exports. BiH needs to develop the potential of the private sector while at the same time it should reduce the signs of the very large and inefficient public sector (World Bank, 2016).

The complex system of state's organization affects mostly the economy. This political and legal framework has caused the existence of overlapping competences, which negatively affects every sector, mostly the economy. It is so because of this political establishment and the fact that in the past two decades, BiH has faced

Fig. 1 Map of Bosnia and Herzegovina. Source: U.S. Department of State (n.d.)

different economic instability while undergoing economic transition from a closed-command economy to an open-market economy. One of those barriers is the rate of the structural unemployment, which means that a high unemployment rate has resulted by structural difficulties that have caused Bosnian's underdeveloped economic system (Mirascic, 2011).

Moreover, some say that it is the Law system that prevents the BiH's companies to develop more. Mr. RusmirHrvić, the general manager of the AS Group, declares that:

> The biggest disadvantages of the economic environment in Bosnia are the laws that limit the development of domestic producers. In many situations, Bosnian producers are not competing not because of their ability, but because of the law regulations. We do not have equal conditions for employment. Foreign producers are in advantage in our trade, which is absurd and directly influences the whole economy and threatens the survivor of actual working places and the ones to come (Personal Interview).

Table 1 Economic indicators of BiH

Economic indicators			
GDP: Gross domestic product (million current US$)	2014	18,491	
GDP growth rate (annual %, const. 2005 prices)	2014	1.3	
GDP per capita (current US$)	2014	4843.7	
Economy: Agriculture (% of GVA)	2014	7.1	Excludes irrigation canals and landscaping care
Economy: Industry (% of GVA)	2014	26.0	Excludes publishing activities, includes irrigation canals
Economy: Services and other activity (% of GVA)	2014	66.9	Excludes repair of personal and household goods. Includes publishing activities and landscaping care
Unemployment (% of labor force)	2014	31.2	Estimate
Labor force participation (female/male pop. %)	2014	34.5/58.2	Estimate
CPI: Consumer price index (2000 = 100)	2014	123	Index base: 2005 = 100
Agricultural production index (2004–2006 = 100)	2014	113	2013
Food production index (2004–2006 = 100)	2014	114	2013
Balance of payments, current account (million US$)	2014	−1451	
Exports (million US$)	2015	5099.1	
Imports (million US$)	2015	8993.9	
Balance (million US$)	2015	−3894.8	
Major trading partners (% of exports)	2015	Germany (15.7), Italy (13.5), Croatia (10.3)	
Major trading partners (% of imports)	2015	Germany (12.1), Italy (11.1), Serbia (10.9)	

Source: UN Data (2016)

Some of the economic indicators of the BiH economy are provided in Table 1. BiH is performing much better in the recent years economically, due to different factors, especially the growth and development of SMEs and the increased exports. World Bank (2016) noted that the BiH's economic growth performed better-than expected in 2015, where net export was the main driver of it. Consumption and investment also performed well. The real GDP has achieved the highest rate in the last 5 years—4.3% year-on-year (y/y) in the second quarter (Q2). The consumer price index declined by 1.3% y/y in December 2015. Export has increased by 3.5% and net export is increasing approximately 3%, and shows rising tendencies.

2.2 *Family Businesses in BiH*

Efendioglu (2001) noted that SMEs create the basement of the European economy. They are an irreplaceable part of the private sector, which contributes significantly to the job creation and plays a very important role in developing the competitiveness on selected markets, including underdeveloped markets (Stevenson, 2010) and transition markets (Dana & Ramadani, 2015). In the Balkans region, as well as in the Europe, most of the SMEs are family owned businesses, owned by one or more members of a family, or more families (Hisrich, Petković, Ramadani, & Dana, 2016; Palalic, 2017; Ramadani & Hoy, 2015). As stated in Zemlic (n.d.), the KPMG in BiH has identified that the family owned-businesses are an important part of country's economy, and they are the wheel of the economic development. Latest analyzes (Dana & Ramadani, 2015; Palalic, Ramadani, & Dana, 2017) show that almost 80% of SMEs in BiH are family owned businesses, whose employees contribute more than 60% of the total employment in the private sector. Family businesses are more focused on the long-lasting operations and success. Also, they continue investing even during an economic crisis or instable periods.

Even though the big businesses in harsh times were still reducing the number of their employees, the governments have been obligated to make strategies and new regulations for the growth of employment rate. Family businesses, seen as heroes in this period, were the job creators and the economic developers (Petković & Tešić, 2013; Ramadani & Schneider, 2013)

Even though family businesses have not been studied enough in BiH, there is a growing need to study them because of the uniqueness the BiH's entrepreneurship offers, and the environment for doing business that is improving every day, even though it is in a so called transitional phase. This phase characterizes the economic environment of every country in the neighborhood (Palalic et al., 2017).

3 The Concept of Relationship Marketing

The concept of a relationship has been used for 100 years, even though it seems that it has not been around for a long time. Before the Industrial revolution, the farmers and craftsmen individually sold their products to their customers in the local markets. Only some of the trades have been organized into groups with relationships between the members, e.g. trade on the silk route (Sheth & Parvatiyar, 1995). Mutual trust was the key element while exchanging. As Šonková and Grabowska (2015) claim, the accomplishments of the Industrial revolution in the nineteenth century have led to both, mass production and consumption of different products. It means that for a relatively low cost, producers could have generated a large amount of goods. In this period, the marketing strategy used the most, was the promotion with regulation of price. This was possible to be realized, because the products of the producers were interchangeable at a high level. One of the most important roles in this period was the middleman's; they stored the big amounts of products and made their transportation to a specified destination.

The most important period for the development of marketing was the twentieth century; starting with mass-marketing (1950s), marketing focused on industrial marketing (1960s), marketing segmentation (1970s) (Buttle, 1996). Maxim (2009) noted that the 1970s and 1980s of the twentieth century, were the years when some authors started to question the validity of transactional marketing approaches, considering that the socio-economic changes have resulted with a change of the marketing efforts from the area of transactions to that of relationships, as the newest one. So, in the beginning of the 1980s of the last century, the first books for the relationship marketing started to appear. In the marketing literature, Berry's "Relationship marketing" in Emerging perspectives on services marketing (1983) is considered the first ever written book about this concept.

There are numerous reasons why this shift on the relationship marketing appeared. Palamtier (2008) identifies two the most important reasons for this shift. Firstly, he argues with the shift of world's orientation of economy to services. Under those circumstances, middleman, who was so important during the industrial revolution, is no longer needed. Sales—people, on the other hand, came into a personal contact with the company's customers. The parties to the transactions are bound on each other again as it was in the beginning and there is a direct relationship line between the customer and the company.

Consequently, Palamtier (2008) says that the relationship marketing is the best alternative for strategy for companies that provide services. It is mostly because, being different from products, services are intangible, and it is therefore more and more important to create powerful relationships to gain trust, and to be able to make their customers believe in the quality of the service.

Thirdly, the advances in technology support the return to the relationship marketing. Thanks to the modern communication channels and all the opportunities that modern media offers, companies are able to communicate with all their customers, no matter where they live or where they work. Consequently, it is much easier for customers to learn about the company and their services from different sources. Customers are well-informed and search for a value. The progress in the technology enables marketers to easily target their customers, as well as to implement the strategy. Once the program is implemented, the modern technology also helps with its evaluation.

Finally, the increase of the global competition is stated as an influential factor on the return of the relationship marketing. Its tools, such as the loyalty programs, help differentiate the company from its competitors. Creating long-lasting relationships is also economically reasonable, since there are lower costs for retaining of customers, than for attracting new ones (Šonková & Grabowska, 2015).

It is generally accepted that it is very important to develop and maintain the long-lasting relationship among companies and customers (as well as other parties involved). An issue that is not well-studied is explain which factors managerially affect those relationships and the mechanisms used. Generally, a customer can have more relational benefits, but they can be grouped into benefits received apart from the products/services they purchase and relationship quality, which focuses on the overall nature of the relationship (Thurau, Gwinner, & Gremler, 2002).

But, what is the relationship marketing and why is it important? At the center of the relationship marketing is an exchange that is profitable to parties involved in that exchange. The concept of those exchanges, as it applies to the relationship marketing, can be viewed at from two dimensions: either a transaction cost analysis approach or a social exchange theory approach (Kangal, 2009; Ratten, 2013). It focuses on efforts of both sellers and buyers to investments in the long-term beneficial partnerships and behaviors.

George Homans (1961) is the first one that has proposed social exchange theory. He said that exchanges of goods and services take place between two parties who are entities with rationality, who act in their own interest and who will perform social action based on rewards and costs. It is not only monetary (material) benefits that take place in the exchange; non-monetary ones seem to be a special part, such as: love, approval, affection or esteem. This is called *social exchange*. The social exchanges involve interaction; interaction occurs when an activity done by one man is rewarded (or punished) by an activity done by another man. The social exchanges respect emotions; emotions are signs of the attitudes and feelings a party takes towards another party. This social exchange theory (Homans, 1961) sets the disciplines of the psychology of behaving and elementary economics in proposing the principles of social exchange. The psychology of behaving in any way derives from the history of behaviors in the past. Based on them, people behave in the present. Between the walls of past and future behaviors, the relationships are built.

There are four types of relationships between buyers and sellers—bilateral relationships, relationships that are maintained by sellers, relationships that are maintained by buyers, discrete exchanges (Dwyer, Schurr, & Oh, 1987). For a firm, a relational exchange could occur with goods suppliers, services suppliers, business units, employees, functional departments, intermediate customers, ultimate customers, competitors, non-profit organizations, governments (Morgan & Hunt, 1994).

According to Berry (1983), which was the first person that mentioned the relationship marketing concept, relationship marketing is attracting, maintaining and—in multi service organizations—enhancing customer relationships. After him, there were a lot of researchers that have given their scientific contribution about the relationship marketing. Sheth and Parvatiyar (1995) define the relationship marketing as the process of developing cooperative and collaborative relations with customers as well as other market actors. Shani and Chalasani (1992) seethe relationship marketing as an effort to identify, create, and develop a network of individual customers, and to empower the network for the mutual benefit of both sides. Furthermore, Andersen (2001) says that the relationship marketing is a group of cumulative phases during which belief and common norms are established with the help of a design of communication means and forms.

Building good and successful relationships has a lot of benefits. As noted by Levitt (1986), relationship marketing is as important in developing the intangible asset known as 'goodwill' as is the hard assets management. The fact that it is probably harder to do is that much more reason that hard effort be expended to do it.

Bruhn (2003), collecting data from different studies, concludes that customer retention offers advantages from a circulation perspective as well as from a costs perspective. Other than maintaining the current circulation level, retention may have a favor approach in both cross-selling and an increase in the frequency of purchases. Furthermore, the customers become less sensitive to price and are willing to accept price premiums in exchange for a reduced risk. The long-lasting relationships also ensure reduction of costs by the experience effect: the operational costs for an old customer are much smaller than those for a new one.

3.1 Specifics of Relationship Marketing

The most important goal of the RM is to identify which are the drivers that affect the outcomes for a firm, as well as to identify correlations among the drivers and outcomes. Until now, in the marketing literature have been used a lot of approaches to identify those correlations and the specific drivers and outcomes of RM, starting from one variable, then continuing to a different number of very specific variables that are still in the process of studying. Every day, a new variable that affect the RM is discovered, thus the system of the RM is becoming more and more important and valued. Based on the review of some past studies and scientific works, we are going to evaluate some indicators and specifics of the RM, which affect mostly or are derivatives of relations in marketing. We will start evaluating the characteristics of each element, starting from loyalty, trust, commitment, satisfaction as well as other indicators and specifics of the RM.

3.1.1 Loyalty

The Merriam Webster Dictionary defines the word *loyal* as: "unswerving in allegiance as faithful in to a cause, ideal, custom, institution, or product". As the RM has been one of the most popular topics over the last years, a lot of studies try to identify the most important aspect of this field, the customer loyalty. The customer loyalty has been named as a marketing goal of the firm (Diller, 1996). The loyalty is the primary goal of the relationship marketing and sometimes even equated with the relationship marketing concept itself (Sheth, 1996). Being loyal to a company, specific brand or a product means to repeat the purchase behavior, believing in them and the company's marketing activities.

One of the focuses of both theoretical and empirical studies has been the connection between the loyalty and the profitability. It has been found that customer loyalty positively influences profitability through. This is arrived with cost reduction effects and increased revenues per customer (Berry, 1995). Cost reduction effects means that retaining the old customers is less expensive than trying to gain new ones, that is why having loyal consumers is more cost effective. On the other side, it influences increased customer revenues along the relationship life cycle, because of cross-selling activities and increased customer penetration rates (Thurau et al., 2002).

If we look at the relationships between suppliers and customers, we will realize that in fact customers' loyalty is the way transactions among them are made and how often they do occur. It is very important that those transactions are qualitative, in terms of the way they are realized and the atmosphere where they take place. Customers will declare themselves very loyal to a supplier, through feelings and perceptions of satisfaction they have, through positive attitudes and through preferences for the supplier. More simply out, customers will want to repeat the purchase from this buyer (Diller, 2000).

Beside the effect of cost reduction for the company and increased revenues for customers, loyalty has a lot of other economic benefits. According to Diller (2000), there are three main benefits associated with customer loyalty: more certainty, more growth and more profit (Table 2). As it can be seen from Table 2, loyal customers bring *more certainty* to an organization, i.e. more stability. More certainty also can offer more customer feedback, which is sincerer when it comes from a loyal customer, than from a not loyal one, because they tend to be more bounded to the company. They can even work together with the supplier in developing customer satisfaction (Hansen & Schoenheit, 1987; Stauss & Seidel, 1998). The feedback received from loyal customers affects marketing, making it more flexible. Also, having loyal relations between customers and suppliers automatically means more trust. On the other side, having close relations with customers may result with disadvantages, such as: inflexibility (failing to adapt to changes in the market structure by being very reliant to loyal customers) and inactivity (in some cases loyal customers may turn the company or supplier to inactivity and carelessness, because they make the supplier feel complacency).

The growth of a company, by trying to maintain the old customers, can be achieved by a deeper customer penetration and more recommendations. The first one means that loyal customers are focused on purchasing by a single supplier or company and the second one means that they will influence to new customers by the good word of mouth, which is considered as the cheapest way to gain new customers. We should always know that there can be a negative word of mouth that could bring the opposite effects of a good word of mouth, as well as the risk of a skewed structure of customers.

In the end, we are going to explain how customer loyalty leads to *more profitability*. More profitability can be achieved by savings on costs on increasing revenues. Costs savings is achieved when the company has a better amortization of acquisition costs and does not have costs that occur while trying to gain new

Table 2 Potential economic effects of customer loyalty

	More certainty	More growth	More profit
+	More stability	Deeper customer penetration	Cost savings
	More feedback	More recommendations	Better amortization of acquisition costs
	More marketing flexibility		Saves costs incurred when gaining new customers
	More trust		Lower costs for customer management
			Increased revenues
			Lower price elasticity
			Cross selling revenues
–	Inflexibility	Skewed customer structure	Cost incurred by bonding activities
	Inactivity	Negative word of mouth	

Source: Based on Diller (2000)

customers. It is estimated that just 15–20% of the amount spent on gaining a new customer needs to be invested to keep this customer's loyalty (Meyer & Blümelhuber, 2000). It has also a lower cost for customer management because customers are already familiar with company's products. Increased revenues are harder to achieve, because loyal customers in mostly of the cases are less sensitive to price changes, but they can also search a discount in price for their loyalty. Loyal customers may bring extra revenues through the cross-buying activities.

According to Meyer and Blümelhuber (2000), there are several indicators of customer loyalty, as shown in the Fig. 2. Analyzing all these indicators and goals of customers' loyalty, we understand that not always the desired results of such a loyalty can be harvested. As Diller (2000) says, sometimes it is the *quality* of this loyalty, not quantity, which determines the effects of this loyalty.

3.1.2 Trust and Commitment

Trust, like loyalty, is one of the most important specifics of the RM, and of the relations in general. To trust, in a way, means to believe in something and what is more important, to believe permanently in what you give and what you are waiting to receive, i.e. the creation of the long-lasting belief and faith in something.

In marketing, the trust exists when the customer believes in the producer or service provider and their product, as well as his/her integrity. The trust is conceptualized by many authors as a necessary component for the long-lasting relationships (Bendapudi & Berry, 1997; Doney & Cannon, 1997). Moorman, Deshpandé, and Zaltman (1993) defines the trust as a will to rely on an exchange partner in whom one has confidence. As Rotter (1967) says, the trust is a generalized expectancy held by and individual that the word of another can be relied on. As we can

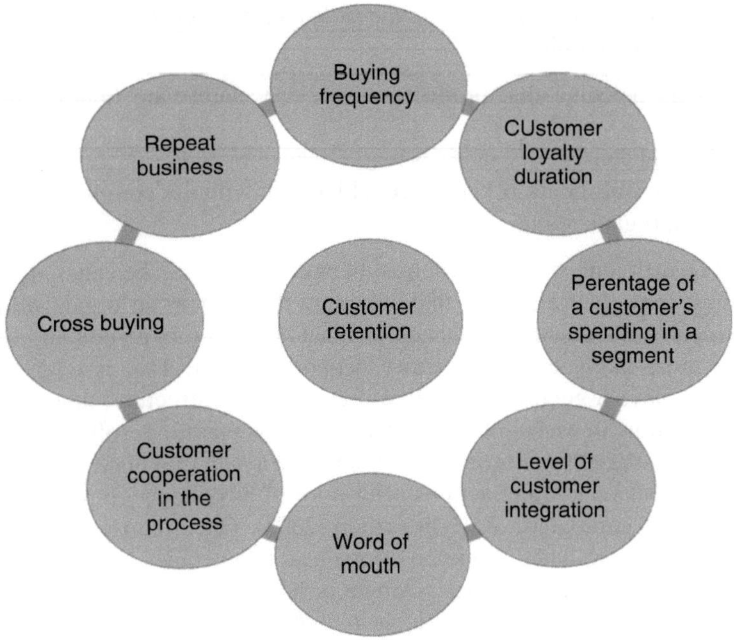

Fig. 2 Selected indicators of customer loyalty. Source: Based on Meyer and Blümelhuber (2000)

see, both definitions rely on *confidence* as one of the most important characteristics of that trust. Murphy, Laczniak, and Wood (2007) says that trust is widely regarded as being an essential element for exchanges moving from a transaction-base to a relationship-base. In the sense of behavioral interpretation, the expectation construct trust results from stimuli originating with the object of the expectation (supplier) and perceived by the person that extends his trust (customer) (Preß, 1997). Anderson and Narus (1990) are focused on the outcomes of trust. They define it the firm's belief that another company is going to perform several actions, which will result in positive results or outcomes for the firm.

The trust is also very important to the relational exchange (Kotler, Dingena, & Pfoertsch, 2015). That is why Spekman (1988) names it as the cornerstone of the strategic partnership. Because of its characteristic of cornerstone, all parties characterized by trust to one other will like to be a part of such relationship, and will always seek only trustworthy partnerships.

Murphy et al. (2007) state that relationship marketing is based on the premise that customers and sellers are long-term partners in a so-called the exchange process that is based on trust and rooted in the marketing concept. The ethical sides of the marketing concept as well as trust are driven by the same elements.

According to Shaw's (1997), *Trust in the Balance*, in order to create a marketplace, three elements are required:

- Consumers perceive that product and service claims are honest and can be relied on.
- Integrity and consistency motives marketplace practices
- Consumer's well-being is kept in equal balance with the competing interests of the selling organization.

Based on different studies on the trust in marketing, it can be concluded that one of the most important elements that stimulate the trust in an organization is the social structure of the same. Organizations that are acting in a good atmosphere of work are more likely to have a trusty network system. That is why, it is very important to have a good and effective organizational structure, that the network will have the trust in each—other, i.e. have better economic results.

Considering these benefits of the trust, let's see a path moving from the trust to a collaborative behavior. Joint actions offer a lot of advantages in problem solving and planning (Claro, Claro, & Zylbersztajn, 2005). Once the trust is established, firms learn that coordinated, common efforts lead to outcomes that exceed what the firm could achieve if it would act as single or had a single role in its own interest (Anderson & Narus, 1990). This suggests that firms that trust one another will exchange information, thereby jointly contributing to problem-solving and planning efforts (Zand, 1972). If the focal company trusts its partner, it will be more willing and worthy to react flexibly to changing conditions or demands of the partner (Morgan & Hunt, 1994).

On the other side, commitment is seen as the long-term orientation, toward creating strong relationships, grounded on both emotional and relational basis. Gundlach and Murphy (1993) identify several characteristics of commitment; such are *stability, sacrifice and loyalty*. On the other side, Söellner (1994) says that the trust is what stimulates the communication, which makes commitment possible. Moreover, Day (1995) states that commitment often involves some managerial actions, which lead to information sharing among partners that is totally open, and thus giving the cooperative arrangements a formal status which is not embodied in the cooperating teams, rather in the organizations themselves.

The commitment represents the intentional element of the attitude of the customer, both positive and intentional, towards the supplier (Jacob, 2015). Moorman, Zaltman, and Deshpande (1992) gives a more precise definition, arguing that the commitment for a relationship is defined as an *enduring desire to maintain a valued relationship*. This includes the will to make short-term sacrifices (Dittrich, 2000).

Explaining the factors that lead to commitment, Söellner (1994, as cited in Kleinaltenkamp, Plinke, & Söllner, 2015) has developed a model of commitment (Fig. 4). Based on this model, commitment is seen as the perceived loyalty from an economic entity or organization compared to another one. But, on the relational exchange processes, commitment is not seen as a solo factor. According to the Model of commitment (Söellner, 1994), in both commitment relations of suppliers and customers, there are two factors (inputs) which lead to relationship success and

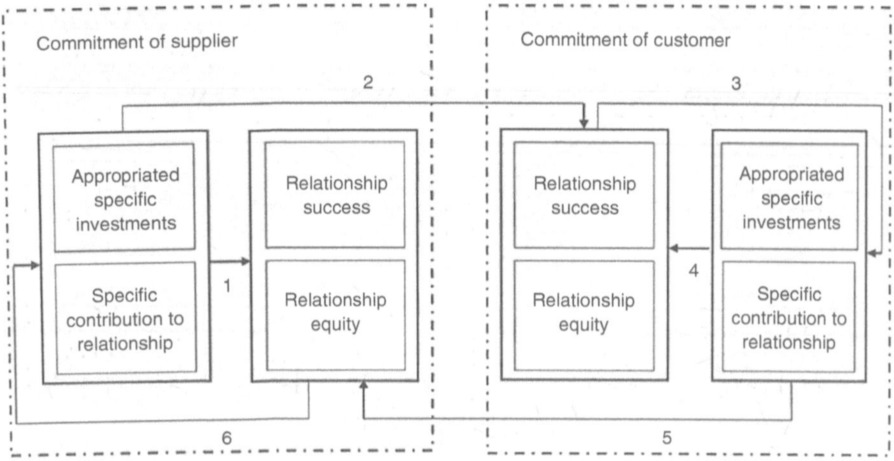

Fig. 3 Commitment model. Source: Based on Kleinaltenkamp et al. (2015, p. 41)

relationship equity (how the success of the relationship is divided between the partners), as outputs (that influence customer's perceived loyalty). These factors are: appropriated specific investments and specific contribution to relationship (loyalty and motivation) (Fig. 3).

Many authors link the trust with the commitment and do give the relational benefits considering them as dependent to each other. Solomon and Flore (2001) indicated that trust is very important or may be even necessary for making commitments. Morgan and Hunt's (1994) commitment-trust theory of the RM gives some relations of these specifics and how do antecedents and outcomes derive. According to him, the commitment and the trust are "key" because they encourage marketers to: (1) work at preserving relationship investments, (2) resist interesting short-term options in favor of the expected long-lasting benefits of staying with old partners, and (3) view potentially actions with a high risk, as being prudent because of the belief that their partners will not act in an opportunistic way.

Therefore, if both commitment and the trust occur together, not just one of them, they produce effective results, productivity, and efficiency. They represent the emotional attitude of the customer while having to evaluate and choose between what the company and its competitors offer. As Jacob (2015) affirms, the positive attitude is attributed to trust in the supplier, meanwhile, it is manifested in commitment to the supplier.

Morgan and Hunt (1994) have developed the *Key Mediating Variable Model* (KMV) of relationship. This model focuses on the relational exchanges of a party, and its relationship commitment and the trust. As shown in Fig. 4, what affects directly commitment are relationship termination costs and relationship benefits, shared values influence both commitment and trust and communication and opportunistic behavior affect trust and across trust, they influence commitment. On the other side, the relationship commitment directly effects acquiescence and

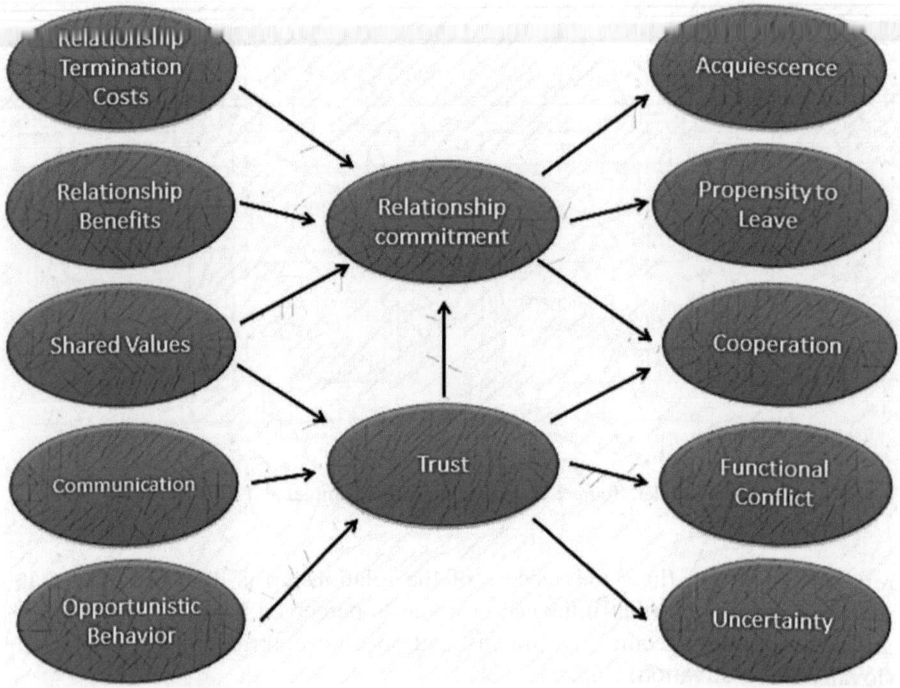

Fig. 4 The KMV Model of Relationship Marketing. Source: Based on Morgan and Hunt (1994)

propensity to leave, as well as both the relationship commitment and the trust, create cooperation. Moreover, trust leads a partner to perceive that future conflictual episodes will be functional (Morgan & Hunt, 1994) and decision making uncertainty.

Jacob (2009) has developed a *Model of Trust and Commitment* in an exchange relationship (Fig. 5), saying that the trust as an expectation of the customer is a determinant of behavior that can be acknowledged as an emergent factor. The form and extent of trust, as a very important component, always remain emergent or implicit. However, some basic correlations to active and systematic trust management can still be posed.

3.2 Satisfaction

When one party in the relational exchange has received the perceived values created before the relational exchange process, there is created a new phenomenon called satisfaction. Satisfaction occurs if the customer's experience fulfills or exceeds his or her expectations (Stauss, 1999). Satisfaction arises when a customer is rewarded for his/her loyalty and trust, in terms of a good quality, good prices and

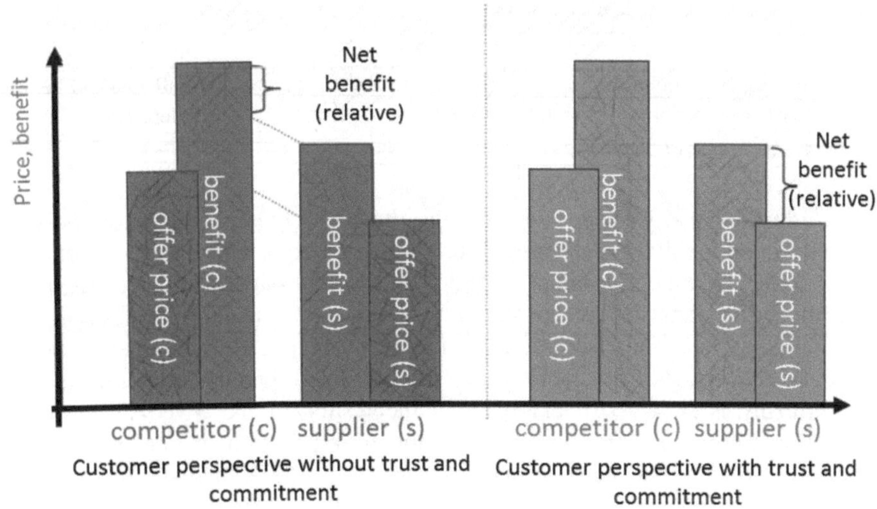

Fig. 5 Trust and commitment in an exchange relationship. Source: Based on Jacob (2015, p. 66)

loyalty in return. The same applies to B2B relation exchanges; a partner is satisfied, only when he gets what expects and what is agreed, and when he is rewarded for his trust and loyalty. There are cases when loyalty may miss, even when there is customer satisfaction. These are situations when there are barriers to close relationships, and normally, parties should work to avoid those kinds of barriers and try to build up the long-lasting and qualitative relationships.

Diller (2000) has developed a model of Customer bonding and satisfaction, based on two variables: *penetration* (high and low) and *satisfaction* (high and low). In Table 3 can be seen four situations of customer penetration and satisfaction.

The most interesting situation in this table is when there is high customer penetration, but low satisfaction. These are situations when there are not any recommendations from customers or friendly feedback from them. This arises when loyalty and satisfaction change in different rates.

The connection between customer satisfaction and customer loyalty can be demonstrated, for example, using the German Customer Satisfaction Barometer (Meyer & Dornach, 1998). The German Customer Satisfaction Barometer (NCSB or DKB) was founded in 1992 with the initiative of the German Marketing Association, and was sponsored by the German Post AG. Starting from then, it has been carried out annually (Hansen & Thurau, 1999). The results of this annual survey make it clear that "dedicated" customers are most proactive and positive with regard to repeat business, recommending the business to others, and cross buying. Customers with "only" a satisfactory opinion are very indifferent in terms of future loyalty to the business and often only recommend the business to others passively (Meyer & Blümelhuber, 2000).

Table 3 Customer bonding and satisfaction

	Low satisfaction	High satisfaction
High customer penetration	Tenuous loyalty	Well-founded loyalty
Low customer penetration	No loyalty	Potential loyalty

Source: Based on Diller (2000)

According to this, we can conclude that there is a linear connection between satisfaction and loyalty, resulting with economic success. Thus, it is important to have not only satisfied customers; it is very important to have dedicated customers and enthusiastic ones. In the terminology of the disconfirmation paradigm, this means far away from the customer expectations (Meyer & Blümelhuber, 2000).

The positive effect of satisfaction and customer loyalty on the economic success of a company is shown, for example, in the results of the Swedish Customer Satisfaction Barometer; an increase in customer satisfaction of one index point, for a period of 5 years, here produced an average 11.3% increase in return on investment (Andreson, Fornell, & Lehmann, 1993). Moreover, according to Reichheld and Sasser (1990), a 5% reduction in customer loss results with increased profits of between 25% and 85%, depending on the branch.

The potential for greater profit for the organization from the lasting customers comes from many factors, such as: higher frequencies of purchasing, invoices with increased amounts, effects of recommendations (word of mouth), willingness to pay more and accept high prices etc. Satisfaction and loyalty is a strategy that offers long-term potential for profit for a business. In the marketing terms, it means that they should focus more on customers' desires, needs and demands, so the business can offer more of what is expected to be received with good quality and resulting with customer satisfaction.

3.2.1 Gratitude

Gratitude is a feeling that arises when an individual or the so called *beneficiary* perceives that an exchange partner or a *benefactor* (which can be person or organization) has acted intentionally to improve the beneficiary's well-being (Fredrickson, 2004). How the beneficiary will react emotionally to this perception or situation, is called the "feeling of gratitude". In order to make gratitude felt, recognition and appreciation are inalienable. Although it is possible to see gratitude when it is not felt (Buck, 2004), we focus only on the actions where there is gratitude.

Gratitude is composed of some components that can be: cognitive, affective and behavioral, as when the beneficiary recognizes a benefit bestowed by a benefactor or cognition, appreciates the benefit, and acknowledges the benefit (Buck, 2004; Steindl-Rast, 2004). The renowned economist, Adam Smith, declared that gratitude is a vital civic virtue, no doubtfully essential for the good and healthy functioning of societies (Emmons, 2004). Bartlett and DeSteno (2006) says that gratitude drives *helping* behavior. Specifically, gratefulness for another's actions, not awareness of society's reciprocity norm or a positive mood, cause participants to engage in helpful behaviors toward both the benefactor and also strangers. Grateful participants reciprocate a favor, even when doing this or working in this way is costly to them (Raggio, Walz, Godbole, & Folse, 2014). These feelings of gratitude can develop future interactions, even when gratitude is only felt and not expressed. (Bartlett & DeSteno, 2006).

Gratitude may be *felt* in commercial exchanges when relational investments are made, which, for example, can include extra effort extended to benefit a buyer, purchases made based on factors beyond merely financial ones, or gifts exchanged (Raggio et al., 2014). Gratitude has not only interpersonal construct (individually), but it can be expressed among companies, when partners express gratitude to each other (B2B relations) or to customers (B2C).

4 Research Methodology

4.1 General Information

This research aimed to emphasize the advantages of using relationship marketing approaches, as one of the best alternatives for having long-term efficient results. The research results are based mostly on the data collected from the interviews held with the marketing managers of two family businesses in Bosnia and Herzegovina: the AS Group and Pharmamed Ltd (Table 4). The interviews were conducted in April 2016 in Bosnia and Herzegovina. Interviews lasted about 60 minutes, and were held in the company's offices of general and marketing managers.

The interviewees are: Mr. Rusmir Hrvić—general manager of AS Group, Mr. Adis Hasaković—marketing manager of AS Group, and Mr. Sanjin Kotlica—general manager of Pharmamed Ltd. The current management positions of the interviewees made it possible to have the most updated information about the companies and the sincerest opinions about relationship marketing and its use in their organizations. Furthermore, the fact that those people are among the decision-makers in their organizations, made it possible not only to have their opinions about the issues studied, but also, they gave the ways how do they reach to such decisions about the marketing activities in their organizations as well as other decision making processes.

AS Group is one of the largest Bosnian private holding companies. It owns and operates in three divisions: food, trade and textile. It is based in Tešanj, a municipality that hosts 13 out of 100 largest companies in Bosnia and Herzegovina. AS Group's first steps were found in 1988. At that time, Sulejman Hrvić, one of the owners of this organization, together with his wife, Azra Hrvić, opened a grocery in Vukovo, BiH. After the devastating war, in 1996 the same owner established "AS", a company for wholesale trading and retail. It has been a small company with only

Table 4 Profile of AS Group and Pharmamed Ltd

	AS Group	Pharmamed Ltd.
Industry	Food, trade and textile	Pharmaceutical
Headquarters	Tesanj, Bosnia and Herzegovina	Travnik, Bosnia and Herzegovina
Established	1988	1996
Employees	3300	97

three employees. Today, AS Group employs around 3300 people. It is a group of nine companies:

1. AS (food trading from Tesanj),
2. Vispak (food producer from Visoko),
3. Klas (flour and baking industry in Sarajevo),
4. Vemal (real estate company),
5. Napredak (clothing manufacturer),
6. Fortitudo (clothing manufacturer),
7. Oaza (water producer),
8. Sprind (flour and baking industry in Sarajevo) and
9. Mill and baker Ljubace (flour and baking industry in Tuzla).

Only in food industry, AS Group has more than 1200 different products, such as: Zlatna Dzezva, Zlatni Puder and Bosanski Lokum. In 2016, Klas was chosen as "The business of the year" at Sarajevo Business Forum. This award, which for the first time was dedicated to a company, was delivered to Rusmir Hrvić, director of AS Group. This was one of the biggest awards that AS Group has gained.

Pharmamed Ltd is placed in Travnik, BiH and it was established in 1996. At the beginning, company's headquarters and production plants were located in a private house, which was organized for the needs of production and sales processes.

Construction of the first production facility began in year 2000, and it was completed in a record time of 3 months. After that, the seat of the company was changed to its present address, Dolac n/L bb, Travnik. Construction of the second production plant, which was conducted in accordance with strict GMP guidelines, started in May 2002 and it was completed in December 2002. The construction of the third and fourth production buildings began in October 2014 and it was completed in May 2015. Today, Pharmamed Ltd has more than 5300 m^2 which is deployed on production, business facilities, storage facility for starting materials and facility for storage finished products.

The business strategy of the Pharmamed Ltd from the very beginning was directed towards their own production. Significant investments in marketing have contributed extremely rapid growth in sales of products from own production program. As strategic products from the assortment of own production can be distinguished:

- Production of medicines and medical devices
- The production of herbal medicines

- Production of dietary products
- Production of cosmetics, cosmetics with special purpose and children's cosmetics
- Production of herbal drops
- Production of filter and bulk teas
- Laboratory services of the physical and chemical control of products

The total range of own production line has more than 210 products. Pharmamed Ltd product portfolio was expanded in 2005, when they received the status of exclusive representative and distributor of production program of Salus-Haus, Germany. The distinctive products to the local market are Alpenkraft syrup, Floradix tonic with iron, and Kindervital multivitamin supplement for children.

Pharmamed's products are sold in Albania, Australia, Azerbaijan, Bosnia and Herzegovina, Montenegro, Egypt, Croatia, Yemen, Kingdom of Jordan, Qatar, Kosovo, Kuwait, Lebanon, Macedonia (FYOM), Morocco, Germany, Oman, Kingdom of Saudi Arabia, United States, Slovakia, Serbia, Turkey and United Arab Emirates.

The company's business started with five employees, mostly family members, while today the company has 97 employees. In the context of human resources policies, Pharmamed Ltd takes care of the continuous education of its employees, and fosters the practice of scholarship personnel who will in future be necessary for further development of the company.

The production is organized in modern facilities that meet strict standards. In their facilities, they pay close attention to the system for conditioning and control of air quality in clean rooms, as well as the production of purified water, and between the individual zones of movement provided the difference in air pressure, which are acquired preconditions for reducing cross-contamination. In order to improve the manufacturing process of strategic products successively in recent years they acquired equipment that their automated and semi-automated operation ensures sufficient capacity to meet current market demands. As a special mechanism to achieve previous targets established they run quality assurance as a first step to the ultimate goal of total quality management (Total Quality Management), which is one of the ultimate strategic goals of the company. Quality assurance (QA) is a systematic approach to quality management that defines and establishes actions that lead to a reduction in the diversity and the introduction of uniformity in the system by monitoring and react to all the factors that can disrupt the system. Good Manufacturing Practice (Good Manufacturing Practice), as part of the Quality Assurance is implemented in Pharmamed Ltd, and ensures that products are consistently produced and controlled to the quality standards, which meet the purpose of the product and quality requirements, as confirmed by the Agency for Medicines and Medical Devices BiH issuing the GMP certificate number INS-M-05-3622-06/287 of 12.06.2013. Parallel with the quality assurance, as complementary, they introduced a system that complies with the requirements of the ISO 9001: 2008. As confirmation of compliance with the new international standards in 2004, Pharmamed Ltd received the ISO 9001: 2008 certificate, from the Bureau Veritas

Company and has been renewing it until today. Product quality has been and remains one of the main strategic goals of the company. With permanent quality control of their products, they established control—analytical laboratory whose primary task is to control raw materials, packaging, semi-finished products, control of intermediates and finished products. The laboratory is staffed and equipped to provide other types of chemical analysis and testing of microbiological safety. Based on this, they have implemented the system ISO 17025:2005, which ranks their laboratory among the laboratories that can do analysis of the approved scope.

The reason why we have chosen different industries for studying is that we can offer more information to our group of interests how the RM approaches work in different industries and not only in one industry or selected industries. It is important to understand that the RM is the new way of doing the marketing strategies, end that everyone, from every industry should know how it can affect them.

5 Research Design

This research is a qualitative approach, an exploratory one, which will help us dive deeper into the marketing issues, especially into the relationship marketing ones. It provides insights into the detailed aspects of the relationship marketing in family businesses, based on case evidence from two big companies, that are part of our study analyzes: AS Group (with the companies that are part of it) and Pharmamed Ltd.

This chapter discusses an inductive approach. The inductive researches are those who will make use of all the coding techniques that are offered by theories that are grounded (Corbin & Strauss, 1990), in the process of development of sensitizing concepts (Dana & Dumez, 2015). We choose the inductive, qualitative approach, because among other advantages, it gives the opportunity to learn directly from the research subject, i.e. reducing measurement errors that are mostly appeared in survey studies. The result is deeper. This approach, also reduces Type III error (asking the wrong question) and Type IV error (solving the wrong problem), because of the interaction between researcher and subject (Dana & Dana, 2005).

Research where there should be studied the behavior, the relations, or other aspects of the inner personality, or actions that derive from inner stimulations, are hard to be studied by quantitative methods. Furthermore, the conceptual tools used in a research, influences what is actually observed (Dana & Dana, 2005). Moreover, Pasquero (1988) suggested that "quantitativists" in many cases let themselves to be carried away by some strict, but very limited methods, and by some assumptions that could not be considered as realistic, so they "miss a true understanding of real-world behaviors in alien cultures" (p. 184).

An alternative to traditional (deductive quantitative research), is the inductive qualitative approach, which is the most used paradigm in anthropological research so far. It is based on naturalistic inquiry, i.e., the research is set naturally with no manipulation by the researcher (Willens & Rausch, 1969).

Qualitative methodology is based on a personal observation of: different situations, numerous events, different types of individuals, B2B and B2C interactions and transactions, as well as analysis of documents (including quantitative data) and open interviews. Qualitative data includes thick description (Geertz, 1973), and direct quotes from different people about attitudes, beliefs, actions and experiences of theirs (Dana & Dana, 2005).

This research is based on the analysis of interviews with marketing managers and directors of AS Group and Pharmamed Ltd, both family owned businesses operating in BiH and abroad. Also, the research includes: a short preface about Bosnian economic situation, family businesses there, the economic and political structure; a deeper analyze of literature review about relationship marketing, transactional marketing; as well as family businesses.

6 Type of Data

This chapter includes qualitative and descriptive data, based on real case studies, two family owned businesses from Bosnia and Herzegovina. The results have derived from the research questions, which helped developing the idea of using relationship marketing in family businesses.

The reason why we chose these companies is that they both offered enough relationship marketing approaches. We chose BiH because it is a good example of entrepreneur and family businesses development in transition conditions, as well as the society with a high level of cultural interactivity and tradition. Thus, it is better to understand how relations among people and businesses work. Moreover, we chose case studies, instead of a generalized sample of family owned businesses, because they seem to be more reliable. Case studies are shown to be appropriate to understand better the behavior within a specific context (Yin, 2003). These case study designs gave more realistic approaches to the relationship marketing, real experiences and a lot of cases experienced among time; which of them motivated a specific behavior, etc.

7 Research Instruments

One–on–one interviews were realized with marketing managers and directors of the companies, since this is both a common and powerful way to try to understand fellow human beings (Denzin & Lincoln, 1998). Qualitative interviews are good because they allow the parties to interact freely and enter deeper into the questions; they are not like quantitative ones, where only numbers and official data can speak itself. Thus, the interviews were designed to research questions, which were the basement, but there was a free space to talk about many other issues that were interesting for researchers, or seemed important to the interviewees and they shared them. Specifically, I was interested on the factors that affected specific behavior in B2B and B2C relations, as well as they ways relationships among them is appeared, such as: trust, commitment, loyalty, satisfaction approaches, the cooperation with competitors etc. Also, interviews covered other areas. They gave us information about the companies themselves, their activity, their history, organization and their plans for the future.

8 Findings

As we have mentioned before, this is a qualitative research based on research questions (interviews), i.e., there is no econometric model or hypothesis that we can test here. The research questions that derive from the above discussion are as follows.

RQ1 Which are the ways that family businesses use to maintain and develop loyalty, trust and commitment, both in B2B and B2C relations?

AS Group

AS Group, the leader of production of food in Bosnia and Herzegovina, bases the creation and maintain of its customer loyalty, trust and commitment on the *development of brands*, especially traditional brands, such as the Bosnian Coffee Zlatna Dzezva, flour Zlatni Puder or traditional Bosnian cookies, called *Bosnian Lokum*. Powerful brands are a guarantee for development. Their target group of interest is the BiH's population and everyone who wants to taste the BiH's tradition and culture.

> Our culture and tradition is very interesting to everyone. Bosnian cuisine is very rich, qualitative and famous, so we try to offer all the products needed to taste this wealth of ours. Bosnians, for many reasons, are much related to their culture and tradition and are very committed and loyal to them. They would not change their Bosanska kafa for any other homemade coffee. Therefore, we always want to offer them and everyone else that wants to taste our culture, the non-changeable traditional products with all the qualitative ingredients needed. So, we make the traditional way of eating and foods, industrialized in order to keep the tradition going on. Except this, we are working on the development of new products, new designs and new fields of activity to satisfy our customers need. But what remain our clients loyal to our products and the way we do things is that we always keep the original recipe. In this way, we are not developing only our company, but the whole industry in Bosnia and Herzegovina—states Mr. Hasaković (Personal interview).

Also, AS Group uses the strategy of educating our customers. They organize different workshops for groups starting from children in elementary schools ("Cooking with our children") to grandparents, in educating them about the importance of use of high quality foods and they really have fun by cooking together. Moreover, AS Group communicates with its customers to create committed customers in a way that is not used by many companies. For example, they have the right of ownership of the biggest coffee pot in the world, which has the Guinness

World Record, as the biggest coffee pot in the world.[1] Whenever there is an important event in BiH or elsewhere, they bring there their coffee pot and cook coffee for about 8000 people. It is a great attraction for the people and a good way to taste the Bosnian coffee, as well as promote this coffee. For 11 years, starting from 2004 in Mostar, the pot has travelled around the world, including: Brazil, China, Turkey, Germany, Austria, Macedonia, Slovenia etc. Last year, another product of Vispak, Bey's soup, entered the Guinness World Record.[2]

Pharmamed Ltd

Pharmamed Ltd representatives think that all of them must work on creating good relationships with their customers, partners, the external environment and the internal one. One of the ways that they use to build good relations with their customers is the so-called "Pharmamed's loyalty club of nature and health" or "Health club", which is about 2 years old. These days, they are working on the following segments of this club:

1. *B2C*—in this group they have around 4000 customers, who by buying a Pharmamed's product and by a symbolic participation of 5 € have become part of the club. Every product they buy has a financial value, which is converted into points. Members of the club collect those points and for a particular number of points, they can choose any of the products in the magazine of Health Club for free. Every member's house address receives the magazine of Health Club, published quarterly. With this magazine, they often include a questionnaire for a new product, its design or their needs in general. Pharmamed Ltd wants to involve their clients in their decision-making process. All the activities that Pharmamed Ltd realizes with their final customers aim to bring them to the pharmacy, i.e. their sales point, using the *pull* strategy.
2. *B2B*—beside the final customers, Pharmamed Ltd has included in the club the pharmacies that they work with. There are about 100 pharmacies that have joined the club, from 1100 pharmacies in total in BiH. Even though they do not work with them directly, because the BiH's Law says that there must be a wholesale channel between a producer and a retailer, they give the retailers the opportunity to join the club with the wholesaler's intermediation. By joining the club, they have the right of financial discount that is given by Pharmamed Ltd,

[1] In 2004, under the Old Bridge in Mostar (BiH), during the jumps from the reopening of the famous Old Bridge after the war of 1992–1996, a total of 650 l of 'Zlatnadzezva' coffee had been made in the largest pot in the world and the citizens of Mostar drank 8000 cups of real Bosnian coffee. This was a world record of coffee made and drunk in the same time. For a single charge of a giant coffee pot takes about 65 kg of coffee. The largest coffee pot in the world was made in the summer of 2004 under the hammer of Bascarsija (Sarajevo) master Nasir Jabucar and his assistants. See URL: http://www.sarajevotimes.com/?p=103703 (Accessed on 02.08.2016).

[2] In 2015, Bey's soup (Begova čorba) was made from 6.00 A.M. by 50 chefs and voulonteers; its weight was 4.120 and was offered to thousands citizens of Sarajevo, as well as tourists who were very glad to be part of the biggest ever made soup that entered in the Guiness World Record book. See URL: http://www.slobodnaevropa.org/a/begova-corba-za-ginisa/26962999.html (Accessed on: 02.08.2016).

but with the intermediation of the wholesalers and they can use the opportunity to have free samples as well as distilled water for free. Moreover, they have the opportunity to host the activities of Pharmamed Ltd held in the pharmacies that are members of the club, which includes free controls of vitamins, minerals and other indicators to the final customers. It is very effective because it brings a lot of people in the pharmacy that end the control by buying a product in the pharmacy.

> By joining the loyalty club, customers have the right of discount in a lot of hospitals and other health institutions. In the Health Club Magazine, customers can find all the objects divided in BiH cantons, where they can reach the right of discount. There are about 40 health institutions that are members of this club. In this way, Pharmamed Ltd has stimulated the doctors and all the other institutions, members of the club, to be loyal to Pharmamed's products and recommend them to their clients. Moreover, doctors that are specialist in a specific field, write different articles for our magazine that could be interesting and useful for customers. Meanwhile, we advertise them in different ways; such as in radio jingles, radio programmers, different kinds of direct promotions etching this way we make loyal customers stay loyal and stimulate new customers to become loyal. Our group of interests is the population of 45+ years old, which means people that are in mostly of the cases affected by any disease. More detailed, our group of interests is the woman, because the woman is the decision maker in the purchase process, especially in pharmaceutics—says Mr. Kotlica (Personal interview).

Beside this, Pharmamed tries to make committed clients to their products with the fact that they are a domestic company, even though in BiH's community there is no developed the culture of buying domestic products. They make their clients believe in their products by setting quality as the primary objective.

RQ2 Which are the ways that family businesses use to maintain and develop customers' satisfaction approaches with special emphasis on motivational and cooperation elements, both in B2B and B2C relations?

AS Group

AS Group always tries to satisfy its client's and partner's needs and demands, by offering them all the requirements in real time, with high quality. They always try to find any ways to communicate in real time with them, using different approaches of direct communication with the customer or by using social media. They are aware that using relationship approaches is more expensive than using transactional ones, but they are also aware that in long-term, relationship approaches give the best results.

> What makes our customers satisfied is also the fact that in mostly of the cases we use direct marketing to present our products in the retail store, with different campaigns where customers can taste the products by themselves or see how they can use them, i.e. pull strategy as the most used relationship marketing strategy and not push strategy, which I would consider as a much transactional marketing approach. Furthermore, we have developed all the modern standards for quality required in the trade, in order to make our clients feel safe when consuming our products. It includes ISO, HACCP, Halal etc. Also, what we consider as one of the most important elements for satisfaction is respect. We are very committed to realize what is said and what is agreed with our customers and partners. We develop our relations as first with people, then with customers, media, competitors or

suppliers. In the foreign market, there are about 28 different that we work with and a big number of buyers. In order to make them satisfied, we have strong controls of the delivering process, the quality of the deliver, the time limit agreed etc. One of the most important factors that influence their satisfaction is that they must be sure that they are exclusive distributors of ours and no one is going to threaten this right of them. We are very conscious about this and we work on keeping our responsibilities in high level every single day with every single partner. (Hasaković, A., 2016, April, Personal interview)

AS Group is focused on the social responsibility, and it is one of the reasons why the customers are satisfied with them. AS Group recruits the best students in BiH universities, from different fields and also offers different scholarships for students in high schools and universities.

We are aware that they are our future and we work with them. Our Foundation created for humanity and social help, works every day in fulfilling as much as needs as we can in our society. (Hrvić, R, 2016, April, personal interview)

Pharmamed Ltd

Pharmamed Ltd is very committed to do everything by strong and strict procedures. Among others, it means that quality is necessary. Pharmamed Ltd possess the certificates by the Agency for Medicines and Medical Devices for Good Manufacturing Practices (GMP certificate), which means not only producing high quality products, but also, ensuring that all the required documentation for quality production is completed. For example, if a pharmacy or a final customer has any complaint about a specific product, they inform the company about it and it is obligated to receive it with all the required strict procedures in order to have the most professional answer. They collect and have strong evidence for every complaint from the market. Usually, they are more often appeared when they change the design or the package of any product. Related to this, Mr. Kotlica argues:

We have launched a free telephone number, where our final customers can call to ask any question about the use of our products. We have professional group of people that gives them the required information. Also, we take care of our clients by using the social media. As tendencies of this kind of media rise, we have a person that works specifically with our clients using the social media and updates the posts of Pharmamed. Moreover, we help good students while their studying period in universities with different scholarships, mostly the pharmaceutical students. (Personal interview)

RQ3 In which way do family businesses cooperate with their competition and which are the benefits they see from relations with them? Is pure cooperation possible?

AS Group

With regards to this question, Mr. Hasaković declared:

Even though that there are not a lot of companies that are our competitors in producing these kinds of products from the Bosnian cuisine, there is still a lot of space for cooperating with those who could compete in other aspects. In retail, there is a lot of space for cooperation with other retail networks, even though we have our own retail centers. For example, we are realizing the programs for cooking together with children in Bingo, which is one of the biggest retail networks in BiH, as well as our competitor and partner. Moreover, we do realize direct marketing promotion of flour Zlatni puder there. Pure cooperation with competitors is not possible totally, but is very effective regarding the state's economy as a whole, in a high level. In order to achieve this kind of cooperation, a lot of work should be done in order to raise the level of responsibilities in our companies. (Personal interview)

Pharmamed Ltd

The general manager of Pharmamed Ltd, Mr. Kotlica says that a pure cooperation could be possible, but not in every situation and in every industry. They think that communication with their competition must be in higher levels, but the problem is that Pharmamed Ltd is the only company of this size and characteristics in BiH that produces these kinds of products, i.e. herbal products.

> We have our laboratory for special analyzes, accredited by the states institutions, which can be used from other companies in this industry. We have agreement with our competition for realizing the service of analyzing their products in our laboratory; hence with our certificate they become a competition to us. Very often, we give some kind of consultancy of how some production processes should be done, because when we receive their products, we can immediately see where the problem is. Moreover, we are open to sell our competition the raw materials that they may need, and we have it. The general statement that we have for our competition is that if we do not cooperate with them, they will surely find a way to compete us because today the information is provided to everyone, today or tomorrow, and that being closed to cooperation is not a way to compete in the trade, there is quality and there is the power of the company. For example, now we are working with the biggest pharmaceutical company in BiH that produces generic products, by giving them our expertise in using the dietary supplement products and other herbal products. (Personal interview)

RQ4 Which are the economic benefits that have derived from using relationship marketing approaches in the industry where they belong instead of traditional marketing ones, both in B2B and B2C relations?

AS Group

Sponsorships have helped the AS Group to reach great economic effects and be famous all around. They sponsor almost all the national teams in: football (soccer), basketball, handball and individual swimmers in their world championships in swimming. They have realized that this is the win-win combination. One of the most effective sponsorship that they have done lately is sponsoring the Football National Team of Federation of BiH, in the World Championship in Football, in Brazil, 2014. The extraordinary thing is that they sent their the biggest coffee pot (in the world) to the World Cup and people from around the world thus had the chance to taste the pride of Bosnian coffee. They labeled our coffee packages with the championship's signs and everyone knew that Bosnia and its *dzezva* are there.

> Two years from then, we have doubled the production of coffee; 2.5 times multiplied the total production of Vispak and reached the top, first place of customer loyalty in BiH from the 12th one in 2010. Meanwhile, we have not changed the prices; prices policy is not very important because we compete with quality and loyalty. Moreover, we develop our brands outside with the exclusive and irreplaceable help of the Bosnian people that live abroad. There about 1 million people that have migrated during the war, unfortunately. They live in almost every corner in the world and for as they are the best promoters. They are loyal and committed clients—concludes Mr. Hasaković (Personal interview).

Pharmamed Ltd
With regards to this question, Mr. Kotlica contended:

> Using traditional marketing in the pharmaceutical industry could mean the cooperation with the doctor, i.e. the pressure made to the doctors for using your products, because they are the ones that give instructions for using a particular medicine. It is the approach used by most of the pharmaceutical companies and it is not a secret. The new approaches include education of the customers and in this way pulling them to our products. In this way, you create a very conscientious buyer that will always know what he needs and what he wants. ROI in using this approach is much bigger comparing to TV advertisement, for example. TV advertisement and other kinds of transactional marketing, as we have analyzed, have a lower level of ROI, comparing to the previous year, because about 70% of the TV watchers change the channel when there is a promotional spot. As we have analyzed, the costs for relationship marketing are much bigger than transactional marketing, but the return of investments in long term is higher. Another way is the use of social media, as we mentioned before. (Personal interview)

RQ5 Do and how the relationship marketing approaches of family businesses change with regards to the cultural differences, both in B2B and B2C relations?

AS Group
Mr. Hasaković, the marketing manager of AS Group says that:

> Because of the nature of the products we produce and sell, there is not very much space to be flexible in our clients' needs from abroad, in regard of their culture. (Personal interview)

They always try to fit to everyone's needs. For example, they always have the opinion of their clients and partners while developing a new product or when they need a new product.

Pharmamed Ltd
Differently from As Group, Mr. Kotlica, the general manager of Pharmamed Ltd claimed:

> The fact that in general we are a small or medium company, gives us the opportunity to be very flexible when we have to react on cultural differences. We try to satisfy all the need of every customer. We let the distributer of a particular state to make the marketing strategy, and based on the specifics that this state has, we try to adjust. Even though two countries may be geographically very near to each other, they may have very different specifics in their needs. We have concluded that in mostly of the cases, we cannot use the practices used in BiH in other countries. For example, in Azerbaijan we sell very big quantities of the product AntiDep, which intends mild depression. It is the opposite in Bosnia and Herzegovina, i.e. we sell very small quantities of this product. Here, this product has reached the end of its life cycle. Or another example could be the sales of royal jelly in Macedonia which has very low sales levels, compared to Bosnia and Herzegovina, where it is one of our most important products. Moreover, our distributor in Macedonia has demanded mountain tea, which is not even known in BiH. In Macedonia, it is a well-known type of tea. In order to satisfy our customer's need, we developed the recipe of this type of tea and started producing it for them.

There are cases when different country's laws force them to be flexible. For example, the same syrup or medicine for coughing in Croatia, i.e. EU, is intended for *oral suspension for the mouth and pharynx*, so coughing cannot be mentioned by new regulative and laws. In BiH it is considered as a dietary supplement and in its package may write *assistance with hash coughing*. Moreover, for the Arab countries, they are making totally different translations and totally different packaging and designs, according to their culture and desires.

9 Conclusion and Discussion

As the environment for doing business all around the globe grows more complicated and more difficult every day, it is very important for every company to know how they should act and how they should do business, and not lose market share to their competitors. Today, when everyone has the information needed in every second, and when any new product can be found in every corner in the world, sales are the hardest part of doing business. Moreover, the price is not anymore the most important determinant. Quality has a lot of cheapest alternatives. What should companies do in these cases? As we saw from all the cases presented in this research, every company should think and develop a new way of doing business; something that is not comparable and competitive to other competitor's strategies. It is: creating the long-lasting relationships with customers and partners in order to have loyal, satisfied, trustworthy and committed ones. In this way, companies will have always their group of interest opened for their products. Normally, it is harder and more expensive alternative, but it is proven that it is the best one if worked and applied as it should be.

By analyzing the RM approaches in AS Group and Pharmamed Ltd, we have confirmed many of the statements of different authors about the RM, mentioned in the literature review, about all the advantages of using the RM tools. Based on the data provided from this research, we can elaborate the outputs regarding the importance of developing good and long-lasting relations, both B2B and B2C relations, i.e. relationship marketing. According to our research questions and their answers, we can see that both companies agree that relationship is the best strategy to have effective results in the long-term. Based on their activities, they have seen these results from using RM approaches:

- They have won loyal customers, which trust them and are committed to their products and companies,
- They have reached a high satisfaction level at their customers and partners, as well as all the other groups of interests,
- RM has given them the opportunity not to be feared of their competition, giving them a lot of ways and alternatives how can they work together with their competitors and how to have effective collaborative programs,
- The economic effects are one of the most important achievements that have derived from this way of working, giving the companies the opportunity to reach the highest levels in their industry; their turnover has doubled, and in many cases, it has experienced up to 300% increase (Mr. Rusmir Hrvic),

- Last, but not least, the RM approaches have opened a new door of modern marketing, giving these companies the opportunity to offer their customers what they need, on the time they want and in the way they want.

10 Limitation of the Research

As this research is among the first ones about relationship marketing in BiH, it has several limitations, mostly because of the fields' nature. On the other side, it is an advantage because it is a rare one talking about the RM. As the first limitation, we would consider the lack of literature review about relationship marketing that cover the Balkans countries. It is obviously that BiH companies are still not very aware of the importance of this approach. Secondly, the sample size used in this research as a sample of two companies cannot definitively show the importance of relationship marketing approaches on the development of family businesses. But as a small sample, they are very important because mostly of family businesses have positive tendencies to increase, as well as are more open to implement new approaches, like the RM. Finally, another limitation is the fact that the both companies covered in this chapter come from a transition country and thereby we cannot come to a general conclusion that would include family businesses from developed and/or developing countries in terms of usage of relationship marketing approaches and their benefits.

11 Recommendations for Future Research

This research is only a water drop in the ocean, as some would say. It is so, because there is a huge area in the relationship marketing, which can be and needs to be studied, especially for the BiH's family businesses. It is obvious that some of the approaches of the RM are used in BiH's family businesses, i.e. in family businesses in transitional economies, but they are not aware of that. Thus, these businesses do not take the needed care for creating the RM strategies while running their activities. Hereby, we would recommend to scholars to emphasize more the role of the RM and make aware companies about this field. For example, a similar study in this field could be how do family businesses from other ex-Yugoslavia countries implement the relationship marketing approaches and compare them with other transitional countries.

References

Andersen, P. H. (2001). Relationship development and marketing communication: An integrative model. *Journal of Business and Industrial Marketing, 16*(3), 167–182.

Anderson, C. J., & Narus, J. A. (1990). A model of distributor firm and manufacturer firm working partnerships. *Journal of Marketing, American Marketing Association, 54*, 42–58.

Andreson, E., Fornell, C., & Lehmann, D. R. (1993). *Customer satisfaction, market share and profitability: Findings from Sweden* (Working paper). Ann Arbor: University of Michigan.

Bartlett, M. Y., & DeSteno, D. (2006). Gratitude and pro social behavior. *Psychological Science, 17*(4), 319–325.

BBC. (2016). *News*. Available at: http://www.bbc.co.uk/news/world-europe-17211937 (Accessed 01.07.2016)

Bendapudi, N., & Berry, L. L. (1997). Customers' motivations for maintaining relationships with service providers. *Journal of Retailing, 73*(1), 15–37.

Berry, L. (1983). Relationship marketing. In L. Berry, G. L. Shostack, & G. D. Upah (Eds.), *Emerging perspectives on services marketing*. Chicago: American Marketing Association.

Berry, L. L. (1995). Relationship marketing of services-growing interest, emerging perspectives. *Journal of the Academy of Marketing Science, 23*(4), 236–245.

Bloom, N., Eifert, B., Mahajan, A., McKenzie, D., & Roberts, J. (2011). *Does management matter? Evidence from India* (NBER Working Paper w16658). National Bureau of Economic Research, Cambridge, MA.

Bloom, N., & Van Reenen, J. (2010). Why do management practices differ across firms and countries? *The Journal of Economic Perspectives, 24*(1), 203–224.

Bruhn, M. (2003). *Relationship marketing: Management of costumer relationships*. Essex/Upper Saddle River: Financial Times/Prentice Hall.

Buck, R. (2004). The gratitude of exchange and the gratitude of caring: A developmental-integrationist perspective of moral emotion. In R. A. Emmons & M. E. McCullough (Eds.), *The psychology of gratitude*. New York: Oxford University Press.

Buttle, F. (1996). *Relationship marketing: Theory and practice*. Thousand Oaks, CA: Sage Publication.

Carrigan, M., & Buckley, J. (2008). What's so special about family businesses? An exploratory study of Irish consumer experiences of family businesses. *International Journal of Consumer Studies, 32*(6), 656–666.

Claro, D. P., Claro, P. B. O., & Zylbersztajn, D. (2005). Relationship marketing strategies: When buyer and supplier follow different strategies to achieve performance. *Brazilian Administration Review, 2*(2), 17–34.

Cooper, M. J., Upton, N., & Seaman, S. (2005). Customer relationship management: A comparative analysis of family and non-family businesses practices. *Journal of Small Business Management, 43*(3), 242–256.

Corbin, J., & Strauss, A. (1990). Grounded theory research: Procedures, Canons and evaluative criteria. *Zeiftchrift fur Soziologie, 19*(6), 418–427.

Dana, L. P., & Dana, T. E. (2005). Expanding the scope of methodologies used in entrepreneurship research. *International Journal of Entrepreneurship and Small Business, 2*(1), 80–86.

Dana, L. P., & Dumez, H. (2015). Qualitative research revisited: epistemology of a comprehensive approach. *International Journal of Entrepreneurship and Small Business, 26*(2), 156–165.

Dana, L.-P., & Ramadani, V. (2015). *Family businesses in transition economies*. Switzerland: Springer International Publishing.

Dashew, L. (1996). Marketing to family businesses checklist. *Journal of Accountancy, 4*(10), 1–42.

Day, G. S. (1995). Advantageous alliances. *Journal of the Academy of Management Science, 23* (4), 297–300.

Denzin, N. K., & Lincoln, Y. S. (1998). *Collecting and interpreting qualitative material*. Thousand Oaks, CA: Sage Publications.

Diller, H. (1996). Customer Loyalty as a Marketing Objective. *Marketing ZPF, 18*(2), 81–94.
Diller, H. (2000). Customer loyalty: Fata Morgana or realistic goal? Managing relationships with customers. In T. H. Thurau & U. Hansen (Eds.), *Relationship marketing: Gaining competitive advantage through customer satisfaction and customer retention*. Berlin: Springer.
Dittrich, S. (2000). *Kundenbindungals Kernaufgabeim Marketing: Kundenpotentialelangfristigausschäpfen*. Verlag Thexis, St. Gallen, Switzerland.
Doney, P. M., & Cannon, J. P. (1997). An examination of the nature of trust in buyer-seller relationships. *Journal of Marketing, 61*(2), 35–51.
Dwyer, F. R., Schurr, P. H., & Oh, S. (1987). Developing buyer – Seller relationships. *Journal of Marketing, 51*(2), 11–27.
Efendioglu, U. (2001). *Technology development and capacity-building for competitiveness in a digital society: A concept note*. UN Commission on Science and Technology: UNCTAD. Accessed November 22, 2016, from http://www.doingbusiness.org/~/media/fpdkm/doing%20business/documents/profiles/country/BA.pdf
Emmons, R. A. (2004). The psychology of gratitude: An introduction. In R. A. Emmons & M. E. McCullough (Eds.), *The psychology of gratitude*. New York: Oxford University Press.
Fredrickson, B. L. (2004). Gratitude, like the other positive emotions, broadens and builds. In R. A. Emmons & M. E. McCullough (Eds.), *The psychology of gratitude*. New York: Oxford University Press.
Geertz, C. (1973). *The interpretation of cultures*. New York: Basic Books.
Gundlach, G. T., & Murphy, P. E. (1993). Ethical and legal foundations of relational marketing exchanges. *Journal of Marketing, 57*(4), 35–46.
Hansen, U., & Schoenheit, I. (1987). Consumer satisfaction and complaints – Strategic challenges for companies and consumer policy organizations. In U. Hansen & I. Shcoenheit (Eds.), *Consumer satisfaction and complaint behavior*. Frankfurt/Main: Campus.
Hansen, U., & Thurau, T. H. (1999). National customer satisfaction indices: A critical investigation from an application perspective. In P. Kunst, J. Lemmink, & B. Stauss (Eds.), *Quality management in services*. Maastricht: Assen.
Hisrich, D. R., Petković, S., Ramadani, V., & Dana, L.-P. (2016). Venture capital funds in transition countries: Insights from Bosnia and Herzegovina and Macedonia. *Journal of Small Business and Enterprise Development, 23*(2), 296–315.
Homans, G. C. (1961). *Social behavior in elementary forms*. New York: Harcourt.
Jacob, F. (2009). *Marketing–Eine Einführungfür das Master-Studium*. Stuttgart: Gabler Verlag.
Jacob, F. (2015). Repeat purchasing in business relationships. In M. Kleinaltenkamp, W. Plinke, & I. Geiger (Eds.), *Business relationship management and marketing, Springer texts in business and economics*. Berlin: Springer Verlag.
Kangal, N. (2009). Role of relationship marketing in competitive marketing strategy. *Journal of Management and Marketing Research, 2*(1), 1–17.
Kleinaltenkamp, M., Plinke, W., & Söllner, A. (2015). Theoretical perspectives of business relationships: Explanation and configuration. In M. Kleinaltenkamp, W. Plinke, & I. Geiger (Eds.), *Business relationship management and marketing, Springer texts in business and economics*. Berlin: Springer Verlag.
Kotler, P., Dingena, M., & Pfoertsch, W. (2015). *Transformational sales: Making a difference with strategic customers*. Cham: Springer.
Levitt, T. (1986). *The marketing imagination*. Ann Arbor, MI: Free Press, The University of Michigan.
Maxim, A. (2009). Relationship marketing – A new paradigm in marketing theory and practice. *Analele Stiintifice ale Universitatii "Alexandru Ioan Cuza" din Iasi – Stiinte Economice, 56*(1), 2897–2300.
Meyer, A., & Blümelhuber, C. (2000). Relationship marketing success through investments in services. In T. H. Thurau & U. Hansen (Eds.), *Relationship marketing: Gaining competitive advantage through customer satisfaction and customer retention*. Berlin: Springer.

Meyer, A., & Dornach, F. (1998). *Yearbook of customer satisfaction in Germany*. Munich: Service Barometer.

Miller, D., Le Breton-Miller, I., & Scholnick, B. (2008). Stewardship vs. stagnation: An empirical comparison of small family and non-family businesses. *Journal of Management Studies, 45*(1), 51–78.

Mirascic, G. (2011). Current economic situation in Bosnia and Herzegovina. *Journal of International and Global Studies, 3*(1), 32–46.

Moorman, C., Deshpandé, R., & Zaltman, G. (1993). Factors affecting trust in market research relationships. *Journal of Marketing, 57*(1), 81–101.

Moorman, C., Zaltman, G., & Deshpande, R. (1992). Relationships between providers and users of market research: The dynamics of trust within and between organizations. *Journal of Marketing Research (JMR), 29*(3), 314–328.

Morgan, M. R., & Hunt, D. S. (1994). The commitment – Trust theory of relationship marketing. *Journal of Marketing, 58*(3), 20–38.

Murphy, P., Laczniak, E., & Wood, G. (2007). An ethical basis for relationship marketing: A virtue ethics perspective. *European Journal of Marketing, 41*(1), 2. doi:10.1108/03090560710718102.

Palamtier, R. W. (2008). *Relationship marketing*. Cambridge, MA: Marketing Science Institute.

Palalic, R. (2017). The phenomenon of entrepreneurial leadership in Gazelles and Mice: A qualitative study from Bosnia and Herzegovina. *World Review of Entrepreneurship, Management and Sustainable Development, 13*(2/3), 211–236.

Palalic, R., Ramadani, V., & Dana, L.-P. (2017). Entrepreneurship in Bosnia & Herzegovina: Focus on gender. *European Business Review, 29*(4), 476–496.

Pasquero, J. (1988). Comparative research: the case for middle-range methodologies. *Research in Corporate Social Performance and Policy, 10*(1), 181–209.

Petković, S., & Tešić, J. (2013). SMEs and Entrepreneurship Development and Institutional Support in Republic of Srpska (Bosnia and Herzegovina). In V. Ramadani & R. C. Schneider (Eds.), *Entrepreneurship in the Balkans: Diversity, support and prospects*. Berlin: Springer-Verlag.

Pope, N., & Voges, K. (2000). The impact of sport sponsorship activities, corporate image, and prior use on consumer purchase intention. *Sport Marketing Quarterly, 9*(2), 96–103.

Preß, B. (1997). Kaufverhalten in Geschäftsbeziehungen. In M. Kleinaltenkamp & W. Plinke (Eds.), *Geschäftsbeziehungsmanagement*. Berlin: Springer.

Raggio, R. D., Walz, A. M., Godbole, M. B., & Folse, J. A. G. (2014). Gratitude in relationship marketing: Theoretical development and directions for future research. *Marketing Faculty Publications, 48*(1), 2–24.

Ramadani, V., & Hoy, F. (2015). Context and uniqueness of family businesses. In L.-P. Dana & V. Ramadani (Eds.), *Family businesses in transition economies*. Cham: Springer International Publishing.

Ramadani, V., & Schneider, R. C. (2013). *Entrepreneurship in the Balkans: Diversity, support and prospects*. Berlin: Springer.

Ratten, V. (2013). Cloud computing: A social cognitive perspective of ethics, entrepreneurship, technology marketing, computer self-efficacy and outcome expectancy on behavioural intentions. *Australasian Marketing Journal, 21*(3), 137–146.

Reichheld, F. F., & Sasser, W. E., Jr. (1990). Zero-defections: Quality comes to services. *Harvard Business Review, 68*, 105–111.

Rotter, J. B. (1967). A new scale for the measurement of interpersonal trust. *Journal of Personality, 35*, 651–665.

Shani, D., & Chalasani, S. (1992). Exploiting niches using relationship marketing. *Journal of Services Marketing, 6*(4), 43–52.

Shaw, R. B. (1997). *Trust in the balance: Building successful organizations on results, integrity, and concern*. San Francisco, CA: Jossey - Bass.

Sheth, J. N. (1996). *Relationship marketing: Frameworks and concepts*. Paper presented at the 1996 International Conference on Relationship Marketing: Development, Management and Governance of Relationships, March 29–31, Berlin, Germany.

Sheth, J., & Parvatiyar, A. (1995). The evolution of relationship marketing. *International Business Review, 4*(4), 397–418.

Solomon, R. C., & Flore, F. (2001). *Building trust in business, politics, relationships, and life*. New York: Oxford University Press.

Söellner, A. O. E. (1994). Commitment in exchange relationships: The role of switching costs in building and sustaining competitive advantages. In J. N. Sheth & A. Parvatiyar (Eds.), *Relationship marketing: Theory, methods and applications*. Atlanta: Emory University.

Šonková, T., & Grabowska, M. (2015). Customer engagement: Transactional vs. relationship marketing. *Journal of International Studies, 8*(1), 196–207.

Spekman, R. E. (1988). Strategic supplier selection: Understanding long-term buyer relationships. *Business Horizon, 31*(4), 75–81.

Srinivasan, S., & Hanssens, D. (2009). Marketing firm value: Metrics, methods, findings, and future directions. *Journal of Marketing Research, 46*(3), 293–312.

Stauss, B. (1999). Customer satisfaction: On the state-of-the-art. *Marketing ZFP, 21*(1), 5–24.

Stauss, B., & Seidel, W. (1998). *Complaint management* (2nd ed.). Munich: Hanser.

Steindl-Rast, D. (2004). Gratitude as thankfulness and as gratefulness. In R. A. Emmons & M. E. McCullough (Eds.), *The psychology of gratitude*. New York: Oxford University Press.

Stevenson, L. (2010). *Private sector and enterprise development*. Northampton, MA: Edward Elgar Publishing.

Thurau, T. H., Gwinner, K. P., & Gremler, D. D. (2002). Understanding relationship marketing outcomes: An integration of relational benefits and relationship quality. *Journal of Service Research, 4*(3), 230–247.

U.S. Department of State. (n.d.). *Bosnia and Herzegovina Country Page*. Accessed December 17, 2016, from http://www.state.gov/p/eur/ci/bk/

UN Data. (2016). *Bosnia and Herzegovina: Overview*. Accessed July 17, 2016, from http://data.un.org/CountryProfile.aspx?crName=Bosnia%20and%20Herzegovina

Veseli, N., Ramadani, V., & Rexhepi, G. (2010). *Direct marketing and small businesses*. Berlin: Lambert Academic.

Ward, J. (1997). Growing the family businesses: Special challenges and best practices. *Family Business Review, 10*(4), 323-337.

Willens, E., & Rausch, H. (1969). *Naturalistic viewpoints in psychological research*. New York: Holt, Rinehart and Winston.

World Bank. (2016). *Country overview – Bosnia and Herzegovina*. Accessed August 15, 2016, from http://www.worldbank.org/en/country/bosniaandherzegovina/overview#4

Yin, R. K. (2003). *Case study research: Design and methods*. Thousand Oaks, CA: Sage Publications.

Zand, D. E. (1972). Trust and managerial problem solving. *Administrative Science Quarterly, 17* (2), 229–239.

Zavod za statistiku Bosne i Herzegovine. (2016), *Popis*. Accessed January 4, 2017, from http://www.bhas.ba/

Zemlic, Z. (n.d.) *KPMG Family businesses blog*. Accessed August 19, 2016, from http://www.kpmgfamilybusiness.com/bosnia-and-herzegovina/

The Gender Question and Family Entrepreneurship Research

Ogechi Adeola, Michael Zisuh Ngoasong, and Olaniyi Evans

Women are the largest untapped reservoir of talent in the World.
Hillary Clinton, former Presidential Aspirant, USA

Abstract Gender in family entrepreneurship is still exploratory and, despite an increase in family entrepreneurship research, most of the studies give little or no information role of gender in family business. Existing research on family entrepreneurship tends to focus only or primarily on men, and the women appear invisible in the studies. However, there is little evidence that of extensive research focus on the issue of family entrepreneurship with the aim of building a cohesive understanding of gender in family entrepreneurship and the interactions existing between the different dimensions and components. Consequently, this chapter examines how gender issues are addressed in family entrepreneurship research. In particular, the chapter provides a critical review of the literature around the gender question in entrepreneurship, focusing on the resource-based view, organizational studies and gender in family entrepreneurship. Based on the review, a gender-aware framework is developed depicting three key areas for understanding the gendered process in family entrepreneurship: the determinants of women's entry into family businesses, their gendered roles and the associated outcomes. Finally, implications and future research opportunities are identified and discussed.

Keywords Gender • Family • Entrepreneurship • Family business

---

O. Adeola (✉)
Lagos Business School, Pan Atlantic University, Lagos, Nigeria
e-mail: oadeola@lbs.edu.ng

M.Z. Ngoasong
Open University, Milton Keynes MK7 6AA, UK
e-mail: michael.ngoasong@open.ac.uk

O. Evans
University of Lagos, Lagos, Nigeria
e-mail: evans@analystman.com

V. Ratten et al. (eds.), *Knowledge, Learning and Innovation*, Contributions to Management Science, DOI 10.1007/978-3-319-59282-4_10

1 Introduction

Described as entities owned and controlled by members of a family (Brockhaus, 2004), family businesses constitute 80% of firms in Europe and Asia, and 80–95% of all businesses in Latin America and the United States (Poza & Daugherty, 2014). Family businesses provide 50% of total employment and more than 50% of developed economies' GDP (Shepherd & Zacharakis, 2000). Family business plays a major role in promoting entrepreneurship, skills training, investing for long-term growth, and the dynamism and strength of the whole economy (Siakas, Naaranoja, Vlachakis, & Siakas, 2014). Therefore, as a vital economic engine, the role of family businesses in the economy cannot be ignored.

Gender is defined by Acker (1992, p. 250) as the "patterned, socially produced, distinctions between female and male, feminine and masculine". Since gender is an important concept for understanding how women face skepticism and suffering in family businesses, the gender question in the family business should inspire great interest and reflection (Staffansson, 2015). Gender in family entrepreneurship is still a new concept in entrepreneurial activity. Research into gender issues in family entrepreneurship or the role and the involvement of women in family firms has been driven (Barrett & Moores, 2009; Benavides Velasco, Guzmán Parra, & Quintana García, 2011; Dugan et al., 2011; Hamilton, 2013a, 2013b), especially in recent years, by a general increase in the visibility of women's work as self-employed, the rising number of women entrepreneurs, and the increasing appreciation of gender as a key analytical variable (Rodríguez-Modroño, Gálvez-Muñoz, & Agenjo-Calderón, 2015).

Though there has been a growing interest in gender in entrepreneurial activity, gender is largely unexplored in family entrepreneurship (Sonfield & Lussier, 2009). Research incorporating gender as a key analytical variable is still insufficient, compared to other issues studied regarding family firms. In most analyses, the family firm is the core of the research rather than the individuals. In most studies investigating individuals, the emphasis is on the owner/manager (Hamilton, 2006), even when individual roles are identified in the family business (Heinonen & Hytti, 2011). This chapter, therefore, focuses on the gender aspect.

Considering the international evidence on the significant changes in women's roles and positioning within family businesses (Cappuyns, 2007), the changing dynamics has started to influence theoretical developments. To this extent, gender theory in family business research has begun to contribute to the theoretical reconstruction of family businesses. However, while continuously evolving, the gender question is still largely under-researched within the family business research (Sonfield & Lussier, 2009). Moreover, the role and involvement of women in family businesses is an issue of great interest. An increasing number of women enter family businesses and face many obstacles to their participation/involvement, such as succession, primogeniture, stereotyped roles and inconspicuousness (Jimenez, 2009).

Thus, this chapter confronts and addresses the gender question in family business research. The gender question explores how family business research faces methodological problems of too much emphasis on firms with male owner-managers as respondents, a faulty gendered process, leading to the neglect of 'familiness' even at the core of family business research. Familiness refers to "... the unique bundle of resources a particular firm has because of the systems interactions between the family, its individual members, and the business" (Habbershon and Williams 1999: 11). It can be a source of competitive advantage, value creation and wealth generation in a firm (Monroy, Solís, & Rodríguez-Aceves, 2015), particularly with positive influence of family involvement (Pearson, Carr, & Shaw, 2008). Dye (2010) described Gendering as 'the process of ascribing characteristics of masculinity or femininity, femaleness or maleness to a phenomenon (i.e., a role, position, concept, person, object, organization, or artifact), usually resulting in power and privilege, voice and neglect, or advantage and disadvantage, as drawn along the lines of sex and gender.' In this case, the gendering process is geared towards the male owner-managers.

The purpose, therefore, is to explore the interface between gendered processes and the family entrepreneurship domain. By exploring the extent to which gendered processes are reinforced in family business research, the study unravels how the literature has contributed to our understanding of gendered in family business. This chapter explores three key areas to understand how to identify and resolve the gender question in family entrepreneurship research. It highlights the gender question in family firms: the barriers faced by women regarding entry or collaboration; the inconspicuousness and lack of recognition of their work and, thus the low compensation it receives; and the gendered roles in these businesses. By focusing on gender, the chapter highlights the decision-making process in the household and the business, and related division of roles and responsibilities. It shows how family business research faces methodological problems of too much emphasis on firms with male owner-managers as respondents and the gendered processes, leading to the neglect of 'familiness' even at the core of family business research.

The chapter is organized into six sections. Following this preliminary introduction, the next section presents the gender order which explains the gender question. To answer the gender question, a review of literature follows which explores women and family entrepreneurship, gender in organizational studies and gender in family business. The concluding chapters discuss the findings and provide suggestions for future research.

2 The Gender Order

"A woman's place is in the home", famously declared Aeschylus in 467 B.C. While this dictum is vigorously rejected by women everywhere, the gender order continues to follow societal norms (Eckert & McConnell-Ginet, 2014). According to Hirdman (1992), the gender order is an obvious pattern in the society on a general level and has segregation and hierarchization as its two primary logics. Segregation suggests the stereotypical segregation between men and women, and between masculinity and femininity. Hierarchization is the formation of a gender-based hierarchy with men and masculinity ascribed higher status than women and femininity. The two logics often lead to female subordination and male domination (Staffansson, 2015).

Though women entrepreneurs are found in most industries, segregation still continues between male- and female-dominated businesses (Bolton & Muzio, 2008), and can be found in the rest of the labour market (Statistics Sweden, 2010). In particular, in welfare states where women's participation in the labour market is high, gender segregation is quite striking, as jobs in health care, care for the elderly and childcare are female gender-labelled and female-dominated (Bolton & Muzio, 2008; Statistics Sweden, 2010).

Broomhill and Sharp (2005, p. 103) states: "although many aspects of the traditional gender order remain intact, it has been profoundly disrupted by restructuring within the labour market and also by the decline of the nuclear family and other socio-economic changes affecting gender arrangements within households." Such changes have led to more complexity in existing gender arrangements. To further complicate the process, changes and continuities in gender order are not evenly experienced, leading to growing polarisation in gender roles and order in different socio-economic groups. Thus, the gender order explains the gender question in family entrepreneurship research. To consider the gender order, a review of literature follows which encompasses women and family entrepreneurship, using the resource-based view, gender in organizational studies and finally gender in family business. Our research focuses on women as 'owner-manager' and not women as 'workers', providing an in-depth review of literature on how gender issues are addressed in family entrepreneurship research.

3 Women and Family Entrepreneurship: Resource-Based View

One of the most widely used theories in the organizational literature, the resource-based view (RBV) is an approach to attaining competitive advantage that emerged in the 1980s, after Wernerfelt's (1984) study on "*The Resource-Based View of the Firm*". The proponents of RBV argue that firms should look inside the firm to find its unique sources of competitive advantage instead of looking for it in the competitive environment (Barney, 1991; Wernerfelt, 1984). Essentially, RBV is a theory that views resources as essential to superior firm performance. Resources can be tangible or intangible. While tangible resources consist of land, capital, and machinery among others, intangible resources comprise skills, knowledge and brand reputation among others (Runyan, Huddleston, & Swinney, 2006).

There are two important assumptions in the RBV. Firstly, resources are immobile. That is, resources do not move from company to company, at least in the short-run. Therefore, rivals' resources and processes cannot be easily replicated. Secondly, resources are heterogeneous. In other words, organizational capabilities and resources differ from one company to another. Therefore, RBV assumes that by using their individual bundles of resources, companies achieve competitive advantage (Jurevicius, 2013). Although having immobile and heterogeneous resources are crucial to attaining competitive advantage, these are not enough in order to sustain competitive advantage. The resources must also be VRIO: valuable, rare, inimitable and organized (Rothaermel, 2013). Only the firms that are capable of exploiting their valuable, rare, inimitable and organized resources can attain sustained competitive advantage (Jurevicius, 2013; Runyan et al., 2006).

A small number of studies have considered family firms from an RBV perspective (Rau, 2014; Zahra, Hayton, & Salvato, 2004). Family firms are such that must rely heavily on the resource of family skills. This is especially true of female small business owners, as 85% of them have no employees other than the female owner (Adler, 1999; Runyan et al., 2006). However, while access to tangible resources may differ by gender (Marlow & Patton, 2005), the facility to exploit intangible resources may equalize women's chances of success in family businesses (Runyan et al., 2006).

3.1 Gender in Organizational Studies

The glass ceiling, a phrase coined in the 1980s, is a metaphor for the invisible and artificial barriers that hinder women from moving up the corporate ladder (Johns, 2013). The Glass Ceiling Commission (1995) reported several barriers to the success of women in reaching the top of the corporate ladder. These included societal barriers such as opportunity and attainment, cultural, gender, and prejudice and bias (Hurley, Hurley, Choudhary, & Choudhary, 2016; Johns, 2013).

However, in contrast to The Glass Ceiling Commission (1995) and other earlier studies, Cole (1997) found that women were neither hindered because of their gender, nor up against the dreaded glass ceiling. The women in Cole's (1997) study had a positive outlook on their careers. They had accessed sectors conventionally viewed as masculine, such as the construction industry. Epstein, Seron, Oglensky, and Saute (2014) argued that Cole's (1997) findings were made possible by the introduction of flexible schedules, which enable women to combine child care and their professional responsibilities (Dumas, 1998; Epstein et al., 2014).

Notwithstanding Cole's (1997) findings, organization theory has mostly ignored gender issues (Staffansson, 2015). Studies such as Calás and Smircich (1996) have argued that organizational scholarship is primarily written by men, for men, and about men. They noted that to make the field more inclusive, feminist theories would have to be seen not as only women's issue. In furtherance of Calás and Smircich (1996), Alvesson and Billing (2009) argued two strong motives for taking an interest in gender, which are injustice and business management. In this regard, the authors suggested that women are strongly underrepresented in higher positions, and have less autonomy and control over work.

In recent decade, increasing attention has been paid to gender in entrepreneurship (Ahl, 2006; Jimenez, 2009; Heinonen & Hytti, 2011; Staffansson, 2015). In entrepreneurship research, gender studies have mainly examined the experiences of women (Bruni, Gherardi, & Poggio, 2014; Henry, Foss, & Ahl, 2016). The key role of the gender perspective in entrepreneurial research is that it shows sundry ways of entrepreneurship and diverse ways of running a business, without constraints of 'arrant' masculinity that grows on risk-taking, technical innovation, full-time employment, and huge ambitions for growth (Pettersson, 2008). Studies such as Bjursell and Melin (2011) have therefore argued for a shift away from the current focus of the entrepreneur as masculine towards appreciating entrepreneurship as a blend of the feminine and the masculine. Viewing entrepreneurial identity as a narrative construction, the authors noted the impact of the move from the family context to the business context on the individual woman's identity process. As a result of gendered expectations, women in family firms may find themselves in circumstances where they are not regarded as potential leaders/owners by the older generation. This is because, in family firms, the construction of meaning and identity among family members are context-influenced by family, business, and gender (Bjursell & Melin, 2011).

In recent years, both in the empirical and theoretical literature in the entrepreneurship domain, scholars are actively introducing gendered analyses which depict the limitations of much of the entrepreneurial literature to date (Ahl, 2006; Marlow & McAdam, 2013; Al-Dajani, Bika, Collins, & Swail, 2014). These analyses portray the contemporary entrepreneurial discourse as fundamentally masculine, and constrains the character of an entrepreneur and the definition of entrepreneurship (Ahl, 2006; Al-Dajani et al., 2014). Thus, women are depicted to be outsiders or intruders to entrepreneurship (Taylor & Marlow, 2009), which diminishes the potential contribution of women, as family business actors and entrepreneurs, to the economy and society as a whole (Al-Dajani et al., 2014). Besides, the outcomes of women businesses are considered as under-par, because they are risk-averse, smaller, and lacking growth orientation (Brush, 1992 as cited in Al-Dajani et al., 2014). In fact, almost any conceivable damaging business term possible has been used to describe the hapless female entrepreneur (Marlow, 2013).

4 Gender in Family Business

The woman in the family is an important role (Staffansson, 2015). Surprisingly, little research has been done on investigating the role of the woman in family entrepreneurship/businesses. Studies of gender in entrepreneurship are increasing, but those devoted to the role of women in family entrepreneurship are still fragmented (Heinonen & Hytti, 2011). Despite the role and the involvement of women in family firms, it is not until recent decades that gender is incorporated as a result of the mix of feminist theories, and social, and business and cultural history (Gálvez, 2004; Rodríguez-Modroño et al., 2015). Moreover, the studies on family firms focus on the role of women in the course of inheritance (Cole, 1997; Dumas, 1992; Vera & Dean, 2005) and on relational family dynamics, underscoring principally three spheres related to the procreative role of women: making the next generation, educating future business leaders, and transmitting values (Dugan et al., 2011), or the linkage between their working experience restricted to a few sectors and their entrepreneurial abilities (Gálvez & Fernández Pérez, 2007).

Historically, women have played important roles in the establishment, management, and expansion of family firms, either visibly or hiddenly (Dumas, 1998; Vera & Dean, 2005). Although women have often and directly been involved in daily management, historically they have received little recognition, either in the form of a management position or a reasonable salary (Hollander & Bukowitz, 1990; Nelton, 1998). The relative invisibility of women in entrepreneurship highlights the need to unravel the differences and the inimitable role of women entrepreneurs (Hamilton, 2013a, 2013b); their unique experiences and their natural, feminine styles. Indeed, the literature has argued that women possess some unique qualities vital for business success, making women a valuable resource (Miller, 2012; Salganicoff, 1990). Studies such as Francis (1999) has suggested that most women have characteristics and skills deemed necessary for the success of managers and leaders. These include the ability to multitask, and to trust instinct and intuition rather than analysis and rationality.

Some authors even adopted the term 'emotional leadership' in reference to women, especially in family firms (Jimenez, 2009; Lyman, 1988; Meroño-Cerdán & López-Nicolás, 2017; Ward, 1987). The view is that women have high emotional intelligence: the ability, or skill to assess and manage the emotions of oneself and of others. In family firms, women are capable of assessing and managing the behaviour of family members and of ensuring consideration for people's feelings. Women have "certain gender characteristics that make them better suited to the roles of caretaker, peacemaker and conflict solver, roles that are fundamental to the success and survival of the family firm" (Salganicoff, 1990, as cited in Staffansson, 2015, p. 1).

For example, Colli et al. (2003, as cited in Rodríguez-Modroño et al., 2015, p. 8), who studied family firms in Italy, Great Britain and Spain in the nineteenth and twentieth centuries, showed that 'women constituted an important hidden resource, although their participation was not formally recorded. Women contributed vital capital resources and access to trusted business and family networks. In nineteenth Century Great Britain, for example, women were under the protection of their spouses and could not inherit until the second half of the nineteenth Century, so that many were de facto partners in a business, but lacked the legal right to the business capital or other properties. This pattern was also fairly common in Europe in the twentieth Century. However, business interests and the family were fully interlinked and the phantom tasks performed by women extended even to finance".

Another study by Parsons and Bales (1956), which adopted traditional functionalist approaches to gender analysis, found that, in a capitalist society, role specialization was necessary within the family, with men involved in the cut-throat world of business and the women carrying out the roles of nurturing. The presumed mutual exclusivity of these roles provided justification for the type of family that became dominant: the 'traditional' or breadwinner/housewife family (Bradley, 2007).

Despite the considerable change in patterns of employment and family composition which have altered the opportunities available for venturing in recent decades, Arber and Ginn (1991) contended that family and work are still independent spheres, with women's advances in market position not commensurate with advances in their family position. In fact, Ahl (2004, p. 167) sums this aptly, "the existence of a line dividing a public sphere of work from a private sphere of home, family and children is also taken for granted in the entrepreneurship literature". Remarkably, there are now approaches in the institutional entrepreneurship literature that integrate these two spheres (e.g. Bika, 2012). Also, the social capital approach to 'familiness construct' and its components is rectifying this deficiency (Pearson, et al. 2008), and thus views the family and the business as intertwined, rather than as separate entities. Though this is auspicious to the field of family entrepreneurship, the leaning in the existing literature is still to abstract women in family business as side-lined through paternalism or patriarchy (Hamilton, 2006).

A stream of the literature also delved into why women's role and involvement in family firms are hidden (e.g. Gálvez & Fernández Pérez, 2007; Rodríguez-Modroño et al., 2015). For example, Gálvez and Fernández Pérez (2007) found that the bulk of women's role and involvement in family firms are executed without a contract, or benefits, and even when women receive some sort of compensation, it is always less than their male counterparts, though the variance is not attributable to differences in productivity. In the nineteenth Century when women often helped out family firms in agriculture and commerce without wages or recognition, many women managed the businesses for years, and yet despite abundant responsibilities, were never accorded as owners. Even in large mercantile cities where women managed the business while the men were away (Fernández, 1996), their participation was dependent on the wishes of their male folks.

Also, in a recent study, Rodríguez-Modroño et al. (2015) identified the reasons why women contributions to family firms have been hidden. First, due to the division of labor between the family and business subsystems, women are usually assigned informal support functions such as assistants, or mediators between the family members (Gillis-Donovan & Moynihan-Bradt, 1990) or sometimes, an emotional leadership role (Salganicoff, 1990). Second, because the cultural and legal framework barred the incorporation of women into the labor market, the management and ownership of business, or sometimes impede the formal recognition of women in family firms (Fernández & Hamilton, 2007; Gálvez & Fernández Pérez, 2007). Thus, the works of women and their roles in business are not only marginalized but repressed, and even purposely distorted (Wiesner-Hanks, 2001).

Using a radical subjectivist view of economics, Canada, Barrett and Moores (2009), in a case study of 16 women in leadership positions in family businesses in the US, the UK, the Middle East, Southeast Asia, and Australia, investigated the various contextual factors of women's entrepreneurship in the family business. The study took the first step away from the limitations of a particular feminist ideology towards creating a gender-aware framework of entrepreneurship in the manner of

Brush, de Bruin, and Welter (2009) by providing a new theoretical direction for exploring gender and family entrepreneurship. The findings concerning the entrepreneurial imagination, self-organization, empathy, and modularity challenge existing ideas of women's entrepreneurship, illustrating how family business prepares rather than encumbers women for entrepreneurship and leadership within, and beyond the family.

Daughter succession is another under-researched area in family entrepreneurship (Al-Dajani et al., 2014). The available studies on succession planning in family businesses show that many family firms still utilize the primogeniture criterion, where the firstborn male child takes over the family firm (Deng, 2015). Glover's (2014) '*Gender, Power and Succession in Family Farm Business*' provides useful insights into how power and gender issues operate in the succession process of small firms, in line with Robert Smith's theory of matriarchy. Applying an ethnographic approach to a family farm in the Midlands of England, the author depicted how one daughter navigated gender issues as she became an eventual successor. "To this extent, Glover's article turns the focus of scholarly enquiry away from the role of traditional farmers' wives and shows how contemporary women enter the farm business through succession rather than marriage in the twenty-first century. In this family business context, gender bias emerges as a determinant of routine farm management but not of strategy" (Al-Dajani et al., 2014, p. 13).

In Deng's (2015) study, only 23% of all single family successors in the sample are females, indicating a high preference for male heirs. "Family successions are significantly more likely to occur when the predecessor has a son. Under specific family structures, such as when both genders are represented among the predecessors' children, the number of female successors decreases to 19% of family successions with one successor. Sons increase the likelihood of CEO succession contest constraints. We observe that the selected female family successors seem to be equipped with higher levels of human capital compared to the selected male family successors" (p. 38). The study thus indicates that male successors are chosen not because of higher human capital but because of the gender preferences for male heirs. The primogeniture criterion frees fathers from the unpleasant task of comparing and choosing between their children (Staffansson, 2015).

Consistent with Cole (1997), one of the real opportunities for women to reach the highest positions in business (i.e. president, a member of the board of directors) are family firms. The family firm is, therefore, an ideal setting to prepare daughters as a leader, in the sense that the father serves as a natural mentor (Dumas, 1998). However, daughters come up against substantial obstacles to gaining power in family firms. Founders are usually reluctant to hand over the running of the firm to their daughter (Jimenez, 2009). Often, daughters join the family firm, especially at times of crisis or when the father has no sons (Dumas, 1998). Vera and Dean (2005) noted that, though the father is the definer of his daughter's position in the firm, a daughter may face many problems once she takes over the running of the firm. The authors added that the daughter could, however, have higher credibility and self-confidence if armed with experience outside of the family firm.

Recent studies have challenged the stereotyped perception of the husband being the lead (male) entrepreneur. For example, Deacon, Harris, and Worth (2014), using a multiple exploratory interview and ethnographic approaches, delved into contemporary gender and entrepreneurship theories to unravel "the division of labour, capitals and capacities and gendered identities within husband and wife heterosexual copreneurial businesses... Expelling the myth of the "male lead entrepreneur", this study found that entrepreneurial identity and roles and responsibilities within a copreneurial business are shared and complementary, and are dependent upon the unique capacities and capitals of each partner. While there is evidence of duties that could be stereotypically described as either "men's work or women's work", there was no apparent role tension between the partners. Thus, no partner's contribution was deemed more valuable than the other" (p. 317). The authors thus suggested that copreneurship is not a process of gender but a gendered process whereby the former designates a fixed physiological typology and the latter a fluidity of psychological application. The study questions the appropriateness of assigning (son/father, mother/daughter) labels to the husband and wife, which have gendered connotations and carry distinct societal expectations (Al-Dajani et al., 2014; McAdam & Marlow, 2010).

It must be noted that the increased recognition of women's work, the social advances towards greater equality, and women's access to formal education have enabled family firms to train women as future managers, and the resulting growth in women entrepreneurs and woman heads of family firms has reduced the gender gap in business (Jimenez, 2009; Rodríguez-Modroño et al., 2015). For example, Jimenez (2009), in a review of 48 articles, 23 books and 3 doctoral dissertations published since 1985 on women and family businesses, found an increase in the involvement and role of women in family businesses.

However, Rodríguez-Modroño et al. (2015) maintained that the important role and involvement of women in family firms is still underappreciated since their participation is not necessarily as owners/managers, but still very often as collaborators and informal leaders. Other studies such as Sharma (2004) and Vadnjal and Zupan (2009) have also shown how women are still under-recorded, therefore unrecognised as business people in the official statistics of companies, and are stereotyped into reproductive, informal and secondary roles. Occupational segregation, underrepresentation in management, and societal expectations restrict women, affect their motivation and goals for their businesses. Jimenez (2009) further highlighted the difficulties or obstacles that women continue to face in family firms, especially the lack of appreciation for their contributions, exemplified by inconspicuousness, stereotyped roles, succession and primogeniture. Indeed, women in family businesses face not only constraints faced by all businesswomen (Starr & Yudkin, 1996), but also problems unique to their situation.

5 Gendered Processes in Family Entrepreneurship

Understanding the Gender Question in Family Entrepreneurship

Based on a critically review of the literature on women and family entrepreneurship from a resource-based view, organizational studies and gender in family business, it has become clear that a thorough conceptual and methodological re-thinking is needed not only to change the focus on male owners/managers as respondents, but also the stereotypical assumptions reinforced in the existing studies. Contemporary entrepreneurial discourse is fundamentally masculine and constrains the character of an entrepreneur. Historically, women have played important roles in the management of family firms, either visibly or hidden, although they have received little recognition. Today there are many women entrepreneurs, yet the dominant model of an entrepreneur is a male. We, therefore, concur with Bjursell and Melin (2011) who argued for a shift away from the current focus of the entrepreneur as masculine towards appreciating entrepreneurship as a mix of the feminine and the masculine. Family entrepreneurship research, policy and practice should be released from the shackles of masculine domination through a reconstruction of the images, narratives and discourses of entrepreneurs, entrepreneurship and entrepreneurial practices.

Three key areas of research highlight the gender question in family firms: the determinants of women's entry into family businesses, the gendered roles in the family business and the associated outcome (Fig. 1). Although Aeschylus's notion that "A woman's place is in the home" is being vigorously rejected by women, Fig. 1 illustrates that the gender order still continues. In terms of determinants, the first key area, an increasing number of women enter family businesses today and face many obstacles to their involvement, such as inconspicuousness, stereotyped roles, succession and primogeniture. They face the glass ceiling of societal barriers such as opportunity and attainment, cultural, gender, and prejudice and bias (Gillis-Donovan & Moynihan-Bradt, 1990; Jimenez, 2009). Identifying these determinants and the extent to which they serve as either incentives or barriers is a starting point to understanding and resolving the gender question in entrepreneurship.

Secondly, the gender order continues to deter women in the labor market, the management and ownership of business, and their formal recognition in family firms. The managerial and operational activities that women undertake in their roles in family businesses are still marginalized, repressed, and even distorted. Their important roles and involvement in family firms are underappreciated and under-recorded, as they are stereotyped into reproductive, informal and secondary roles. In order to resolve the gender order (and the myth of the "male lead entrepreneur"), our proposed gender-aware framework recognizes the resources and support available to help women make informed choices about their roles in family businesses. Indeed, the family firm is an ideal setting to prepare women as leaders. The family business should, therefore, prepare rather than encumber women for entrepreneurship and leadership within, and beyond the family, because the real opportunities

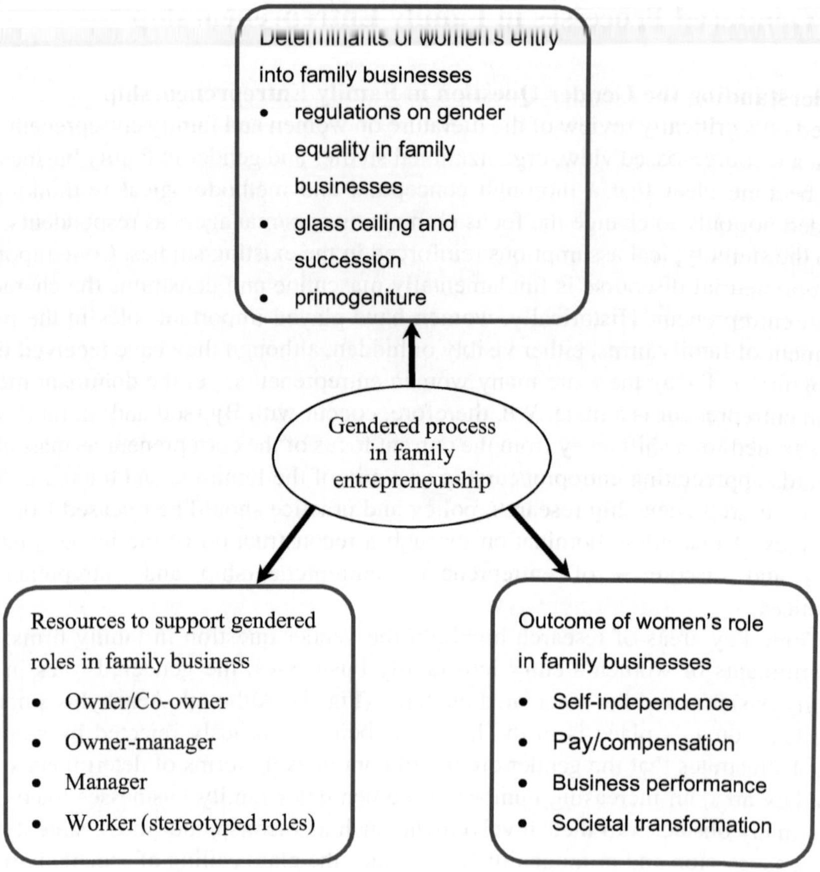

Fig. 1 The gender question in family entrepreneurship

for women to reach the highest positions in business (i.e. president, a member of the board of directors) are family firms.

Thirdly, the outcome for encouraging and supporting women's roles in family businesses is beneficial where it promotes self-independence for the woman, as seen in social and economic independence and wealth creation. It can also serve as a means to achieve societal transformation, for example through successful women in business serving as role models, promoting and empowering other women (Kimbu & Ngoasong, 2016). Thus, the gender question in family entrepreneurship also has to take into account the nature of the outcome of women's involvement in the family business both as an end in itself (business performance and self-independence) but also as a means of encouraging more women entrepreneurs and managers in family businesses.

6 Future Research Opportunities

Progress has been made on gender in family business research, but many important areas and research questions remain. For example, a number of gaps can be identified in the understanding of the gendered processes in family businesses by applying the framework depicted in Fig. 1 to different family businesses in different contexts. The gender factor is believed to be a function of the family business context. In this regard, Staffansson (2015) suggested areas for further research, such as the kind of society, the type of business or industry, the types of customers served, the prevailing gendered processes, and the gendered overlap between family and business. Also, Jimenez (2009) suggested areas for further research in regard to women supposed emotional leadership; succession and primogeniture, and the effects on family business; women's insignificance in the family business; the making of a professional career in the family firm; and the running of the family firm, involvement and motivation. This is related to determinants of women's entry into family businesses and their gendered roles.

Many studies used the essentialist view of men and women to propose the view that women have unique traits; this is limiting and biased towards heterosexuality. Future research should apply Acker (1990, 1992) model of four gendered interactions in the family business context, in order to extend the organizational gendering processes to the family gendering processes. According to Staffansson (2015), Ackers' model is based on the assumption that work and everyday life are separate, though work is the first priority of the worker. It has to be noted that work and family overlap, the gendering processes in business and family must also overlap. As suggested by Kvande (2002) and Staffansson (2015), it would be interesting to explore how women construct femininity in family businesses; how different versions of femininity are constructed through relations with men in family businesses in different industries; how women choose to promote themselves; and how they see themselves as men's equals.

As Hamilton (2013a, 2013b) noted, academic research perpetuates the discourse of entrepreneurship as a form of masculinity. A study of the theory of male-dominated entrepreneurship would be atopic worthy of investigation. Such enquiry would need to challenge the primary discourse that women are inconspicuous. Gender in family entrepreneurship research should focus more on "how gender is accomplished rather than study what it is" (Ahl, 2004, p. 192). There is need to understand the family business as a blend of the feminine and the masculine (Bjursell & Melin, 2011). A more grounded understanding and conceptualization of gender in the entrepreneurial field, as argued by Wharton (2009) and Hamilton (2013a, b), would make family entrepreneurship more inclusive. According to Fletcher's critical theory approach (Fletcher, 2014), there is little understanding of how family settings, business structures and practices create relations of power or asymmetry. Future research should, therefore, question the norms of the gendered processes in family businesses.

Another promising avenue to pursue would be to study the different family businesses inherited and run by women in male-labelled or male-dominated industries, such as the real estate or the construction industry. For example, how do family and business overlap? How do they negotiate femininity while pursuing their career? Is it different from the non-family business?

It is necessary to move beyond conventional molds of the family unit. Al-Dajani et al. (2014) suggested that future research should explore gender in family business, in the context of stepfamilies, single parent families and extended families. This can offer ample research opportunities to exploring gendered processes within the family business from all directions.

There is a need to investigate the complex process of 'familiness' and entrepreneurship with a special emphasis on gender. Further studies would, therefore, need to focus more on capturing the notion of 'familiness' as the focal point in family entrepreneurship.

7 Conclusion

This chapter has explored the gender in family entrepreneurship research and provided insights into how women face inconspicuousness, stereotyped roles, succession and primogeniture in family businesses. It highlights the need to investigate the complex process of 'familiness' and entrepreneurship with a particular emphasis on gender. Research into gender issues in family entrepreneurship has been driven in recent years by a general increase in visibility of women's work as women entrepreneurs, and the increasing appreciation of gender as a key analytical variable. While it can be said that gender theory in family business research has begun to contribute to the theoretical reconstruction of family businesses, gender in family business research is still evolving, as the gender question remains largely under-researched within the family business research. Research incorporating gender as a key factor is still insufficient, compared to other factors studied in family business research.

References

Acker, J. (1990). Hierarchies, jobs, bodies: A theory of gendered organizations. *Gender and Society, 4*(2), 139–158.

Acker, J. (1992). Gendering organizational theory. In A. Mills & P. Tancred (Eds.), *Gendering organizational analysis* (pp. 248–260). London: Sage.

Adler, N. J. (1999). Global entrepreneurs: Women, myths and history. *Global Focus, 11*(4), 125–134.

Ahl, H. (2004). *The making of the female entrepreneur*. Jonkoping International Business School Dissertation Series No. 015. Sweden: Jonkoping University.

Ahl, H. (2006). Why research on women entrepreneurs needs new directions. *Entrepreneurship Theory and Practice, 30*(5), 595–621.

Al-Dajani, H., Bika, Z., Collins, L., & Swail, J. (2014). Gender and family business: New theoretical directions. *International Journal of Gender and Entrepreneurship, 6*(3), 218–230.

Alvesson, M., & Billing, Y. D. (2009). *Understanding gender and organizations*. London: Sage.

Arber, S., & Ginn, J. (1991). *Gender and later life*. London: Sage.

Barney, J. B. (1991). Firm resources and sustained competitive advantage. *Journal of Management, 17*, 99–120.

Barrett, M., & Moores, K. (2009). *Women in family business leadership roles. Daughters on the stage*. Cheltenham: Edward Elgar Publishing.

Benavides Velasco, C. A., Guzmán Parra, V. F., & Quintana García, C. (2011). Evolución de la literatura sobre empresa familiar como disciplina científica. *Cuadernos de Economía y Dirección de la Empresa, 14*, 78–90.

Bika, Z. (2012). Entrepreneurial sons, patriarchy and the colonels' experiment in Thessaly, rural Greece. *Entrepreneurship and Regional Development, 24*(3–4), 235–257.

Bjursell, C., & Melin, L. (2011). Proactive and reactive plots: Narratives in entrepreneurial identity construction. *International Journal of Gender and Entrepreneurship, 3*(3), 218–235.

Bolton, S., & Muzio, D. (2008). The paradoxical processes of feminization in the professions: The case of established, aspiring and semi-professions. *Work, Employment and Society, 22*(2), 281–299.

Bradley, H. (2007). *Gender matters*. Cambridge: Polity Press.

Brockhaus, R. H. (2004). Family business succession: Suggestions for future research. *Family Business Review, 17*(2), 165–177.

Broomhill, R., & Sharp, R. (2005). The changing male breadwinner model in Australia: A new gender order? *Labour and Industry: A Journal of the Social and Economic Relations of Work, 16*(1), 103–127.

Bruni, A., Gherardi, S., & Poggio, B. (2014). *Gender and entrepreneurship: An ethnographic approach*. Abingdon: Routledge.

Brush, C. G. (1992). Research on women business owners: Past trends, a new perspective and future directions. *Entrepreneurship: Theory and Practice, 16*(4), 5–31.

Brush, C. G., de Bruin, A., & Welter, F. (2009). A gender-aware framework for women's entrepreneurship. *International Journal of Gender and Entrepreneurship, 1*(1), 8–24.

Calás, M., & Smircich, L. (1996). From "the woman's" point of view: Feminist approaches to organization studies. In S. Clegg, C. Hardy, & W. Nord (Eds.), *Handbook of organization studies* (pp. 218–257). London: Sage.

Cappuyns, K. (2007). Women behind the scenes in family businesses. *Electronic Journal of Family Business Studies, 1*(1), 38–61.

Cole, P. M. (1997). Women in family business. *Family Business Review, 10*(4), 353–371. doi:10.1111/j.1741-6248.1997.00353.x.

Colli, A., Fernández Pérez, P., & Rose, M. B. (2003). National determinants of family firm development? Family firms in Britain, Spain, and Italy in the nineteenth and twentieth centuries. *Enterprise and Society, 4*(1), 28–64.

Deacon, J., Harris, J., & Worth, L. (2014). Who leads? Fresh insights into roles and responsibilities in a heterosexual copreneurial business. *International Journal of Gender and Entrepreneurship, 6*(3), 317–335.

Deng, X. (2015). Father-daughter succession in China: Facilitators and challenges. *Journal of Family Business Management, 5*(1), 38–54.

Dugan, A. M., Krone, S. P., LeCouvie, K., Pendergast, J. M., Kenyon-Rouvinez, D. H., & Schuman, A. M. (2011). *A woman's place: The crucial roles of women in family business*. New York: Palgrave MacMillan.

Dumas, C. (1992). Integrating the daughter into family business management. *Entrepreneurship, Theory, and Practice, 16*(4), 41–56.

Dumas, C. (1998). Women's pathways to participation and leadership in the family-owned firm. *Family Business Review, 11*(3), 219–228.

Dye, K. (2010). Gendering. In A. J. Mills, G. Durepos, & E. Wiebe (Eds.), *Encyclopedia of case study research* (Vol. 2). Thousand Oaks, CA: Sage.

Eckert, P., & McConnell-Ginet, S. (2014). *Language and gender* (2nd ed.). Cambridge: Cambridge University Press.

Epstein, C. F., Seron, C., Oglensky, B., & Saute, R. (2014). *The part-time paradox: Time norms, professional life, family and gender*. Abingdon: Routledge.

Fernández Pérez, P. (1996). El rostro familiar de la metrópoli. In L. M. Enciso (coord.), *La burguesía española en la edad moderna* (pp. 280–298). Valladolid: Universidad de Valladolid.

Fernández Pérez, P., & Hamilton, E. (2007). Gender and family firms: An interdisciplinary approach. *Documents de Treball de la Facultat de Ciències Econòmiques i Empresarials Collecció*.

Fletcher, D. (2014). Family business inquiry as a critical social science. In L. Melin & M. Nordqvist (Eds.), *The sage handbook of family business*. Thousand Oaks, CA: Sage.

Francis, A. E. (1999). *The daughter also rises: How women overcome obstacles and advance in the family-owned business*. Rudi.

Gálvez, L. (2004). Logros y retos del análisis de género en la Historia Económica de la Empresa. *ICE Historia Empresarial, 812*, 77–89.

Gálvez, L., & Fernández Pérez, P. (2007). Female entrepreneurship in Spain during the nineteenth and twentieth centuries. *Business History Review, 81*(3), 495–515.

Gillis-Donovan, J., & Moynihan-Bradt, C. (1990). The power of invisible women in the family business. *Family Business Review, 3*(2), 153–167. doi:10.1111/j.17416248.1990.00153.x.

Glover, J. (2014). Gender, power and succession in family farm business. *International Journal of Gender and Entrepreneurship, 6*(3), 276–295.

Habbershon, T. G., & Williams, M. L. (1999). A resource-based framework for assessing the strategic advantages of family firms. *Family Business Review, 12*(1), 1–25.

Hamilton, E. (2006). Who's story is it anyway? Narrative accounts of the role of women in founding and establishing family businesses. *International Small Business Journal, 24*(3), 253–271.

Hamilton, E. (2013a). The discourse of entrepreneurial masculinities (and femininities). *Entrepreneurship and Regional Development, 25*(1–2), 90–99.

Hamilton, E. (2013b). *Entrepreneurship across generations: Narrative, gender and learning in family business*. Northampton: Edward Elgar Publishing.

Heinonen, J., & Hytti, U. (2011). *Gender in family firms: A literature review*. University of Turku, School of Economics, TSEEntre1, Pori Unit 2.

Henry, C., Foss, L., & Ahl, H. (2016). Gender and entrepreneurship research: A review of methodological approaches. *International Small Business Journal, 34*(3), 217–241.

Hirdman, Y. (1992). *Den socialistiska hemmafrun och andra kvinnohistorier*. Stockholm: Carlssons Förlag.

Hollander, B. S., & Bukowitz, W. R. (1990). Women, family culture, and family business. *Family Business Review, 3*(2), 139–151.

Hurley, D., Hurley, D., Choudhary, A., & Choudhary, A. (2016). Factors influencing attainment of CEO position for women. *Gender in Management: An International Journal, 31*(4), 250–265.

Jimenez, R. M. (2009). Research on women in family firms – Current status and future directions. *Family Business Review, 22*(1), 53–64.

Johns, M. L. (2013, Winter). Breaking the glass ceiling: Structural, cultural, and organizational barriers preventing women from achieving senior and executive positions. *Perspectives in Health Information Management*.

Jurevicius, O. (2013). *All you need to know about a resource-based view – Strategic management insight* [Online]. Accessed February 22, 2017, from https://www.strategicmanagementinsight.com/topics/resource-based-view.html

Kimbu, A. N., & Ngoasong, M. Z. (2016). Women as vectors of social entrepreneurship. *Annals of Tourism Research, 60*, 63–79.
Kvande, E. (2002). Doing masculinities in organizational restructuring. *NORA – Nordic Journal of Feminist and Gender Research, 10*(1), 16–25.
Lyman, A. R. (1988). Life in the family circle. *Family Business Research, 1*(4), 383–398.
Marlow, S. (2013). Conclusion: Setting research agendas. In M. McAdam (Ed.), *Female entrepreneurship* (pp. 94–107). Abingdon: Routledge.
Marlow, S., & McAdam, M. (2013). Gender and entrepreneurship: Advancing debate and challenging myths; exploring the mystery of the under-performing female entrepreneur. *International Journal of Entrepreneurial Behaviour and Research, 19*(1), 114–124.
Marlow, S., & Patton, D. (2005). All credit to men? Entrepreneurship, finance and gender. *Entrepreneurship Theory and Practice, 29*, 717–736.
McAdam, M., & Marlow, S. (2010). *Gender practices and practicing gender in copreneurial teams*. London: Institute for Small Business and Entrepreneurship Conference.
Meroño-Cerdán, Á. L., & López-Nicolás, C. (2017). Women in management: Are family firms somehow special? *Journal of Management & Organization, 23*(2), 224–240.
Miller, J. B. (2012). *Toward a new psychology of women*. Boston: Beacon Press.
Monroy, V. I. B., Solís, E. R. R., & Rodríguez-Aceves, L. (2015). Familiness and its relationship with performance in Mexican family firms. *Academy of Strategic Management Journal, 14*(2), 1.
Nelton, S. (1998). The rise of women in family firms: A call for research now. *Family Business Review, 11*(3), 215–218. doi:10.1111/j.1741-6248.1998.00215.x.
Parsons, T., & Bales, R. F. (1956). *Family socialization and interaction process* (Vol. 7). Psychology Press.
Pearson, A. W., Carr, J. C., & Shaw, J. C. (2008). Toward a theory of familiness: A social capital perspective. *Entrepreneurship Theory and Practice, 32*(6), 949–969.
Pettersson, K. (2008). Hur påverkas kvinnors företagande av familj och privatliv? In P. Larsson, U. Göransson, & M. Lagerholm (Eds.), *Sesam öppna dig! Perspektiv på kvinnors företagande*. Stockholm: Vinnova.
Poza, E. J., & Daugherty, M. S. (2014). *Family business* (4th ed.). Mason, OH: South-Western Cengage Learning.
Rau, S. B. (2014). Resource-based view of family firms. In L. Melin, M. Nordqvist, & P. Sharma (Eds.), *The sage handbook of family business* (pp. 321–340). London: Sage.
Rodríguez-Modroño, P., Gálvez-Muñoz, L., & Agenjo-Calderón, A. (2015). *The hidden role of women in family firms* (No. 15.01).
Rothaermel, F. (2013). *Strategic management: Gaining and sustaining competitive advantage, concepts and cases* (2nd ed.). New York: McGraw-Hill.
Runyan, R. C., Huddleston, P., & Swinney, J. (2006). Entrepreneurial orientation and social capital as small firm strategies: A study of gender differences from a resource-based view. *The International Entrepreneurship and Management Journal, 2*(4), 455.
Salganicoff, M. (1990). Women in family businesses: Challenges and opportunities. *Family Business Review, 3*(2), 125–137.
Sharma, P. (2004). An overview of the field of family business studies: Current status and directions for future. *Family Business Review, 17*(1), 1–36.
Shepherd, D. A., & Zacharakis, A. (2000). Structuring family business succession: An analysis of the future leader's decision making. *Entrepreneurship: Theory and Practice, 24*(4), 25–25.
Siakas, K., Naaranoja, M., Vlachakis, S., & Siakas, E. (2014). Family businesses in the new economy: How to survive and develop in times of financial crisis. *Procedia Economics and Finance, 9*, 331–341.
Sonfield, M., & Lussier, R. N. (2009). Gender in family business ownership and management: A six-country analysis. *International Journal of Gender and Entrepreneurship, 1*(2), 96–117.
Staffansson Pauli, K. (2015). Gender theory and the family business. In M. Nordqvist, L. Melin, M. Waldkirch, & G. Kumeto (Eds.), *Theoretical perspectives on family businesses* (pp. 191–210). Cheltenham: Edward Elgar Publishing. doi:10.4337/9781783479665.00018.

Starr, J., & Yudkin, M. (1996). *Women entrepreneurs: A review of current research* (Vol. 15). Wellesley Centers for Women.

Statistics Sweden. (2010). *Women and men in Sweden 2010*. Örebro: Statistics Sweden.

Taylor, S., & Marlow, S. (2009). *Engendering entrepreneurship: Why can't a woman be more like a man?* Paper Presented at the 26th EURAM Conference, Liverpool, UK.

The Glass Ceiling Commission. (1995). *Good for business: Making full use of the nation's human capital*. US Department of Labor.

Vadnjal, J., & Zupan, B. (2009). The role of women in family businesses. *Economic and Business Review, 11*(2), 159–177.

Vera, C. F., & Dean, M. A. (2005). An examination of the challenges daughters face in family business succession. *Family Business Review, 18*(4), 321–346.

Ward, J. L. (1987). *Keeping the family business healthy: How to plan for continuing growth, profitability, and family leadership*. San Francisco, CA: Jossey-Bass.

Wernerfelt, B. (1984). A resource-based view of the firm. *Strategic Management Journal, 5*, 171–180.

Wiesner-Hanks, M. A. (2001). Response to women and business in eighteenth- and nineteenth-century northwestern Europe. *Social History, 34*(68), 371–375.

Wharton, A. S. (2009). *The sociology of gender: An introduction to theory and research*. Wiley.

Zahra, S. A., Hayton, J. C., & Salvato, C. (2004). Entrepreneurship in family vs. non-family firms: A resource-based analysis of the effect of organizational culture. *Entrepreneurship Theory and Practice, 28*(4), 363–381.

A Composite Index Approach to Detecting Reporting Quality: The Case of Female Executives in Family Firms

Gianluca Ginesti, Carlo Drago, and Riccardo Macchioni

Abstract In this chapter, we offer a composite index approach to detect firms' information quality. Our interest coincides with recent moves among scholars in analysing the quality and understandability of corporate disclosure practices. We test our measure of information quality using a sample of annual reports of Italian family listed firms. We find a positive association between non-family female executives and firms' information transparency. These findings support the argument that non-family female executives are more likely to reduce agency problems with a net benefit for the information quality. Our study may help policy makers and managers in looking at how to make corporate disclosures easier and more meaningful.

Keywords Composite disclosure index • Information transparency • Textual analysis • Female executives

1 Introduction

In this chapter we provide an overall index of corporate reporting quality based on the Fog index (Fog) and the Flesch Reading Ease index (Flesch) and the corporate document file size (File_Size). The main explanation for this interest is related to the

---

While all authors contributed to this study, Dr. Ginesti mainly focused on the development of the research idea, design and hypothesis, Dr. Drago focused primarily on the econometric models and the statistical results and Prof. Macchioni predominantly covered the discussion and implications of this study in relation to the literature.

G. Ginesti (✉)
University of Naples "Federico II", Napoli, Italy
e-mail: gianluca.ginesti@unina.it

C. Drago
University of Rome "Niccolò Cusano", Roma, Italy
e-mail: Carlo.drago@unicusano.it

R. Macchioni
University of Campania "Luigi Vanvitelli", Caserta, Italy
e-mail: riccardo.macchioni@unicampania.it

V. Ratten et al. (eds.), *Knowledge, Learning and Innovation*, Contributions to Management Science, DOI 10.1007/978-3-319-59282-4_11

concerns about the negative effects of corporate documents complexity for stakeholders and the investor decision-making process (Lawrence, 2013; Lehavy, Li, & Merkley, 2011; Lo, Ramos, & Rogo, 2017; Miller, 2010; Rennekamp, 2012).Our interest coincides with recent moves among policy makers who perceive the increasing needs for enhancing the quality and understandability of corporate disclosure practices (Guay et al., 2016; Hooghiemstra, Kuang, & Qin, 2017; Lundholm, Rogo, & Zhang, 2014).

Our main objective is to devise a model that may be useful for analysing the information quality in different fields of research and activities (Zhang, Sun, & Jara, 2015). In particular, we test our disclosure index by using as an experimental setting the business case of board gender diversity, which has become an important issue in current policy and academic debate (Adams, de Haan, Terjesen, & Van Ees, 2015). To improve diversity on corporate boards, several European countries have promoted the introduction of gender quotas for publicly traded companies (Labelle, Francoeur, & Lakhal, 2015).[1] Not surprisingly, the literature on board gender diversity is enormous and examines a wide range of aspects such as board functioning and monitoring financial disclosures and the capital market consequences (Adams et al., 2015; Carter, D'Souza, Simkins, & Simpson, 2010; Gul, Srinidhi, & Ng, 2011). However, the role of female executives in family firms has attracted a limited amount of research (Al Dajani, Bika, Collins, & Swail, 2014). Therefore, there is an empirical question concerning whether family firm dominance may affect the relationship between board composition in terms of gender and reporting communication style. Leveraging a sample of 192 annual reports of Italian listed family firms and data for over 450 board members we provide evidence that non-family female executives have a positive impact on information quality.

This study makes several contributions to the literature. First, we offer an intuitive measure to capture the information transparency which may help researchers gain a better understanding of corporate reporting practices.

Second, we extend prior research on board gender diversity has overlooked the field of family business (Al Dajani et al., 2014) and we use of data from European civil law countries, such as Italy, where efforts at improving board gender diversity have recently been outlined by policymakers and academics (Bianco, Ciavarella, & Signoretti, 2015; Gordini & Rancati, 2017).

Finally, our paper may help policymakers in reducing the costs of processing information of corporate documents by offering a potential tool to detect more transparent financial information. In addition, our measure may be useful to guide managers in producing higher quality documents.

The remainder of this study is structured as follows. The next section reports the literature and hypothesis. We then describe the research methodology. This is followed by a section that illustrates the results. Finally we present some conclusions and implications of our study.

---

[1]Italy's law 120/2011 requires to Italian listed companies to gruadually increase the gender quota since 2012. In particular, the law prescribes that gender quota should increase up by 2015.

2 Literature Review

Scholars claim that board gender diversity raises interesting issues and new developmental challenges for research (Adams et al., 2015; Hillman, 2015). In particular, several empirical studies have suggested that board diversity is beneficial for board functioning and monitoring (Anderson, Reeb, Upadhyay, & Zhao, 2011; Ararat, Aksu, & Tansel Çetin, 2015; Carter, Simkins, & Simpson, 2003; Terjesen, Barbosa Couto, & Morais, 2015). For instance, empirical studies have revealed that firms with greater female board participation exhibit higher performance (Campbell & Minguez-Vera, 2008; Ho, Li, Tam, & Zhang, 2015; Srindhi, Gul, & Tsai, 2011; Terjesen et al., 2015). Nevertheless, there is empirical evidence of a negative—on average—association between board gender diversity and firm performance (Adams & Ferreira, 2009), or a non-significant link between firm performance and female board representation (Carter et al., 2010; Chapple & Humphrey, 2014).

In general, research uses different theories to analyse whether gender-based differences on corporate boards are able to improve legitimacy and effective communication and increase the oversight of management (Adams et al., 2015). From the agency perspective scholars suggest that a more diverse board may enhance monitoring of managers, thereby aligning principals' and agents' interests (Bear, Rahman, & Post, 2010; Ben Amar et al., 2013; Carter et al., 2003; Hillman & Dalziel, 2003). This is because the stronger leadership ability and stricter ethical values of women directors may improve the corporate governance system (Eagly & Johnson, 1990; Ho et al., 2015). For instance, some empirical research has shown that the presence of women on boards increases board independence, which in turn can determine improvements in financial reporting quality and the information environment (Gul et al., 2011; Srindhi et al., 2011). The benefit of having woman directors has been explained using other perspectives. Some studies suggest that females are more conservative and less risk averse than men (Jianakoplos & Bernasek, 2007; Vandergrift & Brown, 2005) and they are able to increase firm's moral legitimacy by enhancing the salience of stakeholder claims (Zhang, Zhu, & Ding, 2013). However, there are mixed results from emprical evidence on the coercive approach to promoting board gender equality by external authorities (Labelle et al., 2015). According to Casey, Skibnes, and Pringle (2011), critics argue that gender quotas would lead to enforcing negative views on the merit of the women competence appointed as directors in terms of their competence.

The case of family firms is interesting given that ownership is usually shared between a block-holding family and non-family investors (Carney, Van Essen, Gedajlovic, & Heugens, 2015; Gomez-Mejia, Nuñez-Nickel, & Gutierrez, 2001; Schulze, Lubatkin, Dino, & Buchholz, 2001) and controlling families are often in conflict with regard to the choice of hiring a family member or unrelated directors (Anderson & Reeb, 2004; Bennedsen, Nielsen, Perez-Gonzalez, & Wolfenzon,

2007). Therefore, whether the appointment of family female directors or unrelated female directors has an impact on corporate disclosure quality is an empirical question.

As suggested by Mitchel et al. (2003) and Klein and Bell (2007), non-family executives play a significant role in family businesses. The advantages of employing non-family executives in a family business are explained in the literature. For instance, Dyer (1989) claims that non-family managers compared to family managers have broader professional abilities in terms of world view a job experiences. Indeed, family members may serve as directors not because of their expertise and but because of their family representation role (Ramón-Llorens, García-Meca, & Duréndez, 2017). In addition, non-family managers are generally more economically oriented and less prone to family emotions (Cortena, Steijversa, & Lybaer, 2017). As a family firm takes on more non-family female executives, it will encourage better monitoring of boards and limiting managerial opportunism (Abbott, Parker, & Presley, 2012), we expect that non-family female executives will be able to exert influence on management decisions to increase the transparency of corporate disclosures. Thus we posit the following hypothesis:

Hypothesis 1 The percentage of non-family female executives on corporate boards is positively associated with the firms' information quality.

3 Methodology

3.1 Data and Sample

Our study requires each firm English annual report. We begin our analysis with the list of Italian listed companies, over the period 2010-2013, analyzed in Ginesti et al. (2017).

To identify a firm as family, we followed Cascino, Pugliese, Mussolino, and Sansone (2010), which considers either the equity ownership at least of 50% of the voting rights or outstanding shares held by the family and the board representation by family members. This criterion leaves a final sample of family listed firms, which comprises 192 annual reports for the period 2010–2013. We use Amadeus dataset for accounting variables and Italian Security Commission (CONSOB) dataset for goverannce data. In particular we manually collected individual data on all members of the boards (over 450 different individuals) from CONSOB database.

3.2 Variables

Disclosure Index

A number of prior studies have examined company reporting focusing on the proxies for corporate disclosure or using measures obtained by inspecting original disclosure documents (Hassan & Marston, 2010). This latter strand of studies has focused on individual measures of disclosure, such as the disclosure index and textual analysis techniques (Jones & Shoemaker, 1994; Marston & Shrives, 1991). The Literature claims that the disclosure index is an instrument that assists scholars in measuring the quality of disclosure on the basis of the amount of information released by the firms on specified topics (Beattie, McInnes, & Fearnley, 2004; Marston & Shrives, 1991). To identify the items to be included in the index, researchers have mainly used a content analysis technique, which involves subjective judgment (Beattie et al., 2004). Over the years, the relevance of the writing style of financial documents has led to an increase in readability studies and linguistic approach in the accounting and finance literature (Loughran & Mcdonald, 2014; Lundholm et al., 2014; Cho, Roberts, & Patten, 2010). Several papers support the argument that readability studies are an important field of research to detect the quality of financial disclosure and its implication for investors (Hooghiemstra et al., 2017; Lehavy et al., 2011; Lundholm et al., 2014; Rennekamp, 2012; You & Zhang, 2009). To undertake readability analysis, scholars have used formula-based approaches which take into account the attributes of the language used , such as sentence and word length, syllables and other vocabulary elements (Courtis & Hassan, 2002; Li, 2008).

In line with this strand of research we offer an analysis of the corporate disclosure by exploiting an aggregate measure of information quality that considers three main measures.

While there are many approaches to measuring textual disclosure quality (De Franco, Hope, Vyas, & Zhou, 2015; Guay, Samuels, & Taylor, 2015; Brennan, Guillamon-Saorin, & Pierce, 2009), in this article, we use the File_Size as one of the three components of our composite index. As suggested by Loughran and Mcdonald (2014), the File_Size has the advantage of an easy calculation and is not prone to the measurement errors. In addition, this approach could reduce the potential biases that analysts and researchers ascribe to the disclosure indices based on the content analysis (Beattie et al., 2004).

Fog and Flesch are considered the most popular indices used in accounting literature (Courtis & Hassan, 2002; Laksmana, Tietz, & Yang, 2012; Li, 2008; Subramanian, Insley, & Blackwell, 1993).

The Fog index is calculated as follows: 0.4 * (words_per_sentence + percent_of_complex_words). Where complex words are defined as words with three syllables or more. Lower values for the Fog index denote clearer text.

The Flesch index is calculated as follows: $206.835 - 0.846WL - 1.015SL$. Where WL is the number of syllables per 100 words and SL is the average sentence length. Higher values for the Flesch indicate greater readability of text.

File_Size is a novel measure that may be important and more consistent to identify the quality of annual reports related to the activities adopted by companies to revamp their financial disclosures. As suggested by a recent survey by Ernest and Young (2016), companies are increasing their efforts to make their annual report more understandable by employing more infographics (EY, 2016). As a result, when the annual reports contain a substantial amount of tables, charts and graphs, the File_Size may increase.

Therefore we expect that firms with a larger File_Size are more likely to provide better information quality, by streamlining disclosures and introducing greater use of graphics for investor needs (Lang & Lawrence, 2015). However, we acknowledge that a positive link between File_size and reporting quality is not to be considered as an univocal prediction, but as suggested by Loughran and McDonald (2014), firms may often obscure results in longer documents. Therefore, it is important to highlight that this prediction may assume different directions from this study on the basis of the business case analysed.

To create our aggregate measure of information quality, we adopted the following steps.

First, we multiplied the Fog by −1 to align it with Flesch and File_Size. Second, we standardized Fog, Flesch and File_Size and then used a single weight for all the above components and we multiplied the same weight for the components, summing the total obtained. Therefore, higher value of our disclosure index denotes higher quality of the annual report.

Independent Variables

As gender variables, we first consider the percentage of women on the board of directors and the presence of female chairmen (Campbell & Minguez-Vera, 2008; Gul et al., 2011). In doing so, we distinguish between family female directors and unrelated female directors. In addition to these variables, we include the following set of controls variables.

Size Size of the firms is often used as control variable for explaining the firm's disclosure policy (Inchausti, 1997). Empirical evidence on impact of firm size on the disclosure policy has been offered in several studies (Beretta & Bozzolan, 2004; Lang & Lundholm, 1993; Raffournier, 1995; Wallace, Naser, & Mora, 1994).

Leverage Leverage has been considered as possible factor affecting the level of text manipulation and readability of corporate reporting (Davis & Tama-Sweet, 2012; Lundholm et al., 2014). This is because firms more leveraged may be motivated to disclose better information in order to satisfy the needs of investors, improving the opportunities to acquire external financing (Wallace et al., 1994).

Profitability Prior research suggests that profitability may affect the amount and the quality of corporate disclosure practices (Inchausti, 1997; Jeanjean, Stolow, Erkens, & Yhon, 2015). For instance, Subramanian et al. (1993) and Li (2008) indicate that firms with a high level or more persistent profitability have annual reports that are easier to read.

Table 1 reports a complete description of the variables used in the analysis.

Table 1 Description of the variables

Variables	Measurement
D_INDEX	Index composed by Fog index, Flesch and the file size of annual report
SIZE	Natural logarithm of the total assets
LEV	Long-term debt to total assets
PROFIT	Net income to total assets
%FAM_FEMALE	Percentage of female directors who are members of the family owner
% NON_FAM_FEMALE	Percentage of female directors who are not members of the family owner

3.3 *Regression Analysis*

We employ the Hausman test (HT) and Breusch-Pagan Lagrange Multiplier test (BP) to choose among a fixed-effects model, a random-effects model, or a pooled OLS model. We use the HT to decide whether an FE model or an RE model should be used and BP test to choose between an OLS model or RE model.

Since the HT is insignificant, we performed the BP test. The BP is significant and thereby the random-effects model is more efficient. For the sake of clarity, we report all regression models in Table 4.

4 Results

Table 2 presents the sample descriptive statistics for all variables. The mean of the D_INDEX index is 0, indicating that Italian family listed firms generally exhibit a low level of disclosure quality in their annual reports. Table 2 also shows that the percentage of family female board members is around 39%, while the level of unrelated female directors is about 49%. These results suggest that the number of female directors in our sample is not underweighted.

Table 3 reports the Pearson correlation matrix for all variables, showing that the D_INDEX is statistically correlated with size (+) and the percentage of non-family female directors (+).

Table 4 shows the results of the OLS pooled model, fixed—effects model and random—effects model. These results show that the D_INDEX is positively associated with TASSET ($P < 0.001$ and $P < 0.05$) in model (1) and in the model (3), confirming that the level of disclosure transparency is highly influenced by size (Beretta & Bozzolan, 2004). The results for the other control variables show no significant association with D_INDEX.

An interesting result is derived from the gender variables related to female directors. Specifically, Table 4 shows that %NON_FAM_FEMALE is positively associated with D_INDEX in all models ($P < 0.01$ and $P < 00.5$ respectively), confirming our expectation incorporated in the hypothesis 1. In contrast the variable %FAM_FEMALE is not associated with D_IDEX. This result may denote the

Table 2 Descriptive statistics

Variables	No. of observations	Mean	Standard Deviation	Minimum	Maximum
D_INDEX	192	0	0.726	−1.870	2.23
D_INDEX components					
Fog	192	14.83	1.961	10.8	20.6
Flesch	192	39.08	6.326	20.08	55.6
File_size	192	1.32	0.744	−0.44	3.28
Firm-specific characteristics					
TASSET	192	13.939	1.394	11.397	18.247
PROFIT	192	3.115	5.885	−13.887	19.36
LEV	192	0.206	0.145	0	0.751
Gender variables					
%FAM_FEMALE	192	0.039	0.063	0	0.25
% NON_FAM_FEMALE	192	0.046	0.078	0	0.04

Refer to Table 1 for variables description

significant role that non-family female directors play in improving the corporate disclosure transparency (Ben Amar et al., 2013; Huse & Solberg, 2006). Conversely, family female directors may not be sufficient in terms of taking actions to improve governance systems and therefore influence disclosure quality.

5 Conclusions

This study offers a composite index approach based on three main measures of disclosure transparency. We test this measure by using as an experimental setting the business case of the link between female executives and the corporate disclosure of Italian family firms, which has been overlooked in the literature. We include in our composite index File_Size as a novel determinant of the quality and effectiveness of disclosures (Loughran & Mcdonald, 2014). However, to moderate the potential biases derived from an absolute use of File_size, we also employ in our index, the Fog and Flesch indices. We acknowledge that we cannot prove that our index is the best measure for detecting the disclosure textual quality, but we believe that it is a first attempt in advancing research on the disclosure quality index. In particular, the advantage of our measure is the intuitive calculation and easy application for academic research and professional activities in all fields of disclosure analysis.

Our findings contribute to the current academic debate on measuring disclosure quality by shedding light that non-family female executives are more likely to engage in better disclosure transparency and are less prone to using the impression management techniques. These findings support the argument that non-family female executives are more likely to reduce agency problems, moderate the

Table 3 Pearson coefficient correlation matrix

	D_INDEX	TASSET	ROA	LEV	%FAM_FEMALE	%NON_FAM_FEMALE
D_INDEX	1					
TASSET	0.270*	1				
ROA	0.082	−0.016	1			
LEV	−0.0349	0.373*	−0.231*	1		
%FAM_FEMALE	−0.106	−0.272*	0.145*	−0.300*	1	
%NON_FAM_FEMALE	0.149*	0.089*	−0.123	0.156*	−0.093	1

Table 4 Regression results

D_INDEX	OLS pooled Model (1)	Fixed effects Model (2)	Random effects Model (3)
TASSET	0.158***	0.153	0.155**
ROA	0.009	−0.009	0.000
LEV	−0.883	−1.119	−0.957
%FAM_FEMALE	−0.830	3.382	−0.149
%NON_FAM_FEMALE	1.403*	2.043**	1.932**
INTERCEPT	−2.089***	0.244	−2.043**
No. of Obs.	192	192	192
R2_Adj	0.09	0.09	

Refer to Table 1 for variables description
*$P < 0.1$; **$P < 0.05$; ***$P < 0.01$

preferences of family directors and protect the interests of the non-family shareholders, with a net benefit for information enviroment transparency. Moreover, we also believe that as the general number of women on a board increases, the presence of non-family female directors becomes more assertive (Bear et al., 2010; Konrad, Kramer, & Erkut, 2008) leading to several benefits for firms' outcomes.

Our findings also have policy and practical implications. First, this study may help regulators and standards setters at looking at how they might financial reporting more effective, potentially employing a novel metric of analysis to address the emerging needs of investors and/or analysts. Second, our measure may be useful for managers in producing information that are easier to process, allowing investors to make more informed decisions.

This study is subject to variuos limitations. First, our aggregate measure of information quality does not take into account the incremental information content that companies may decide to disclose in their annual reports. Second, this measure is subject to the limitations of the readability formulae and thus we call for further research to validate its effectiveness and reliability.

Appendix: Examples of Fog and Flesch Application

Example of article	Readability level	Education level
Title: "Independent US oil producers increase hedges for 2017" US independent oil producers have taken advantage of the recent bump in crude prices to lock in future revenues, building up derivatives positions for 2017. In third-quarter earnings reports over the past three weeks, several US exploration and production companies said they had hedged significantly more		

(continued)

Example of article	Readability level	Education level
of their expected oil sales for the coming year than they had done at the equivalent point of 2015 in preparation for this year. The additional protection from hedges will support cash flows and investment plans even if crude prices continue to weaken, helping to sustain US oil production. ***Financial Times 10, November 2016.****		
Index score:		
Flesch: 28.07	Very difficult	College Graduates
Fog score: 19.47	Very difficult	High level of professional and school background

References

Abbott, J., Parker, S., & Presley, T. (2012). Female board presence and the likelihood of financial restatement. *Accounting Horizons, 26*(4), 607–629.

Adams, R., de Haan, J., Terjesen, S., & Van Ees, H. (2015). Board diversity: Moving the field forward. *Corporate Governance: International Review, 23*(2), 77–82.

Al Dajani, H., Bika, Z., Collins, L., & Swail, J. (2014). Gender and family business: new theoretical directions. *International Journal of Gender and Entrepreneurship, 6*(3), 218–230.

Anderson, R. C., & Reeb, D. M. (2004). Board composition: Balancing family influence in S&P 500 firms. *Administrative Science Quarterly, 49*, 209–237.

Anderson, R., Reeb, D., Upadhyay, A., & Zhao, W. (2011). The economics of director heterogeneity. *Financial Management, 40*, 5–38.

Ararat, M., Aksu, M. H., & Tansel Çetin, A. (2015). How board diversity affects firm performance in emerging markets: Evidence on channels in controlled firms. *Corporate Governance: An International Review, 23*, 83–103.

Bear, S., Rahman, N., & Post, C. (2010). The impact of board diversity and gender composition on corporate social responsibility and firm reputation. *Journal of Business Ethics, 97*(2), 207–221.

Beattie, V. A., McInnes, B., & Fearnley, S. (2004). A Methodology for analyzing and evaluating narratives in annual reports: A comprehensive description profile and metrics for disclosure quality attributes. *Accounting Forum, 28*, 205–236.

Bennedsen, M., Nielsen, K., Perez-Gonzalez, F., & Wolfenzon, D. (2007). Inside the family firm: The role of families in succession decisions and performance. *Quarterly Journal of Economics, 122*, 647–691.

Beretta, S., & Bozzolan, S. (2004). A framework for the analysis of firm risk communication. *The International Journal of Accounting, 39*(1), 265–288.

Bianco, M., Ciavarella, A., & Signoretti, R. (2015). Women on corporate boards in Italy: The role of family connections. *Corporate Governance: An International Review, 23*(2), 129–144.

Brennan, N., Guillamon-Saorin, E., & Pierce, A. (2009). Impression management: Developing and illustrating a scheme of analysis for narrative disclosures – A methodological note. *Accounting, Auditing and Accountability Journal, 22*(5), 789–832.

Campbell, K., & Minguez-Vera, A. (2008). Gender diversity in the boardroom and firm financial performance. *Journal of Business Ethics, 83*(1), 435–451.

Carney, M., Van Essen, M., Gedajlovic, E. R., & Heugens, P. P. (2015). What do we know about private family firm performance? A meta-analytical review. *Entrepreneurship Theory and Practice, 39*(3), 513–544.

Carter, D., D'Souza, F., Simkins, B., & Simpson, W. (2010). The gender and ethnic diversity of US boards and board committees and firm financial performance. *Corporate Governance: An International Review, 18*(5), 396–414.

Carter, D. A., Simkins, B. J., & Simpson, W. G. (2003). Corporate governance, board diversity, and firm value. *Financial Review, 38*, 33–53.

Cascino, S., Pugliese, A., Mussolino, D., & Sansone, C. (2010). The influence of family ownership on the quality of accounting information. *Family Business Review, 23*, 246–265.

Casey, C., Skibnes, R., & Pringle, J. K. (2011). Gender equality and corporate governance: Policy strategies in Norway and New Zealand. *Gender, Work and Organization, 18*(6), 613–630.

Chapple, C., & Humphrey, J. E. (2014). Does board gender diversity have a financial impact? Evidence using stock portfolio performance. *Journal of Business Ethics, 122*, 709–723.

Cho, C. H., Roberts, R. W., & Patten, D. M. (2010). The language of US corporate environmental disclosure. *Accounting Organizations and Society, 35*(4), 431–443.

Cortena, M. B., Steijversa, T., & Lybaer, N. (2017). The effect of intrafamily agency conflicts on audit demand in private family firms: The moderating role of the board of directors. *Journal of Family Business Strategy, 8*(1), 13–28.

Courtis, J. K., & Hassan, S. (2002). Reading ease of bilingual annual reports. *Journal of Business Communication, 39*(4), 394–413.

Davis, A. K., & Tama-Sweet, I. (2012). Managers' use of language across alternative disclosure outlets: Earnings press releases versus MD&A. *Contemporary Accounting Research, 29*, 804–837.

De Franco, G., Hope, O. K., Vyas, D., & Zhou, Y. (2015). Analyst report readability. *Contemporary Accounting Research, 31*(1), 76–104.

Dyer, W. G., Jr. (1989). Integrating professional management into a family owned business. *Family Business Review, 2*, 221–235.

Eagly, A. H., & Johnson, B. T. (1990). Gender and leadership style: A meta-analysis. *Psychological Bulletin, 108*, 233–256.

Ernest and Young. (2016). *Disclosure effectiveness in action: Companies make great strides*. Available at http://www.ey.com/gl/en/services/assurance/ey-disclosure-effectiveness

Ginesti, G., Sannino, G., & Drago, C. (2017). Board connections and management commentary readability: The role of information sharing in Italy. *Corporate Governance: The International Journal of Business in Society, 17*(1), 30–47.

Gomez-Mejia, L. R., Nuñez-Nickel, M., & Gutierrez, I. (2001). The role of family ties in agency contracts. *The Academy of Management Journal, 44*(1), 81–95.

Gordini, N., & Rancati, E. (2017). Gender diversity in the Italian boardroom and firm financial performance. *Management Research Review, 40*(1), 75–94.

Guay, W., Samuels, D., & Taylor, D. (2015). Guiding through the fog: Financial statement complexity and voluntary disclosure. *Journal of Accounting and Economics, 62*(2), 234–269.

Gul, F., Srinidhi, B., & Ng, A. C. (2011). Does board gender diversity improve the informativeness of stock prices. *Journal of Accounting and Economics, 51*, 314–344.

Hassan, O., & Marston, C. (2010). *Disclosure measurement in the empirical accounting literature: A review article* (Economics and Finance Working Paper Series, Brunel University, Working Paper No. 10–18). doi:10.2139/ssrn.1640598.

Hillman, A. (2015). Board diversity: Beginning to unpeel the onion. *Corporate Governance: An International Review, 23*(2), 104–107.

Hillman, A. J., & Dalziel, T. (2003). Boards of directors and firm performance: Integrating agency and resource dependence perspectives. *Academy of Management Review, 28*, 383–396.

Ho, S. S. M., Li, A. Y., Tam, K., & Zhang, F. (2015). CEO gender, ethical leadership, and accounting conservatism. *Journal of Business Ethics, 127*, 351–370.

Hooghiemstra, R., Kuang, Y. F., & Qin, B. (2017). Does obfuscating excessive CEO pay work? The influence of remuneration report readability on say-on-pay votes. *Accounting and Business Research, 47*(6), 695–729.

Huse, M., & Solberg, A. G. (2006). Gender-related boardroom dynamics: How Scandinavian women make and can make contributions on corporate boards. *Women in Management Review, 21*(2), 113–130.

Inchausti, B. G. (1997). The influence of company characteristics and accounting regulation on information disclosed by Spanish firms. *European Accounting Review, 6*, 45–68.

Jeanjean, T., Stolow, H., Erkens, M., & Yhon, T. L. (2015). Evidence on the impact of adopting english as an external reporting language on foreign investment, information asymmetry, and analyst following. *Journal of International Business Studies, 46*, 180–205.

Jianakoplos, N., & Bernasek, A. (2007). Are female more risk averse? *Economic Inquiry, 36*(4), 620–630.

Jones, M. J., & Shoemaker, P. A. (1994). Accounting narrative: A review of empirical studies of content and readability. *Journal of Accounting Literature, 13*, 142–184.

Konrad, A., Kramer, V., & Erkut, S. (2008). Critical mass: The impact of three or more women on corporate boards. *Organizational Dynamics, 37*(2), 145–164.

Labelle, R., Francoeur, C., & Lakhal, F. (2015). To regulate or not to regulate? Early evidence on the means used around the world to promote gender diversity in the boardroom. *Work, Gender and Organization, 22*(4), 339–363.

Laksmana, I., Tietz, W., & Yang, Y. M. (2012). Compensation discussion and analysis (CD&A): Readability and management obfuscation. *Journal of Accounting and Public Policy, 31*, 185–203.

Lang, M., & Lawrence, L. S. (2015). Textual analysis and international financial reporting: Large sample evidence. *Journal of Accounting and Economics, 60*, 110–135.

Lawrence, A. (2013). Individual investors and financial disclosure. *Journal of Accounting and Economics, 56*, 130–147.

Lehavy, R., Li, F., & Merkley, K. (2011). The effect of annual report readability on analyst following and the properties of their earnings forecasts. *The Accounting Review, 86*, 1087–1115.

Li, F. (2008). Annual report readability, current earnings, and earnings persistence. *Journal of Accounting and Economics, 45*(2-3), 221–247.

Lo, K., Ramos, F., & Rogo, R. (2017). Earnings management and annual report readability. *Journalof Accounting and Economics, 63*, 1–25.

Loughran, T., & Mcdonald, B. (2014). Measuring readability in financial disclosure. *The Journal of Finance, 69*(4), 1643–1671.

Lundholm, J. T., Rogo, R., & Zhang, L. J. (2014). Restoring the tower of Babel: How foreign firms communicate with U.S. investors. *The Accounting Review, 89*, 1453–1485.

Marston, C. L., & Shrives, P. J. (1991). The use of disclosure indices in accounting research: A review article. *British Accounting Review, 23*(3), 195–210.

Miller, B. P. (2010). The effects of reporting complexity on small and large investor trading. *The Accounting Review, 85*(86), 2017–2143.

Raffournier, B. (1995). The determinants of voluntary financial disclosure by Swiss listed companies. *The European Accounting Review, 4*(2), 261–280.

Ramón-Llorens, M. C., García-Meca, M., & Duréndez, A. (2017). Influence of CEO characteristics in family firms internationalization. *International Business Review, 26*(4), 786–799.

Rennekamp, K. (2012). Processing fluency and investors' reactions to disclosure readability. *Journal of Accounting Research, 50*, 1319–1354.

Schulze, W. S., Lubatkin, M. H., Dino, R. N., & Buchholz, R. A. (2001). Agency relationships in family firms: Theory and evidence. *Organization Science, 12*, 99–116.

Srindhi, B., Gul, F. A., & Tsai, J. (2011). Female directors and earnings quality. *Contemporary Accounting Research, 28*, 1610–1644.

Subramanian, R., Insley, R. G., & Blackwell, R. D. (1993). Performance and readability: A comparison of annual reports of profitable and unprofitable corporations. *Journal of Business Communication, 30*, 49–61.

Terjesen, S., Barbosa Couto, E., & Morais Francisco, P. (2015). Does the presence of independent and female directors impact firm performance? A multi-country study of board diversity. *Journal of Management and Governance, 23*(2), 77.

Vandergrift, D., & Brown, P. (2005). Gender differences in the use of high-variance strategies in tournament competition. *Journal of Socio-Economics, 34*(6), 834–849.

Wallace, R. S. O., Naser, K., & Mora, A. (1994). The relationship between the comprehensiveness of corporate annual reports and firm characteristics in Spain. *Accounting and Business Research, 25*, 41–53.

You, H., & Zhang, X. (2009). Financial reporting complexity and investor underreaction to 10-K information. *Review of Accounting Studies, 14*(4), 559–586.

Zhang, J., Sun, Y., & Jara, A. J. (2015). Towards semantically linked multilingual corpus. *International Journal of Information Management, 35*, 387–395.

Zhang, J. Q., Zhu, H., & Ding, H. (2013). Board composition and corporate social responsibility: An empirical investigation in the post Sarbanes-Oxley era. *Journal of Business Ethics, 114*, 381–392.

Influencing Factors in Customers' Intention to Re-visit Resort Hotels: The Roles of Customer Experience Management and Customer Value

Bachruddin Saleh Luturlean, Ratih Hurriyati, Lili Adi Wibowo, and Grisna Anggadwita

Abstract Tourism is one of the sectors that contribute to a country's economy. Creative tourist activities form part of the strategy to increase public interest in this industry. The tourism sector is related to the hospitality industry, whose expansion cannot be separated from its development and vice versa. The hospitality industry's rapid development has resulted in competitive rivalry between hotels over attracting customers to stay and use their facilities. This study aims to identify factors that influence the increase in hotel customers' intention tore-visit by exploring customer experience management and customer value. The research focus is a themed resort hotel with distinctive characteristics. The sampling technique used a non-probability variety involving use of an accidental sampling approach. A total of 500 respondents participated in the questionnaire exercise. This study used a quantitative method employing Structural Equation Modeling (SEM) analysis techniques to test the hypothesis with Lisrel 8.8 used as the data processing tool. The findings of the research indicate that customer experience management exerts a significant influence on re-visit intention through customer value. The article's later sections discuss recommendations, implications, and suggestions for future research.

Keywords Customer experience management • Customer value • Hotel industry • Resort hotel • Revisit intention • Tourism industry

B.S. Luturlean
School of Postgraduate Studies, Indonesia University of Education, Bandung, Indonesia
e-mail: bachruddin_saleh@yahoo.com

R. Hurriyati • L.A. Wibowo
Faculty of Economics and Business Education, Indonesia University of Education, Bandung, Indonesia
e-mail: ratih@upi.edu; liliadiwibowo@upi.edu

G. Anggadwita (✉)
School of Economics and Business, Telkom University, Bandung, Indonesia
e-mail: grisnamailbox@yahoo.co.id

V. Ratten et al. (eds.), *Knowledge, Learning and Innovation*, Contributions to Management Science, DOI 10.1007/978-3-319-59282-4_12

1 Introduction

Indonesia is a country seeking to boost its economy through an increase in tourism and one enjoying great potential to develop this particular sector. The Indonesian tourist industry's current upward trend has earmarked it as a major potential investment opportunity. The tourism sector is expected to significantly support the economic growth of both the country and, by extension, its people. Creative tourism has been seen as a strategy for the development of physical, cultural and social resources, while contributing to the local economy and introducing the society and culture of the particular country concerned to outsiders (Chang, Backman, & Chih Huang, 2014; Salman, 2010). The creative tourism sector's activities in Indonesia have become one of the strategies for improving the economic situation of its people. Based on 2013 Central Statistics Agency (BPS) data, the number of foreign tourist arrivals in the country totaled an impressive 9.5 million, a marked increase on those of 2012 which amounted to only 5.9 million. According to Travel and Tourism Index statistics (WEF, 2013), Indonesia ranked 70th out of 140 countries in the world, while in the Asia Pacific region, it occupied 12th place in the rankings which were headed by Singapore.

The tourism sector is inexorably related to the hospitality industry since the development of the latter is inter-dependent with that of tourism in general. The hospitality industry is a service industry engaged in the provision of accommodation and lodging. The Indonesian hospitality industry ranks 21st on the global scale, with the strength of its hotel industry being that of competitive room rates (WEF, 2013). The hospitality industry's rapid development has provoked intense competition in attracting potential customers to take advantage of the facilities provided by hotels. Table 1 shows the annually-increasing number of 5-star hotels in Indonesia.

Table 1 shows the number of star-rated hotels experiencing year-on-year growth. West Java is one of the regions that has the highest number of hotels with an annual growth rate of 10%. Bandung is the city within the province with the highest number of hotels, as many as 104 (BPS, 2015). Total visitor arrivals can be calculated on the basis of hotel occupancy levels. Room occupancy rates at star-rated hotels in West Java are presented in Table 2.

Table 2 shows the fierce competition in the hospitality sector in West Java resulting in low re-visit levels at a specific establishment. The intensity of customer visits did not represent a major benchmark for measuring hotel performance. However, if such intensity increases, the management of a hotel will be able to optimize its use of available resources. Resort hotels have become major tourist destinations offering, according to Pendit (1999), a variety of special facilities related to leisure activities, exercise and sight-seeing in an environment of natural beauty. Features of such hotels include; golf courses, tennis courts, spa, jogging tracks and hiking routes. In another definition proposed by O'Shannessy et al. (2001), a tourist resort meets five criteria comprising; accommodation, recreational facilities, sales outlets, entertainment, and food and beverage

Table 1 Total rated hotels in Indonesia, Period 2010–2014

Provinces	2010	2011	2012	2013	2014
Aceh	16	18	22	22	17
North Sumatera	70	76	83	96	106
West Sumatera	28	36	45	50	56
Riau	33	36	41	45	53
Jambi	18	20	20	23	25
South Sumatera	31	35	46	50	56
Bengkulu	5	5	5	7	8
Lampung	8	13	9	9	11
Bangka Belitung Islands	13	18	23	23	29
Riau Islands	49	69	70	76	79
DKI Jakarta	160	162	175	185	205
West Java	174	199	208	229	253
Central Java	119	131	139	166	186
DI Yogyakarta	34	42	52	61	74
East Java	84	90	98	113	127
Banten	39	46	42	43	52
Bali	170	199	218	227	249
Nusa Tenggara Barat	32	36	43	47	54
Nusa Tenggara Timur	13	16	15	18	19
West Kalimantan	14	18	25	28	31
Central Kalimantan	5	7	9	11	8
South Kalimantan	26	32	35	41	45
East Kalimantan	32	43	43	42	50
North Sulawesi	28	26	28	25	25
Central Sulawesi	3	3	3	5	6
South Sulawesi	63	58	57	57	75
Southeast Sulawesi	1	8	10	12	17
Gorontalo	1	1	1	3	6
West Sulawesi	–	1	6	7	7
Maluku	13	19	19	21	24
North Maluku	3	3	3	3	3
West Papua	9	10	11	11	13
Papua	12	13	19	22	27
Total	1306	1489	1623	1778	1996

Source: BPS (2015)

services. Table 3 shows the percentage rates of customer re-visits at resort hotels in West Java on which this study focuses.

Resort hotels generally set themselves a minimum average target customer re-visit rate of 5–6%.The gap between management expectations and reality is, therefore, an interesting focus of study. The data indicates that re-visit rates at resort hotels in West Java remain low, a fact potentially impacting the economic condition of the province's population which depends on tourism, especially the hospitality

Table 2 Room occupancy rate at star-rated hotels in West Java, 2010–2015

Month/Year	2010	2011	2012	2013	2014	2015
Jan	48.40	49.57	50.15	39.45	40.48	46.26
Feb	46.62	48.91	49.10	41.29	43.54	40.59
March	49.47	48.74	49.17	47.49	47.00	43.52
April	48.39	48.40	48.37	46.83	47.42	44.30
Mei	49.03	49.76	49.79	47.22	45.46	49.47
June	52.44	52.93	56.19	53.05	51.06	50.40
July	53.66	59.59	47.85	41.99	41.20	49.82
August	41.50	39.22	42.97	42.59	47.38	52.61
Sept	48.50	43.47	49.03	45.75	47.10	50.88
Oct	49.20	48.51	45.01	44.61	48.31	51.37
Nov	48.02	43.68	50.97	50.50	51.05	52.38
Dec	55.90	56.15	57.56	51.14	49.14	52.75

Source: BPS (2015)

Table 3 Re-visit Rate at Resort Hotels in West Java

Hotel	Percentage
Hotel B, West Bandung District	3.3
Hotel C, Garut District	2.5
Hotel F, Bandung District	2.5
Hotel E, Sukabumi District	2.3
Hotel A, Subang District	2.0
Hotel D, Bogor District	1.8

sector. Re-visit intention is an important factor in market competition within the tourism industry, although neither the specific reasons underlying it, nor the customer characteristics of those individuals who harbor re-visit intentions are known (Mat Som, Marzuki, Yousefi, & AbuKhalifeh, 2012). Previous research suggests that several factors influence tourist behavior in realizing re-visit intentions, including customer value (Bigne, Sanchez, & Andreu, 2009; Chen & Tsai, 2007; Petrick, Morais, & Norman, 2001; Um, Chon, & Ro, 2006) and customer experience (Klaus & Maklan, 2013). Indeed, previous customer experience is one of the major considerations that can increase tourist re-visits (Chen & Gursoy, 2001; Kozak, 2001; Petrick et al., 2001). The nature of tourists' experience during their initial stay at a hotel will greatly influence their decision about whether to return to the same establishment in the future. Similarly, customers involved in any activities that provided a unique and rewarding experience once, usually harbor the desire to undertake them again. The more they do so, the more enthusiastically they will participate in building the brand and promote it through word-of-mouth (Hasan, 2013). According to Tajeddini and Ratten (2017), brand orientation consists of a company's unique selling proposition (USP), image and experience in providing a high-quality product that differentiates it from the competition.

Previous research suggests that customer value resulting from travel experience or a stay at a particular hotel also determines tourists' re-visit intention (Bigne et al., 2009; Chen & Tsai, 2007; Petrick et al., 2001; Um et al., 2006). Several previous studies also confirmed customer value to be an important hotel strategy in enhancing the ability to encourage tourists to re-visit or extend their current stay. The academic literature related to hotel industry re-visit rates remains comparatively limited in scope, rendering the subject an engaging and valid one for further study. The investigation reported here seeks to complement past research in order to identify factors promoting an increase in customer re-visit intention within the hotel industry sector by exploring customer experience management and customer value. The focus of this research is the themed resort hotel as a tourist visit destination.

2 Literature Review

2.1 *Resort Hotels*

A themed resort hotel is built in a tourist location as accommodation facilities for related activities possessing unique characteristics compared to those of analogous establishments. Salient characteristics of themed resort hotels include market segment, location, facilities, architecture and atmosphere (indonesia.tripcanvas.co). Operating within their target market segment, the accommodation facilities located in the tourist area will target potential customers intending to take a vacation, enjoy a period of leisure time and have fun. The design of a viable resort hotel should cater to customers' needs, equipped with facilities enabling them to be entertained, have fun, and refresh themselves. Generally, resort hotel locations offer significant tourism potential, for example, beautiful natural scenery such as beaches, mountains, river banks, lake shores, or special places away from the bustle of the city.

The facilities provided at a resort hotel fall within two main categories, namely; public facilities meeting general needs, including; accommodation, services, entertainment, relaxation and additional facilities at specific locations which exploit the natural resources available at the site and the immediate surrounding area for leisure activities and contribute to the resort's specific character. For example, the geographical features of the seaside comprise sandy beaches, weather ideal for sunbathing or playing beach volleyball and the ocean for swimming, surfing and diving. These traits can also be considered as characteristic of a resort hotel (Department of Culture and Tourism of West Java Province, 2017). Visitors to resort hotels tend to seek accommodation with unique architecture and a natural atmosphere, different to that of other types of hotels. In addition, tourists staying at resort hotels are more likely to favor buildings and spaces which combine natural or traditional themes with an ethnic interior decor. The design of the building should preferably have a memorable rather than generic, business-like appearance.

The diversity of international tourist areas affects the variety of resort hotels in West Java based on their location and facilities. Such hotels can be classified as follows: (1) Beach Resort Hotel: a resort located in a coastal area, capitalizing on its natural potential and the attractiveness of the sea. (2) Marine Resort Hotel: a marine resort (sea port) whose design exploits the region's main potential. (3) Mountain Resort Hotel: a resort located in a mountainous area. Beautiful mountain scenery represents such a location's strength and is used as the resort's design feature. (4) Health Resort and Spa: a resort hotel built in an area of natural potential that can be utilized for health-improvement purposes. (5) Rural Resort and Country Hotel: a resort hotel constructed in a rural area far from busy commercial districts. (6) Themed Resort: a resort of this type is designed around a specific theme and offers special attractions. (7) Sight-seeing Resort Hotel: a resort hotel situated in an area of outstanding natural beauty or a place of special interest such as a shopping center, historical site, entertainment venue, etc.

2.2 *Customer Experience Management, Customer Value, and Re-visit Intention*

One of the elements that contribute significantly to the success of a company is marketing. According to Kotler and Keller (2009), this is the art and science of selecting target markets and securing, retaining and increasing customers to create, deliver, and communicate the advantages of customer value. Marketing is the activity of creating, communicating, providing and exchanging processes that are useful for the organization and the wider community (Dibb, Simkin, Pride, & Ferrell, 2005). The American Marketing Association defines marketing as an activity, a function and a series of organizational processes for creating, communicating and delivering value to customers, clients, partners and the wider community as a means of managing customer relationships (Kotler & Keller, 2009). The appropriate marketing strategy is a combination of promotional activities designed to secure access to the target market. Customer behavior as one facet of marketing studies is defined as behavior in using, evaluating and buying products and services according to consumers' needs and expectations. Such behavior is expected to satisfy these needs and expectations (Schiffman & Kanuk, 2012).

From a tourism marketing perspective, visitor behavior is divided into three phases, namely; (1) the choice of destination (2) subsequent evaluation (3) future intended visitor behavior (Chen & Tsai, 2007). The subsequent evaluation focuses on the specific travel experience of, or value received by, visitors as a whole. Future behavior intention refers to visitors considering a return to the same destination and their willingness to recommend it to others (Yuniawati & Finardi, 2016).

Customer experience is defined as direct or indirect client exposure to the service process, companies, facilities and method of customer interaction with the company and other customers (Walter, Edvardsson, & Ostrom, 2010). This, in turn, will provoke certain cognitive responses, emotions, and customer behavior. Furthermore, it will leave customers with memories of pre-, during and post-visit experiences. A study conducted by Diller, Shedroff, and Rhea (2006) and supported by that of Luturlean and Anggadwita (2015), suggested that customer experience management can be measured by five core dimensions including: (1) product/service (2) service interface (3) price and promotion (4) communication channels and (5) brand relationship. Experience consists of those components enabling a company to avoid mistakes and know-how to expand and enrich customer experience (Luturlean & Anggadwita, 2016). Through their experiences, customers implicitly generate various psychological assessments to measure the value that can be obtained from the experiential service provided by the company (Vera & Trujillo, 2013).Customer value is rooted in potential customers' evaluation of the perceived benefits and costs of alternative offers (Kotler & Keller, 2009). Customer experience can be located within the context of the customer's life to produce consistent values or patterns of thinking. These succeed in attracting the interest of customers, leaving a positive impression, creating income and enhancing corporate reputation (Bruhn, Schnebelen, & Schalfer, 2014). Based on the literature, customer experience can positively affect customer value. According to Sweeny and Soutar (2001), the dimensions within which customer value is established are emotional value, social value, performance value, and the value of money. Chen and Chen (2010) found that customer value and customer experience positively influence consumer behavior post-purchase. This study attempts to identify the relationship between customer experience management and customer value on the basis of the following hypothesis:

H1 Customer experience management significantly influences customer value at themed resort hotels in West Java

Re-visit intention centers on the possibility of repeating an activity or a visit to a destination (Weng, Ha, Wang, & Tsai, 2012). A purchase decision occurs when a customer decides to re-purchase a product based on the belief that it meets his/her requirements (Schiffman & Kanuk, 2012). According to Yi and La (2004), re-visit intention can be measured by means of two indicators. The first is a re-purchase intention within which customers harbor a firm desire to return. The second is re-purchase probability defined as the likelihood that consumers will return. Each transaction requires marketers to create advantages for customers interested in buying their products. In order to create those advantages, marketers need to understand customer behavior. There is a focus on customer behavior in marketing management services consisting of three schemes, namely; customer choice, customer experience and post-experience evaluation (Zeithaml, Binter, & Gremler, 2009). Creating and managing an effective process and experience is an important management task for service sector companies. Other research has found that customer experience can positively influence buying intention (Luo, Chen, Ching, & Liu, 2011). In addition, such experience also positively affects customer satisfaction and buying intention (Chen & Lin, 2014). Cronin, Brady, and Hult (2000) examined six service industries and found a significant link between customer value and behavioral intention. Thus, the hypotheses proposed in this study are as follows:

H2a Customer experience management has direct influence on, and significance for, customer re-visit intention at themed resort hotels in West Java.

H2b The inter-relationship between customer experience management, customer value and customer re-visit intention is more significant and exerts greater influence than that between customer experience management and customer re-visit intention at themed resort hotels in West Java.

3 Methodology

The methodology used in this study was quantitative in nature. Quantitative research methods were applied "... to explain the phenomenon by collecting numerical data which were analyzed using a method based on math (especially statistics)" (Aliaga & Gunderson, 2000). The variables within this research consisted of re-visit intention as the dependent variable, customer value as an intervening variable, and customer experience management as an independent variable.

The population featured in this study were all customers of a themed resort hotel in West Java and, consequently, in determinant in number. This study used structural equation modeling (SEM), a form of study that Hair, Black, Babin, Anderson, and Tatham (1998) suggested requires a sample size consisting of at least 200 samples. The exact number of subjects within the study population was not known with certainty. Therefore, the researchers calculated it as being approximately 5–10 times the total of the items in the observed variables (Bentler, 1990; Hair et al., 1998). The questionnaire designed for this study contained approximately 49 questions (items), the number of samples used therefore being at least 490 respondents. The sampling technique used was of a non-probability form combined with an accidental sampling technique. Since the focus of this research was that of themed resort hotels, the researchers only collected and investigated data derived from respondents at the time of ongoing research activities to ensure their appropriate selection.

The sources of data/information within this study can be classified as primary and secondary in nature. Primary data was collected directly through questionnaires administered to customers of West Java-based themed resort hotels. Other primary data on the business development of the hotel industry was gathered by means of interviews with hotel managers conducted either directly or via telecommunication devices (mobile phones and e-mail). Secondary data included observation, documentation, literature reviews, and hotel industry and government regulation-related supporting documents. The research instrument included a questionnaire consisting

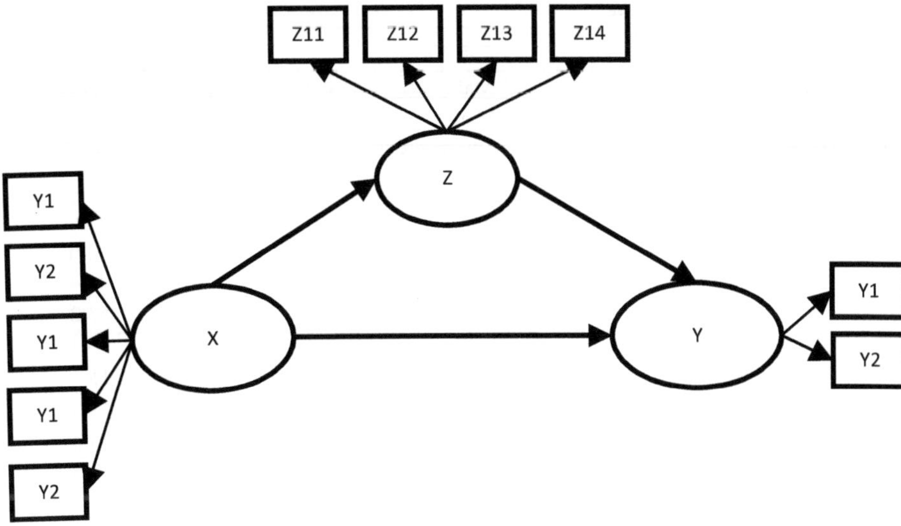

Fig. 1 Conceptual model

of four sections; the first containing an overview of respondent profiles, the second evaluating the customer's perspective on customer experience management, the third measuring customer perceived value, and the last assessing the customer's decision to re-visit. The scale of measurement used an ordinal scale with Likert method. The Five-Likert scale employed in this study is as follows: 1 = Strongly Disagree; 2 = Disagree; 3 = Neutral; 4 = Agree; 5 = Strongly Agree. The adopted analytical method tested the data obtained by means of questionnaires using an SEM approach incorporating several stages (Hair et al., 1998), namely; the measurement model fit, the overall model fit, and the structure model fit. Figure 1 is a conceptual model of the study described here.

4 Result and Analysis

4.1 Profile of Respondents

Data, collected by means of a questionnaire to identify the characteristics of the respondents, is presented in the table.

Table 4 shows the profile of respondents as visitors to a number of resort hotels in West Java. With regard to gender, of the 500 respondents surveyed as many as 285 (57%), were male, whereas females as accounted for 215 (43%).The results of this study support previous research findings on customer gender at resort hotels, while other investigations also suggest that customer gender was taken into consideration when preparing the hotel building concept, plan programs, and even the facility to be provided by management (Andriani, 2015; Asanah, 2012).

Table 4 Profile of respondents

No.	Profile description	Category	Frequency	Percentage
1	Gender	Male	285	57
		Female	215	43
2	Respondent's age	<25 years	175	35
		26–35 years	189	37.8
		36–45 years	113	22.6
		>45 years	23	4.6
3	Marital status	Single	232	46.4
		Married	266	53.2
		Others	2	0.4
4	Educational background	Senior High School	78	15.6
		Diploma	64	12.8
		Bachelor Degree	229	45.8
		Master Degree	103	20.6
		Doctoral Degree	26	5.2
5	Respondent's job	Entrepreneur/Self-employed	125	25
		Government Employees	78	15.6
		Private Employees	174	34.8
		Teacher/Lecturer	61	12.2
		Military/Police	3	0.6
		Others	59	11.8
6	The average income per month (IDR)	≤5 million	198	39.6
		5–10 million	202	40.4
		10–15 million	67	13.4
		15–20 million	29	5.8
		20–25 million	2	0.4
		> 25 million	2	0.4
7	Domicile	Java Island	421	84.2
		Outside of Java Island	26	5.2
8	Frequency of stay	1 time	96	19.2
		2–3 times	316	63.2
		4–5 times	73	14.6
		>5 times	15	3
9	Purpose of stay	Business purposes	104	20.8
		Family purposes	78	15.6
		Vacation/recreation	312	62.4
		Others	6	1.2
10	Expenditure incurred during stay	≤2 million	89	17.8
		2.1–3.5 million	203	40.6
		3.6–5 million	130	26
		>5 million	78	15.6

(continued)

Table 4 (continued)

No.	Profile description	Category	Frequency	Percentage
11	Hotel facilities used	Restaurant	332	66.4
		SPA/Salon	105	21
		Laundry	13	2.6
		Fitness	31	6.2
		Others	19	3.8

Meanwhile, an analysis of customer age showed that 175 people (35%) were under 25,189 (37.8%) were 26–35 years old, 113 (22.6%) were between 36 and 45, and 23 (4.6%)were more than 45 years old. The results also supported previous research showing that young professionals in the 35-year age range prefer to travel and visit or stay at a resort hotel compared with older counterparts (Attubel, 2013).

As far as marital status is concerned, 232 people (46.4%) were single, 266 (53.2%) married, and 2 (0.4%) 'other'. The educational background of the respondents was as follows; 78 individuals (15.6%) were high school graduates, 64 (12.8%) were educated to diploma level, 229 (45.8%) held bachelor degrees, 103 (20.6%) a master's qualification, and 26 (5.2%) doctorates. In addition, with regard to occupation, 125 people (25%) were entrepreneurs/self-employed, 78 (15.6%) were government employees, 174 (34.8%) were private employees, 61 (12.2%) were teachers/lecturers, 3 (0.6%) were military/police, and 59 (11%) had other jobs. Turning to respondents' total monthly income, of 198 people (39.6%) earned less than IDR5 million, 202 (40.4%) enjoyed a monthly income of IDR5–10 million, 67 (13.4%) had one of IDR10–15 million, 29 (5.8%) earned IDR15–20 million, 2 (0.4%) had a monthly income IDR20–25 million, and 2 (0.4%) had one above IDR25 million.

The profile of respondents, based on their domicile, showed that 421 (84.2%) came from Java, 26 (5.2%) were resident outside Java, while 10.6% did not respond. Meanwhile, data relating to the frequency of stay confirmed that 96 people (19.2%) were first-time guests, 316 (63.2%) had previously stayed on 2–3 occasions, 73 (14.6%) 4–5 times and 15 (3%) more than 5. As far as the purpose of stay is known, the following reasons were cited; 104 people (20.8%) business purposes, 78 (15.6%) family reasons, 312 (62.4%) vacation/recreation and 6 (1.2%) other purposes.

Feedback on expenditure during their stay indicated that 89 people (17.8%) spent less than IDR2 million, 203 (40.6%) IDR2.1–3.5 million, 130 (26.0%) IDR3.6–5 million, and 78 (15.6%) more than IDR5 million. Based on this data, it is clear that most respondents expended IDR2.1–3.5 million during their stay at the hotel. Meanwhile, as far as facilities use by respondents is concerned 332 people (66.4%) visited the restaurant, 105 (21%) frequented the SPA/salon, 13 (2.6%) used the laundry, 31 (6.2%) availed themselves of the fitness center and19 (3.8%) utilized other facilities.

Table 5 Measurement of observed variables

Latent Variables	Manifest variables	SLF	t-value	CR	VE
Customer experience management (CEM)	Promotion (X1)	0.41	8.94	0.865	0.565
	Price (X2)	0.55	12.62		
	Product (X3)	0.80	20.13		
	Distribution (X4)	0.64	15.08		
	Service (X5)	0.85	22.21		
Customer value (Cust_Va)	Rational (Z1)	0.85	22.92	0.752	0.923
	Emotional (Z2)	0.82	21.73		
	Experience (Z3)	0.89	24.67		
	Spiritual (Z4)	0.66	16.21		
Revisit intention (Rev_Int)	Repeat purchase intention (Y1)	0.60	12.95	0.798	0.887
	Repurchase probability	0.83	17.54		

Table 6 Goodness of fit index for the structural equation model

χ^2	df	RMSEA	SRMSR	NFI	CFI	AGFI
164.27	41	0.078	0.050	0.97	0.98	0.91

4.2 Hypothesis Result

Table 5 shows the measurement of conceptual model adopted in this study. There are four indicators of customer experience management latent variables that have passed the validity test due to their meeting the requirements of SLF ≥ 0.50 and t-value ≥ 1.96. However, indicator Y4 did not satisfy the requirements because of the SLF value of <0.50. Although the t-value indicator X1 exceeded 1.96, it did not meet the value standards of SLF. Consequently, this indicator was removed due to its under-representing of customer experience management. The reliability test of customer experience management produced an impressive value: CR 0.8655 ≥ 0.70, while VE was 0.565 ≥ 0.50. Therefore, the customer experience management variable demonstrated a high degree of consistency.

The result shows that all the customer value variable indicators have an SLF value ≥ 0.50. In addition, the overall t-value is above 1.96, confirming the overarching indicator for these variables as valid. Meanwhile, the reliability test results show values of CR ≥ 0.70 and VE ≥ 0.50. Therefore, all of the latent variables proved to be reliable and demonstrated considerable consistency.

The validity test result of the re-visit intention variable shows that two indicators passed the validity test because these indicators met the requirements of an SLF ≥ 0.50 and t-value ≥ 1.96. The reliability test of the psychological characteristics variable produced CR ≥ 0.70 and VE > 0.50. As a result, the re-visit intention variables can be said to have a high degree of consistency.

Table 6 shows the overall model fit of this study. The latter's results showed that the NFI and CFI were ≥ 0.90, confirming a good fit. The RMSEA results were

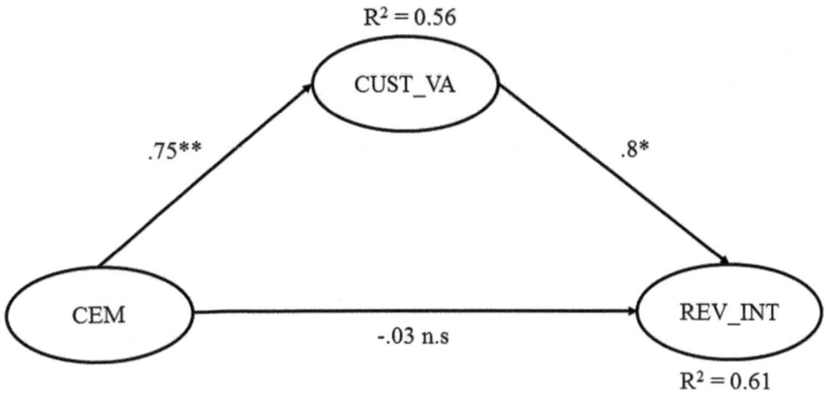

Fig. 2 Structure model (Notes: Standardized coefficients, two-sided significance tests; *$p < 0.1$; **$p < 0.05$; ***$p < 0.001$)

$0.078 \leq 0.08$, which indicated a good fit. The AGFI value was $0.90 \leq 0.90$. AGFI values of $0.80 < \text{AGFI} \leq 0.90$ showed a marginal fit (Jöreskog & Sörbom, 1996). Since the SRMSR value was $0.05 \leq 0.05$, this suggested an encouraging fit. Overall, it is feasible to conclude that overall model fit existed.

Figure 2 represents the structure model of this study showing the results of the hypotheses that have been proposed. With regard to Hypothesis 1, customer experience management was largely proven to influence customer value ($\beta = 0.75$, $p < 0.05$). Thus, the hypothesis can be regarded as valid. Hypothesis 2a that customer experience management exerts a significant influence on re-visit intention ($\gamma = -0.03$ ns) was not validated. Given the loading factor value of $-0.03 \leq 0.50$, the hypothesis was rejected. Meanwhile, Hypothesis 2b that customer experience management is proven to have an indirect influence on re-visit intention through customer value constituted an intervening variable ($\beta = 0.6$, $p < 0.1$). The indirect effect of customer experience management on re-visit intention through customer value was 0.6 (0.75×0.8). Since this value was greater than the coefficient of direct relationships (-0.03), Hypothesis 2b was accepted.

5 Discussion and Conclusion

Customer experience management (CEM) is one of the most promising marketing approaches (Homburg, Jozi, & Kuehnl, 2015), because it can create a long-term competitive advantage for the company. Moreover, it can also result in customer satisfaction and customer loyalty through positive word-of-mouth, creating an ongoing relationship with customers, as well as reducing the incidence rate of customer complaints. CEM dimensions in this study included; promotion, price, product, distribution and service. This study illustrates uniqueness in a range of areas including; promotion conducted, prices offered, product range and the comfort level of resort hotels' service products. Based on the research findings, the dimension of promotion does not meet SLF value criteria standards. Therefore, CEM is better described by product.

This study used the concept of customer value considered to be very important, especially for marketing success. Customer value can form an emotional customer-company bond, while adding value. According to Plewa and Quester (2006), customer value is a consumer-perceived quality judged in relation to the prices of products produced by a company. It is suggested that the emotional connection created between customers and company can create reciprocal positive impact. The creation concept and added value require the full attention of management. The fundamental issue around attracting and retaining customers is recognizing the potential for added value and providing it to them (Hassan, Purnama, & Ridwanudin, 2014). Studies conducted by Al (2004), divide customer value dimensions into functional value, economic value, emotional value and sacrifice value. If the four components are present in an integrated form, the resulting higher customer value will have a positive impact in increasing customer satisfaction. Furthermore, the latter creates an integrated functionality through customer value. The function and support within a framework built on relationships and interactions emerging from a customer value understanding of customers' expectations and desires acts as the basis for achieving an effective strategy to defeat the competition. This study used four dimensions including; rational, emotional, experiential, and spiritual as measured by high or low levels of each dimension with their respective indicators. Based on the study, experience dimensions obtained the highest average scores, while spiritual ones obtained the lowest. The study also showed that inter-dimensional ratings do not differ greatly. Meanwhile, the concept of re-visit intention is described in two dimensions, repeat purchase intention and re-purchase probability, both of which describe customers' desire to sample again resort hotels' facilities, their intention to book another stay thereby enjoying a unique and unforgettable experience and, lastly, their intention to recommend the resort to others.

The present study found that customer value is significantly influenced by customer experience management. The magnitude of the effect of X on Z is one of 0.75 or 56%. The results support those of several previous researchers describing the influence of customer experience management on customer value Prior research described the hotel industry model which is influenced by the existence of customer experience management in delivering customer value (Mohajerani & Miremadi, 2012).

The study also found that customer experience management has no direct influence on re-visit intention but, rather, an indirect one through customer value. Its findings support those of previous empirical studies of the hotel industry (Weng et al., 2012; Dominici & Guzzo, 2010) which discussed customer experience management's role in delivering customer value and customer satisfaction within the hotel industry. The findings show that 61% of the re-visit intention variable can be jointly explained by customer experience management and customer value. The remaining 39% consists of the influence of other variables not described in the model. This study shows that customer experience management and customer value are capable of influencing re-visit intention and is able to provide a performance assessment of any existing dimension. This study supports previous research describing the factors that affect the onset of recurrence (Mat Som et al., 2012), a phenomenon capable of producing impact or influence thereby increasing recurring arrival (Chao-hui, Lin, & Qiao-yun, 2011).

The results also suggest that West Java-based resort hotels, in an effort to increase customer re-visit intentions, need to make improvements in customer experience management that will, ultimately, enhance customer value. The study also recommended that resort hotels make additions to, and improvements in, their products and services so as to provide a high level of customer value. It is expected that every future effort will stimulate customer re-visit intention with regard to resort hotels in West Java.

References

Al, W. (2004). Cytogenetic characterization and fael genevariation in progenies. *National Research Council Canada, 47*, 724–731.

Aliaga, M., & Gunderson, B. (2000). *Introduction to quantitative research. Doing quantitative research in education with SPSS* (pp. 1–11). Thousand Oaks, CA: Sage.

Andriani, E. (2015). Implementasi Konsep "Pretensious Moment" Tradisional Lombok Pada Perancangan Interior Lobby Dan Area Komersil "The Lombo" Hotel Resort Di Lombok. *Intra, 3*(2), 310–319.

Asanah, M. Y. A. (2012). *Perancangan hotel resort di Batu: Green architecture*. Doctoral dissertation, Universitas Islam Negeri Maulana Malik Ibrahim.

Attubel, M. M. (2013). Pengambilan Keputusan Wisatawan Berkunjung di Nusatenggara Timur Melalui Bauran Pemasaran Jasa Pariwisata. *Jurnal Ilmiah Pariwisata, 18*(3), 216–230.

Bentler, P. M. (1990). Comparative fit indexes in structural models. *Psychological Bulletin, 107* (2), 238.

Bigne, J. E., Sanchez, I., & Andreu, L. (2009). The role of variety seeking in short and long run revisit intentions in holiday destinations. *International Journal of Culture, Tourism and Hospitality Research, 3*(2), 103–115.

Bruhn, M., Schnebelen, S., & Schalfer, D. (2014). Antecedents and consequences of the quality of e- customer-to customer interactions in B2B brand communities. *Industry Market Management, 43*, 164–176.

Central Statistics Agency, Indonesia (BPS). (2013, 2015). Statistic Publication. [Online] Official website: https://www.bps.go.id/

Chang, L.-L., Backman, F. K., & Chih Huang, Y. (2014). Creative tourism: A preliminary examination of creative tourists' motivation, experience, perceived value and revisit intention. *International Journal of Culture, Tourism and Hospitality Research, 8*(4), 401–419. doi:10.1108/IJCTHR-04-2014-0032.

Chao-hui, W. A. N. G., Lin, L., & Qiao-yun, X. I. A. (2011). Tourists' perception value and behavior intention in mega-events based on structural equation model (SEM): A case study of 2010 Shanghai World Expo. *地理研究, 30*(4), 735–746.

Chen, C. F., & Chen, F. (2010). Experience quality, perceived value, satisfaction and behavioral intentions for heritage tourists. *Tourism Management, 31*, 29–35.

Chen, J. S., & Gursoy, D. (2001). An investigation of tourists' destination loyalty and preferences. *International Journal of Contemporary Hospitality Management, 13*(2), 79–85.

Chen, S., & Lin, C. (2014). Technological forecasting & social change the impact of customer experience and perceived value on sustainable social relationship in blogs: An empirical study. *Technological Forecasting and Social Change*. doi:10.1016/j.techfore.2014.11.011
Chen, C. F., & Tsai, D. (2007). How destination image and evaluative factors affect behavioral intentions? *Tourism Management, 28*(4), 1115–1122.
Cronin, J. J. J., Brady, M. K., & Hult, G. T. M. (2000). Assessing the effects of quality, value and customer satisfaction on consumer behavioral intention in service environments. *Journal of Retailing, 76*(2).
Dibb, S., Simkin, L., Pride, W. M., & Ferrell, O. C. (2005). *Marketing: Concepts and strategies* (p. 850). Abingdon: Houghton Mifflin.
Diller, S., Shedroff, N., & Rhea, D. (2006). *Making meaning: How successful business deliver meaningful customer experience*. Berkeley, CA: New Riders.
Dominici, G., & Guzzo, R. (2010). Customer satisfaction in the hotel industry: A case study from Sicily. *International Journal of Marketing Studies, 2*(2), 3–12.
Hair, J. F., Black, W. C., Babin, B. J., Anderson, R. E., & Tatham, R. L. (1998). *Multivariate data analysis* (5th ed.). Upper Saddle River, NJ: Pearson Prentice Hall.
Hasan, A. (2013). *Marketing dan Kasus-Kasus Pilihan*. Yogyakarta: CAPS (Center for Academic Publishing Service).
Hassan, S. M. I. P., Purnama, R., & Ridwanudin, O. (2014). Pengaruh customer value Dalam Meningkatkan Kepuasan Wisatawan Di Saung Angklung Udjo (Survei terhadap Wisatawan Nusantara Individu di Saung Angklung Udjo). *Tourism and Hospitality Essentials (THE) Journal, 4*(1), 725–732.
Homburg, C., Jozi, D., & Kuehnl, C. (2015). Customer experience management: Toward implementing an evolving marketing concept. doi:10.1007/s11747-015-0460-7
Jöreskog, K. G., & Sörbom, D. (1996). *LISREL 8: User's reference guide*. Scientific Software International.
Klaus, P., & Maklan, S. (2013). Towards a better measure of customer experience. *International Journal of Market Research, 55*(2), 227–246. doi:10.2501/IJMR-2013-021.
Kotler, P., & Keller, K. L. (2009). Marketing management. *Organization, 22*. doi:10.1080/08911760903022556
Kozak, M. (2001). Repeaters' behavior at two distinct destinations. *Annals of Tourism Research, 28*(3), 784–807.
Luo, M., Chen, J. S., Ching, R. K., & Liu, C. C. (2011). An examination of the effects of virtual experiential marketing on online customer intentions and loyalty. *Service Industry Journal, 31*, 2163–2191.
Luturlean, B. S., & Anggadwita, G. (2015). *A framework for conceptualizing customer experiences management in the hotel industry*. In 3rd International Seminar and Conference on Learning Organization, Yogyakarta, Indonesia.
Luturlean, B. S., & Anggadwita, G. (2016). Customer experience management in the hotel industry: Principles, theory and practice. *Advances in Economics, Business, and Management Research, 15*, 460–463. Atlantis Press.
Mat Som, A. P., Marzuki, A., Yousefi, M., & AbuKhalifeh, A. N. (2012). Factors influencing visitors' revisit behavioral intentions: A case study of Sabah, Malaysia. *International Journal of Marketing Studies, 4*(4), 39–50. doi:10.5539/ijms.v4n4p39.
Mohajerani, P., & Miremadi, A. (2012). Customer satisfaction modeling in hotel industry: A case study of Kish Island in Iran. *International Journal of Marketing Studies, 4*(3), 134–152.
O'Shannessy et al. (2001). *Accommodation services*. Hospitality Press.
Pendit, N. (1999). *Ilmu Pariwisata*. Jakarta: Akademi Pariwisata Trisakti.
Petrick, J. F., Morais, D. D., & Norman, W. C. (2001). An examination of the determinants of entertainment vacationers' intentions to revisit. *Journal of Travel Research, 40*(1), 41–48.
Plewa, C., & Quester, Q. (2006). Satisfaction with University industry relationship: The impact of commitment, trust and championship. *International Journal of Technology Transfer and Commercialization, 5*(1), 79–101.

Salman, L. (2010). *Analisis Perencanaan Program Komunikasi Pemasaran Visit Lombok Sumbawa 2012*. Surakarta: Universitas Sebelas Maret.

Schiffman, L. G., & Kanuk, L. L. (2012). *Consumer behavior*. Upper Saddle River, NJ: Pearson Education.

Sweeny, J. C., & Soutar, G. N. (2001). Consumer perceived value: The development of a multiple item scale. *Journal of Retailing, 77*(2), 203–220.

Tajeddini, K., & Ratten, V. (2017). The moderating effect of brand orientation on inter-firm market orientation and performance. *Journal of Strategic Marketing*, 1–31.

TripCanvas Indonesia. (2017). Find hotels. [Online] Accessed April, 2017, from https://indonesia.tripcanvas.co

Um, S., Chon, K., & Ro, Y. (2006). Antecedents of revisit intention. *Annals of Tourism Research, 33*(4), 1141–1158.

Vera, J., & Trujillo, A. (2013). Service quality dimensions and superior customer perceived value in retail banks; an empirical study on Mexican customers. *Journal Retail Consumer Service, 20*, 579–586.

Walter, U., Edvardsson, B., & Ostrom, A. (2010). Drivers of customers' service experiences: A study in the restaurant industry. *Managing Service Quality, 20*(3), 236–258.

Weng, M., Ha, J.-L., Wang, Y., & Tsai, C.-L. (2012). A study of the relationship among service innovation, customer value and customer satisfaction: An empirical study of the hotel industry in Taiwan. *International Journal of Organizational Innovation, 4*, 98–113.

World Economic Forum. (2013). *The travel and tourism competitiveness report 2013*. Geneva: WEF. Retrieved April 1, 2017, from WEF Web site: http://www3.weforum.org/docs/WEF_TT_Competitiveness_Report_2013.pdf

Yi, Y., & La, S. (2004). What influences the relationship between customer satisfaction and repurchase intention? Investigating the effects of adjusted expectations and customer loyalty. *Psychology and Marketing, 21*(5), 351–373.

Yuniawati, Y., & Finardi, A. D. I. (2016). Gunung Tangkuban Perahu Pengaruh Customer Experience Terhadap Revisit Intention di Taman Wisata Alam Gunung Tangkuban Perahu. *Tourism and Hospitality Essentials (THE) Journal, 6*(1), 983–994.

Zeithaml, V. A., Binter, M. J., & Gremler, D. D. (2009). *Services marketing: Integrating customer focus across the firm* (p. 15). New York: McGraw Hill.

MIX
Papier aus verantwortungsvollen Quellen
Paper from responsible sources
FSC® C105338

If you have any concerns about our products,
you can contact us on
ProductSafety@springernature.com

In case Publisher is established outside the EU,
the EU authorized representative is:
Springer Nature Customer Service Center GmbH
Europaplatz 3, 69115 Heidelberg, Germany

Printed by Libri Plureos GmbH
in Hamburg, Germany